COOKING WITH ALCOHOL

Cover design: **Peter Barnfather**
Editor: **Paige Henderson**
Photography, typesetting and design: **Aaron Rickard and Susannah Rickard**

First published in 2021 by Lendal Press
Woodend, The Crescent, Scarborough, YO11 2PW
an imprint of Valley Press
lendalpress.com

ISBN 978-1912436958

Cat. no. LP0003
Copyright © Lendal Press 2021

All rights reserved. No part of this publication may be reproduced, stored in a retrieval system or transmitted in any form by any means, electronic, photocopying, mechanical, recording, or otherwise, without the prior written permission of the publishers and copyright holders.

The rights of Aaron Rickard and Susannah Rickard to be identified as the authors of this work have been asserted in accordance with the Copyright, Designs and Patents Act 1988.

A CIP record is available from the British Library.

Printed and bound in the EU by Pulsio, Paris.

COOKING WITH ALCOHOL

OVER 100 RECIPES EXPLORING THE FLAVOURS OF ALCOHOL

AARON & SUSANNAH RICKARD

Contents

Introduction	9
Using this book	12

14 Starters and Light Meals

Chorizo in Red Wine and Honey	18
Prawn, Feta and Ouzo Saganaki	20
Jamaican Rum Chicken with Mango Hot Sauce	22
Parsnip and Cider Soup	24
Mushroom and White Wine Soup	26
Irish Onion Soup	28
Cheese Fondue Tear-and-Share Bread	30
Tequila Fish Tacos with Pink Onions	32
Tempura Aubergine with Unagi Sake Sauce	34
Bloody Mary Prawn Cocktail	36
Chicken and Brandy Pâté	38
Mussels in Stout, Bacon and Whisky	40

44 Mains

Slow Cooked

Beef and Ale Stew with Ale Dumplings	50
Bourbon Brined Beef Short Ribs	52
Chicken with Brandy and Apricots	54
Coq au Cidre	56
Dark Beer and Aubergine Chilli	58
Lamb, Gin and Juniper Stew	60

Roasted and Grilled

Mojito Chicken	64
Rickard Family Jägermeister Chicken	66
Sweet and Spicy Tequila Lime Pork	68
Trout with Dill and Ouzo	70
Sangria Chicken	72

Pan Fried

Philly Cheese Steak with Beer Sauce	78
Salmon with Cava Sauce and Crushed Lemon Potatoes	80
Sticky Cider Sausages with Mustard Mash	82
Tequila and Habanero Salmon with Salsa Fresca and Black Beans	84
Dark Rum and Orange Pork Chops	86

Pasta and Rice

Port Pesto with Rigatoni	92
Fennel and White Wine Tagliatelle	94
Mushroom and Sherry Pasta	96
Tomato, Gin and Rosemary Pasta	98
Cheddar and Stout Risotto	100
Chicken, Amaretto and Saffron Biryani	102
Red Wine Risotto with Roasted Aubergine	104

Pies and Pastry

Mushroom and Stout Pasties	108
Parsnip and Cider Tarte Tatin	110
White Wine Chicken Pot Pie	112

114 Side Dishes and Condiments

Side Dishes

Potato and Beer Dauphinoise (Beerphinoise)	120
Cider Braised Leeks	122
Shallots Glazed in White Wine	124
Beer Basmati	126
Bourbon and Bacon Corn-on-the-Cob	128
Spiced Rum Barbecue Pineapple	130
Gin Slaw	132
Prosciutto, Melon and Sherry Salad	134
Port Marinated Olives	136
Bourbon Glazed Carrots	138
Sherry and Lemon Gravy	139

Condiments

Cider Mustard	144
Red Wine and Caramelised Onion Chutney	146
Red Wine Salt	148
Ale Pickled Eggs	150

152 Hot Desserts

Sloe Gin and Blackberry Cobbler	156
Roasted Apricots in Madeira	158
Rhubarb and Gin Crumble	160
Pear and Amaretto Frangipane Tart	162
Chocolate and Rum Fondants with Raspberry Sauce	164
Red Wine Chocolate Fudge Pudding	166
Whisky Sticky Toffee Pudding	168

170 Cold Desserts

Alcoholic Chocolate Mousse	174
Tequila Key Lime Pie	178
Crema Catalana con Madeira	180
Amaretto and Ginger Cheesecake	182
Rum, Raisin and Pistachio Posset	184
Chocolate and Amaretto Ganache Pots	186
Gin, Lime and Elderflower Cheesecake	188
Prosecco Panna Cotta	190
Aperol Spritz Jellies	192
Rosé and Raspberry Trifles	194
Orange and Tequila Sorbet	196
Piña Colada Sorbet	198
Roasted Plum and Port Ripple Ice Cream	200

202 Savoury Baking

Three Cheese and Onion Vodka Tarts	206
Cider Crust Pork Pie	208
Goat's Cheese and Port Canapés	212
Cider Soda Bread	214
Stout and Rye Bread	216
Red Wine Focaccia	220

222 Sweet Baking

Cider Apple Cake	230
Chocolate Stout Cake	231
White Wine Pound Cake	234
Baileys Muffins	236
Limoncello Polenta Cake	238
Dark 'n' Stormy Cake	242
Plum and Brandy Cake	244
Coconut Rum and Raspberry Cupcakes	246
Whisky and Maple Cupcakes	248
Peanut Butter and Bourbon Cookies	250
Whisky Shortbread	252
Lemon and Ouzo Cookies	254
Salted Caramel Spiced Rum Brownies	256
Chocolate and Port Tiffin	260
Alcoholic Bakewell Tart	261
Limoncello Tart	264
Beer and Baileys Doughnuts	266
Kahlua Fudge	270
Apple Cider Pancakes with Cider Caramel	272
Orange and Spiced Rum Marmalade	274
Apricot and Amaretto Jam	278
Apple and Bourbon Butter	280

Index — Recipe difficulty	284
Index — Ingredient	286
Acknowledgements	291

Introduction

What if we used alcohol as an ingredient?

Sometimes, ideas pop into your head and just won't leave. They float into your consciousness and, before you know it, your mind is racing with possibilities. You just can't get that idea out of your head, no matter how much you think about it, and the more you do think about it, the more you get carried away, and the more excited you become.

So, when the idea of cooking with alcohol captured our minds, we just couldn't figure out why it wasn't more popular already. Alcoholic drinks are delicious, and they have been fermented or distilled primarily for flavour and enjoyment. Just think of how many spices you have in your cupboard, and then think of all the drinks you've seen at the grocery store or along the back of a bar - each of those ingredients could bring a lot to the table. We started cooking, determined to discover how alcohol could be used in food.

We are experimental cooks - and always have been. Aaron spent his childhood tasting marinades with his dad, and inventing sandwich combinations that never should have existed. As a teenager Susannah gamified mashed potato with her brother, flavouring it a different way each week, and after university went to work for a spice recipe kit company, simply because spices are fun! Cooking is a joyful and creative process for us, and we're always experimenting to make our home cooking as delicious as possible.

Can we make our food taste like alcohol, in a good way?

We began experimenting with alcohol by creating recipes that used *similar flavour pairings* (similar flavour characteristics between the food and the alcohol). Both chorizo and red wine can be smoky and spicy, so we paired these together in our very first recipe, **Chorizo in Red Wine and Honey**, where they get along beautifully. In another recipe in this book, we adapted our own dark, rich beef stew to include dark, rich ale in a **Beef and Ale Stew with Ale Dumplings**. Over time, we worked this same principle of flavour pairings into sweet dishes, too - the perfect peanut butter cookie should be rich, warming and with hints of vanilla, so they are the perfect place to include sweet and buttery bourbon, which we've done in our **Peanut Butter and Bourbon Cookies**.

As we continued to create and test recipes, we became fascinated by the ways that alcohol can enhance food in *complementary flavour pairings*. We began thinking about using alcohol as a seasoning or garnish, adding depth and complexity that might otherwise be missing from a dish, or take hours to develop with traditional cooking. A white wine might be described as zesty or buttery, and when we bring it into the kitchen, these flavours can enhance a recipe where zestiness or butteriness are desired - an example of this is our **Fennel and White Wine Tagliatelle**.

We also considered these flavour pairings the other way around: *How can we use that bottle of ouzo?* We wanted to create something that would benefit from a hint of anise or fennel flavour, and hit on our lovely **Lemon and Ouzo Cookies**. Creating these balanced flavour pairings is a little like making a cocktail - we might garnish a sloe gin cocktail with a blackberry, so our **Blackberry Cobbler** is the perfect place for a splash of sloe gin, which lifts the flavour and adds beautiful plummy aromas.

We have found that, over time, it becomes second nature to use the alcohol shelf as an extension of the spice cabinet. We truly hope that this book will inspire you to transform your favourite dishes using the incredible flavours of alcohol, and a significant part of this book is devoted to explaining how building alcohol into a dish will impact the flavour.

In pursuit of flavour, however, we found that alcohol was impacting our cooking in entirely new ways. You'll find that there's almost always another effect - perhaps in the texture, caramelisation, gluten formation, acidity, or in something else entirely. An example of this is our **Cider Crust Pork Pie**, a recipe we developed from the desire to create *hot cider crust* instead of *hot water crust pastry*. Cider adds a gentle apple flavour to the robust pork pie pastry - but the cider also adds sugars to the pastry, which caramelise in the oven for a deeper, richer golden brown colour.

In truth, the functional side of cooking with alcohol has been the most fascinating part of the journey over the last few years, when every question that we asked brought another to light. Aside from being immensely interesting to research, test and discover these topics, we've ended up with rather eclectic internet search histories:

How does alcohol act on yeast?
What pH is gin?
Why does beer make a good batter?
….and an endless string of other questions!

Our eureka moment writing this book happened when we discovered the recipe for our **Alcoholic Chocolate Mousse**, a truly wonderful yet puzzling creation, which uses just chocolate and alcohol to create a rich, light mousse. The fact that you can make a mousse from two ingredients is incredible - the fact that one of them can be alcohol is truly delightful. This mousse is a true marriage of flavour and function, as the alcohol provides flavour and sweetness, while also being the base that will emulsify with the chocolate.

The *Savoury and Sweet Baking* chapters were the most challenging to develop - *how can you add alcohol to something that needs to end up solid, like a cake or cookie?* We needed to consider carefully how classic baking techniques might be adapted to incorporate the flavours of alcohol. For example, recipes for sticky ginger cake often add melted ingredients to dry ingredients to give a runny batter, ensuring a rich and moist cake. Our **Dark 'n' Stormy Cake** uses this same melted method with the winning combination of ginger, dark spiced rum, treacle and lime - these are traditional techniques, but adapted in an innovative way.

Each chapter has its own detailed introduction where we present the common principles and discuss how alcohol is used there - the techniques needed for *Starters* are completely different to those that we use for *Cold Desserts*, and we've done our best to make each lesson self-contained. In each recipe blurb, we talk about what alcohol is doing in that specific recipe for both flavour and function. In this way, we have aimed to bring you on our journey of discovery, and we sincerely hope that you enjoy it as much as we have.

What if we used alcohol as an ingredient?

It was such a little question, but it's taken us on a delightful journey of discovery and learning. Over five years later, we bring you this book, with over 100 recipes that use alcohol as a key ingredient. We've delved into the science of how alcohol affects our food in the cooking process, created dishes that bring out and deepen flavours in subtle and bold ways by using alcohol, and experimented with all manner of recipes that are better for having alcohol in them.

However, this book isn't just about recipes. It's also about encouraging you to think about alcohol as more than a drink, by showing you how the flavours and functions of alcohol can help to create some truly amazing food - we firmly believe that alcohol deserves a place in your kitchen, as well as in your glass.

Happy cooking!

Aaron and Susannah

Using this book

We aren't trained professional chefs - just two people who are passionate about creating great food at home, and who believe that the process needn't be overly complicated. We hope that you'll find this a very approachable cookbook. It contains everything from easy midweek dinners, ready in 30 minutes, to more complicated dishes that can be the highlight of your weekend, and we've done our best to write them as clearly and concisely as possible.

Recipe difficulty

To help you navigate this book, and to know what to expect before cooking, there's a difficulty rating at the top of each recipe.

❶ Recipes rated as a "1" will be uncomplicated, usually suitable for a busy weeknight. These recipes require basic kitchen skills, and don't involve too many steps. These recipes will be suitable for a novice cook.

❷ Recipes rated as a "2" will require a bit more skill or time, with a few more steps or techniques involved. These recipes are suitable for an established home cook.

❸ Recipes rated as a "3" are more complex - they either have a few different component parts or steps, or use techniques that we wouldn't have energy for on a weeknight. These are best suited to a confident or accomplished home cook.

Equipment - All our recipes were created, developed, tested (and tested again) at home in our flat, and while the recipes vary in complexity and technique, they are all achievable in a normal kitchen with normal equipment. We assume that you have some sharp knives, stirring utensils, weighing scales, a chopping board, an oven, and a stove. All other required equipment is indicated in the recipe.

Ingredients - You won't see anything in this cookbook that you can't buy at a normal, well-stocked grocery store. We're based in the UK, so this may vary a little depending on your country or region.

We assume that you have a small amount of table or kosher salt, black pepper and cooking oil at home. Freshly ground pepper is always best and, unless otherwise specified, we suggest you use a neutral flavoured oil for cooking - sunflower, vegetable or canola oils all work well. Virgin olive oil burns at a lower temperature than many other oils, so it's not so good for frying and can leave a bad taste on the food.

Always taste and adjust - During the cooking, the aroma compounds in your food will mingle and get to know each other, so tasting at the end is vital. Make sure you taste your food before serving, because your taste buds are different to anyone else's (and your opinion is the most important!). Does it need a pinch of salt, sugar, or a little acidity, perhaps?

Timings - Preparation and cooking times are indicated at the top of each recipe. In calculating these times, we assume a 'home cook' level of kitchen skill - we don't expect that you're a professional chef, but we do assume that it's not your first time chopping an onion.

Prep time includes an estimate for chopping your ingredients (if relevant), mixing things together, preparing baking tins, and anything else before you begin cooking.

Cook time includes any time where you are actively cooking, like frying or baking. Sometimes you will continue prep while something else is cooking, in which case we've assumed a bit of overlap.

Not included is the time it takes to locate your ingredients or utensils, any interruptions, or washing the dishes!

CHORIZO IN RED WINE AND HONEY, PAGE 18

STARTERS AND LIGHT MEALS

Chorizo in Red Wine and Honey	18
Prawn, Feta and Ouzo Saganaki	20
Jamaican Rum Chicken with Mango Hot Sauce	22
Parsnip and Cider Soup	24
Mushroom and White Wine Soup	26
Irish Onion Soup	28
Cheese Fondue Tear-and-Share Bread	30
Tequila Fish Tacos with Pink Onions	32
Tempura Aubergine with Unagi Sake Sauce	34
Bloody Mary Prawn Cocktail	36
Chicken and Brandy Pâté	38
Mussels in Stout, Bacon and Whisky	40

We start with a chapter of very adaptable recipes - whether you're cooking for a celebratory occasion, a light midweek dinner or an informal sharing spread, there's something here for all occasions. Along the way we'll give you an introduction to the art and science of cooking with alcohol, with an exploration of savoury flavour pairings, and the techniques of simmering, searing and sauces.

Recipes that require simmering - that is, bubbling something gently in a liquid to tenderise food and deepen flavours - are a natural place to begin incorporating the flavours of alcohol. In some cases, we choose an alcohol that matches the qualities of other ingredients, and we see this in the **Chorizo in Red Wine and Honey**. Rich, spicy Rioja wine is paired with smoky, spicy chorizo to make a tapas dish with intense flavour and a lingering sweetness of honey. But we might also choose an alcohol that will add something contrasting to a dish, like in our **Mussels in Stout, Bacon and Whisky**. Here, creamy, briny mussels are given an intense savoury flavour from a quick simmer in dark, rich stout, while a splash of Scotch whisky in the sauce enhances the smokiness of the bacon.

Searing food in a hot pan creates deep savoury flavours, and deglazing a pan with a little liquid helps to pick up these delicious flavours. Here, we tend to use spirits. These high proof alcohols have an intense flavour which, like seasoning, can be used in small quantities to add flavour to the surface of the ingredient being fried.

The bright, tart notes of silver tequila are perfect for seasoning delicate white fish in our **Tequila Fish Tacos with Pink Onions**, while the lingering note of brandy adds warmth to pan-fried chicken livers for a rich pâté. And, like seasoning, the alcohol chosen should have flavour notes that enhance your ingredients. Silver tequila is a natural match for zesty lime, while warming, aromatic brandy enhances fragrant herbs pungent mustard.

On occasion, we also use alcohol in a sauce to accompany other ingredients - for example, in the **Bloody Mary Prawn Cocktail**. Here, only a small quantity of alcohol is needed as a seasoning in the Marie Rose sauce. A splash of neat vodka increases the sensation of spiciness and acidity in the sauce, while also lending its own surprisingly delicious flavour. Exploring which flavours should go together is a central part of this book, and we start introducing these pairings here.

STARTERS AND LIGHT MEALS

Prawn, Feta and Ouzo Saganaki

Serves 4 as a starter or 2 as a main — Prep time 10 minutes — Cook time 35 minutes Difficulty ❷

Ingredients

50ml ouzo

2 tbsp olive oil

400g raw shelled king prawns (frozen and defrosted are fine) - patted dry

4 cloves of garlic - peeled, and crushed or finely chopped

1 large white onion - finely chopped

1 tsp chilli flakes

1 tbsp balsamic vinegar

1 x 400g jar passata (or a can of chopped tomatoes, blended until smooth)

100g feta cheese - diced or crumbled

Salt

Crusty bread, lemon wedges and fresh parsley to serve

Equipment

Ovenproof frying pan

Saganaki refers to the small heavy-bottomed frying pan that is used in Greece to cook a wide variety of meze dishes. Here, we're frying prawns in plenty of garlic, adding a splash of ouzo, and then baking it all in a spicy tomato sauce topped with feta cheese. The combination of salty cheese, freshly fried prawns and the savoury tomato sauce makes it incredibly moreish. Saganaki is traditionally a starter, but we also love to cook this as a midweek meal for two.

Ouzo is flavoured with anise, which is in the same aromatic family as fennel and tarragon - these sweet herbs all contain similar essential oils, and go beautifully with rich tomato sauces. You can make a delicious vegetarian version of this dish by substituting the prawns for chopped aubergine, fried until golden brown.

- Preheat the oven to 180C / Gas Mark 4 / 350F
- Heat 1 tbsp olive oil in an ovenproof frying pan over a medium-high heat. Add the prawns and cook for 3 minutes, stirring occasionally, then add the garlic and cook for a further minute
- When the garlic has softened, add the ouzo and cook for 2-3 more minutes until most of the alcohol has evaporated. Remove the prawns from the pan and set to one side
- In the same pan, heat a further 1 tbsp olive oil and cook the chopped onion over a medium heat for 5 minutes until soft. Stir in the chilli flakes, balsamic vinegar, tomato passata and ½ tsp salt
- Simmer for 5 minutes to allow the sauce to thicken a little, then sprinkle the prawns on top, followed by the crumbled feta cheese
- Place the pan in the oven and bake for 15 minutes or until the mixture is bubbling and the feta is brown around the edges
- Serve with crusty bread, lemon wedges and fresh parsley to add at the table

TIP: If you don't have an ovenproof frying pan, just transfer the mixture into an ovenproof dish before adding the prawns and feta cheese

STARTERS AND LIGHT MEALS

Jamaican Rum Chicken with Mango Hot Sauce

Serves 4 as a starter — Prep time 20 minutes — Cook time 15 minutes — Difficulty ❷

Ingredients

6 tbsp dark rum (2 tbsp for the sauce, 4 tbsp for the chicken)

1 fresh mango - peeled, stoned and roughly chopped (or a tub of fresh mango pieces in juice)

½ tsp chilli flakes, or more if you like it spicy!

1 tsp white sugar

½ lime - juiced (or 1 tbsp bottled lime juice)

1 clove of garlic - peeled, and crushed or finely chopped

½ tsp dried thyme

1 tsp allspice berries - ground in a pepper grinder or pestle and mortar (or ½ tsp ground allspice)

1 tbsp + 1 tsp dark soft brown sugar

2 tsp oil

3 skinless, boneless chicken thigh fillets or 2 chicken breasts (approx. 300g total) - chopped into bite size pieces

1 red pepper - chopped into bite size pieces

Salt and freshly ground black pepper

Equipment

Blender

2 x mixing bowls

Pepper grinder or pestle and mortar

8 skewers

Grill (broiler) or barbecue (grill)

Dark rum is generally distilled from molasses and aged in charred wooden barrels, and this production process creates complex flavours of spice and dried fruit, with subtle caramel notes. These sweet flavours make dark rum a perfect match for recipes where meat or sugar are caramelised over a high heat, as in these sticky, flavoursome skewers. We're also using another key Caribbean ingredient, allspice, which adds a wonderful warm, rich fragrance and spice.

On the side, we're making a fresh and fruity mango hot sauce - it keeps well in the fridge, so you can make it a day ahead of time if needed.

For the mango sauce

- Combine the mango, chilli flakes, white sugar, 2 tbsp dark rum, ½ tsp salt and the juice of ½ a lime in a blender. Blend until smooth, then add extra salt, sugar or chilli flakes to taste

For the chicken

- Preheat a grill or barbecue to a very high heat

- In a mixing bowl, stir together the garlic, thyme, allspice, ½ tsp black pepper, 1 tsp brown sugar, 2 tsp oil, ½ tsp salt and 1 tbsp dark rum to make a paste

- Add the chopped chicken into the bowl and rub the spice paste all over the chicken, then thread the chicken pieces onto skewers alternately with pieces of chopped red pepper

- In a separate small bowl, mix the remaining 3 tbsp rum with 1 tbsp brown sugar - this will be used to baste the chicken while it cooks

- Grill or barbecue the skewers for 5-8 mins, brushing or drizzling them liberally with the rum and sugar mixture every few minutes and turning occasionally. You're aiming to cook the meat as quickly as possible, and for the outside to turn sticky and brown

- Serve the chicken skewers with the mango sauce alongside for dipping

TIP: If you can't get hold of allspice, substitute for equal parts cinnamon, nutmeg and cloves

COOKING WITH ALCOHOL

STARTERS AND LIGHT MEALS

Parsnip and Cider Soup

Serves 4 — Prep time 10 minutes — Cook time 40 minutes — Difficulty ❶

Ingredients

500ml dry apple cider

1 white onion - finely chopped

1 clove of garlic - peeled, and crushed or finely chopped

A small piece of fresh ginger - peeled and finely chopped to make approx. 1 tbsp

500g parsnips - scrubbed, trimmed and finely chopped

1 medium potato (approx. 200g) - scrubbed and finely chopped

2 bay leaves

1 tsp dried thyme

500ml vegetable stock

Salt

Oil

Crusty bread and stilton cheese, or other crumbly blue cheese, to serve

There's nothing better on a cold day than a warming soup, and this is sure to be a favourite. The earthy sweetness of parsnips works beautifully with the fresh crisp flavours of apple cider and ginger, topped with a sprinkle of sharp stilton cheese. It's one of our favourites to take to work for lunch during the winter.

Make sure to use a dry cider here, as a sweet sparkling cider could overpower the flavours. For further cider-based nourishment, serve with the Cider Soda Bread on page 214.

- Heat a splash of oil in a large saucepan and fry the onion over a medium heat for 5 minutes or until soft and translucent
- Stir in the garlic and ginger, and cook for a further 2 minutes until fragrant
- Stir in the chopped parsnips and potato, bay leaves, thyme, cider, vegetable stock and ½ tsp salt. Bring to the boil, then cover and cook gently for 20-30 minutes until the vegetables are soft
- Remove the bay leaves, then blend the soup until smooth
- Serve with stilton cheese crumbled over the top, and some crusty bread

Equipment

Large saucepan

Blender

STARTERS AND LIGHT MEALS

Mushroom and White Wine Soup

Serves 4 — Prep time 10 minutes — Cook time 40 minutes — Difficulty ❶

Ingredients

200ml white wine

1 tbsp butter

400g mixed mushrooms (e.g. chestnut and button mushrooms) - sliced

120g fresh shiitake mushrooms - caps and stems sliced separately

2 white onions - finely chopped

1 tbsp plain flour

1L vegetable stock

1 tbsp light soy sauce

150ml milk

Salt and freshly ground black pepper

This simple mushroom soup is elevated with the gentle background note of white wine, and using a few types of mushrooms. Each variety of mushroom has a slightly different flavour - shiitake mushrooms have a complex buttery, meaty flavour, with a firm texture. This intensity comes from the delicious amino acid, glutamate, which occurs naturally in foods like shiitake mushrooms, soy sauce and parmesan cheese.

A full-bodied white wine, such as a buttery Chardonnay, will be the best partner for the savoury mushrooms, but feel free to use whatever wine you have available.

- Melt the butter in a large heavy bottomed pan, and stir in the chopped mushrooms and onions. Turn the heat to high and cook without stirring for 5 minutes until the mushrooms are turning a deep golden brown on one side. Stir well and then cook for a further 5-10 minutes, stirring occasionally, until the mushrooms are golden brown all over

- Turn the heat down low. Sprinkle the flour over the mushrooms and add a splash of the white wine, stirring well to de-glaze the pan and scrape up any brown bits from the bottom of the pan. Gradually add the rest of the wine, stirring as you go so that the flour is evenly incorporated, then add the vegetable stock and soy sauce

- Bring the soup to a boil and simmer uncovered for 15 minutes, then remove from the heat and stir in the milk

- Blend the soup until fairly smooth, but leaving a few chunks of mushroom

- Season with salt and freshly ground black pepper to taste, then serve

Equipment

Large heavy bottomed pan

Blender

Irish Onion Soup

Serves 4 — Prep time 15 minutes — Cook time 1 hour 20 minutes — Difficulty ❷

Ingredients

250ml stout

2 tbsp butter

8 large white onions (approx. 1.2kg) - thinly sliced

2 cloves of garlic - peeled, and crushed or finely chopped

1 tbsp white sugar

1 tbsp plain flour

800ml beef stock (or use 800ml vegetable stock plus 1 tbsp marmite)

2 tsp wholegrain mustard

1 tsp marmite or vegemite

200g strong cheddar cheese - grated

4 slices of crusty bread or baguette

Salt

Traditional French onion soup contains white wine and is topped with gruyère cheese. Our 'Irish' version uses ingredients that we are more likely to have at home - strong cheddar cheese, and a bottle of stout. We find that the creamy bitterness of stout pairs beautifully with the sweet caramelised onions and salty cheese.

The onions in this soup are caramelised for around 45 minutes until they are deep, rich brown with an incredible depth of flavour. It's a perfect dish for a chilly day - simply top with crusty bread and strong cheese, pop it under the grill, and enjoy.

- Melt the butter in a large deep saucepan. Add the onions then turn the heat up high and cook for 5 minutes, stirring occasionally, until the onions are browning around the edges
- Turn the heat down low, and stir in the garlic and sugar. Cook for a further 35-45 minutes without a lid on, stirring occasionally, until the onions are very soft, deep brown and fragrant. Don't be tempted to try and hurry this step, as slow, gentle caramelisation is vital to the sweet and rich flavour of the soup. If the pan starts to dry out before the onions are fully browned, add a splash of water
- Stir in the flour along with a splash of the stout, then slowly add the rest of the stout and the stock, scraping all the oniony bits off the bottom of the pan. Stir in the mustard, marmite and ½ tsp salt
- Put the lid on, bring the soup to a simmer and cook on a low heat for a further 15 minutes until slightly thickened
- Preheat the grill to high and arrange 4 soup bowls on a heatproof tray
- Divide the soup between the bowls and top each with a slice of crusty bread. Sprinkle liberally with the grated cheddar, then place the whole tray under the grill and cook until the cheese is golden and bubbly
- Serve immediately - **be careful not to burn yourself on the hot bowl!**

Equipment

Large deep saucepan

Grill (broiler)

Soup bowls

Heatproof tray

STARTERS AND LIGHT MEALS

Cheese Fondue Tear-and-Share Bread

Serves 4 as a starter — Prep time 15 minutes — Cook time 25 minutes — Difficulty ❶

Ingredients

125ml dry white wine

1 tbsp kirsch

1 loaf of crusty bread (approx. 400g)

1 tsp cornflour (cornstarch)

1 clove of garlic - peeled, and crushed or finely chopped

125g gruyère cheese - grated

125g emmental or edam cheese - grated

Freshly ground black pepper

A selection of cornichons, sweet pickled onions, fruit and cured meat to serve

Equipment

Foil

Small bowl

Medium saucepan

Whisk

Baking tray

This dish has all the distinctive flavours of classic Swiss cheese fondue in a delicious sharing bread showstopper - rich, savoury gruyère cheese is melted with zesty white wine and a hint of garlic, then slathered on crusty bread to be baked. It's quick to make, fun to eat, and perfect for a movie night or as a starter.

Wine is a key ingredient in a cheese fondue, as it helps to create the perfect smooth consistency. The acidity of white wine ensures that the cheese doesn't split, and this acidity also helps to balance the taste of salt and fat, making it incredibly moreish! You'll definitely taste the wine here, so make sure it's one you like (it's ok if the bottle has been open for a while). Kirsch is a traditional ingredient in fondue, but you can substitute it for brandy or vodka.

You can prepare this bread a few hours ahead of time if needed - just wrap the cheesy bread in foil and store in the fridge, then bake when you're ready.

- Preheat the oven to 180C / Gas Mark 4 / 350F, and prepare a piece of foil that's large enough to wrap your bread up completely - you may need to crimp two pieces of foil together into a square

- Carefully slice the bread into thick 2cm / 1 inch slices in both directions, cutting almost all the way through but not quite, so that you have a grid with all the squares joined together at the bottom. Place the bread in the centre of the foil

- In a small bowl, mix the cornflour with a splash of wine to make a smooth, runny paste

- Put the wine and garlic into a medium saucepan, and cook on a low heat until nearly boiling. Whisk in the cornflour paste and then stir in the grated cheeses, heating gently until melted and smooth

- Add the kirsch and a generous grinding of black pepper, stir well, then remove the pan from the heat

- Carefully spoon about two thirds of the sauce between the slices in the bread - it's worth taking time to be thorough so that each bite comes out cheesy. Spoon the remaining mixture over the top of the bread

- Wrap the foil around the bread to cover it completely, then place it on a baking tray and bake for 15 minutes. Unwrap the top of the foil and place the partly-wrapped bread back in the oven for a further 10 minutes until the top is crisp and golden

- Serve with a selection of cornichons, sweet pickled onions, fruit and cured meat

COOKING WITH ALCOHOL

STARTERS AND LIGHT MEALS

Tequila Fish Tacos with Pink Onions

*Serves 4 as a starter or 2 as a main — Prep time 25 minutes — Cook time 15 minutes
Difficulty ❷*

Ingredients

4 tsp silver tequila

250g of white firm-fleshed fish fillets (eg. haddock or basa) - sliced into fingers approx. 1cm (½ inch) wide

1 red onion - thinly sliced

1 avocado - stoned, peeled and roughly chopped

2 tomatoes - diced

2 limes - 1 ½ juiced, ½ sliced into wedges

A small bunch of fresh coriander (cilantro) (approx. 10g) - leaves picked and roughly chopped

½ tsp chilli powder

4 small flour tortillas

Sugar

Salt and freshly ground black pepper

Oil

Equipment

Small saucepan

Small bowls for the taco toppings

Large mixing bowl

Frying pan

Tacos are a great way to start a meal - everyone can get stuck in choosing their own toppings, which takes away any formality, and the vibrant flavours and textures make them a delight to eat. To make these tacos, white fish is seasoned simply with tequila and lime before frying it on a high heat. It's paired with a South American side dish of tangy pink onions known as cebollas encurtidas, which are really simple to make and so pretty. Red onions are boiled quickly to take away the bitterness, then the addition of tequila, salt and lime turns them bright pink.

Silver tequila has a bright and strong flavour of agave, which is a great partner for citrus and spice - you'll only need a little bit so that the flavour doesn't overwhelm the dish. Tequila gets mellower and sweeter as it is aged, so an older, darker colored reposado or añejo tequila would be better paired elsewhere with subtler flavours.

For the taco toppings

- Bring a small pan of water to the boil. Add the sliced onion, boil for 2 minutes then drain. Rinse the onion with cold water and drain again

- Scoop the drained onion into a bowl and stir in the juice of 1 lime, 2 tsp tequila, the chilli powder, a large pinch of sugar and 2 large pinches of salt. Leave to one side for at least 15 minutes to marinate

- Separately, prepare small bowls each of chopped avocado, diced tomato and chopped coriander

For the fish

- In a large mixing bowl combine the juice of ½ a lime, 2 tsp tequila, ½ tsp salt and a good grinding of black pepper. Stir in the sliced fish to coat in the liquid and seasoning

- Heat a frying pan over a high heat and add a splash of oil. Fry the fish for 5 minutes until golden brown, turning half way, then remove from the pan

Bringing it together

- Carefully toast the tortillas for a few minutes over a gas hob or in a dry frying pan, turning occasionally, until lightly browned. Cover with a plate or foil to keep warm and soft

- To build the tacos, spoon about a quarter of the fish onto each warm tortilla. Top with a spoonful of the pink onions and a sprinkling of chopped avocado, tomato and coriander

- Serve with extra lime wedges

STARTERS AND LIGHT MEALS

Tempura Aubergine with Unagi Sake Sauce

Serves 4 as a starter — Prep time 25 minutes — Cook time 25 minutes — Difficulty ❸

Ingredients

200ml chilled lager

80ml sake (30ml for the sauce, 50ml for the batter)

60ml light soy sauce

60ml mirin

35g white sugar

2 tsp rice wine vinegar (or substitute cider or white wine vinegar)

1 egg yolk

120g plain flour + 4 tbsp

80g cornflour (cornstarch)

2 medium aubergines (approx. 700g total) - de-stalked and sliced into long strips about ½ cm (¼ inch) thick

500ml vegetable or sunflower oil

Salt

Equipment

Small saucepan

Large bowl

Sieve

Shallow dish

A wide deep saucepan e.g. stock pot, or a deep fryer

Food thermometer (optional, but very helpful)

Slotted spoon

Metal draining rack or kitchen roll

Tempura is a Japanese method of frying vegetables or seafood in a light, crispy batter - and it's incredibly delicious! Here we're serving the crisp tempura aubergine with an *unagi* sauce made with soy, mirin and sake for a rich sticky flavour. Unagi sauce is usually served with freshwater eel (unagi), but it also pairs beautifully here with aubergine.

The key to great tempura is in the batter - mix the batter as little as possible to keep the texture light. The bubbles in chilled lager or sparkling water help to keep the batter crisp, while the alcohol in sake helps avoid chewy gluten formation. You can also use this method for frying king prawns, thin slices of courgette or other summer veg.

Some tips on deep frying

A food thermometer is helpful for maintaining the right oil temperature. If the temperature is too high, the outside of the food will cook faster than the inside, but if it's too low, the batter will absorb some oil so the aubergine will taste a little oily. If you don't have a food thermometer, drop a tiny bit of the batter into the oil when you think it's hot enough - the batter should sizzle and fry immediately. If the oil starts to smoke, turn it off.

Don't leave the room while you're cooking, as hot oil can be dangerous.

For the unagi sauce
- Combine the soy sauce, mirin, sugar, rice wine vinegar and 30ml of the sake in a small saucepan. Cook over a low heat for 10 minutes until the sauce has reduced by half and coats the back of a spoon. Set to one side

For the aubergine
- To make the batter, lightly beat the egg yolk in a bowl then sift over 120g plain flour, the cornflour and 2 pinches of salt. Whisk in the chilled lager and remaining 50ml sake until the batter is barely combined (it's ok if there are a few lumps), then place the batter in the fridge until you are ready to start frying

- In a shallow dish, toss the aubergine slices in 4 tbsp plain flour until they are lightly coated on both sides

- Fill a wide deep saucepan with 500ml of oil, making sure the saucepan is no more than ⅓ full

- Heat the oil until it reaches 180C / 350F, and take your batter out of the fridge

COOKING WITH ALCOHOL

- Dip a few slices of aubergine into the batter then place gently into the hot oil - be careful to avoid splashing. Fry for about a minute on each side, turning with a slotted spoon, until the batter is pale golden brown and crispy all over. Remove from the oil and drain on a rack or kitchen roll, fishing out any little bits of batter from the oil
- Ensure that the oil returns to 180C / 350F before frying the next batch of aubergine
- Serve the tempura aubergine with a small bowl of the unagi sake sauce for dipping or drizzling

TIP: Serve leftover unagi sauce with sushi rice and a fried egg for a simple dinner. It's worth making the sauce on its own, even if you don't fancy deep frying - it's a fridge staple for us, and keeps very well

STARTERS AND LIGHT MEALS

Bloody Mary Prawn Cocktail

Serves 4 as a starter — Prep time 15 mins — Cook time 20 mins — Difficulty ❶

Ingredients

1 tbsp vodka

150g mayonnaise

½-1 tsp tabasco sauce (depending on how spicy you want it!)

1 tsp horseradish sauce or fresh grated horseradish

1 ½ tsp Worcestershire sauce

2 tsp tomato paste

1 lemon - ¼ juiced for the sauce, ¾ sliced into wedges to garnish

12 cherry tomatoes - 4 very finely chopped for the sauce, 8 halved to garnish

2 sticks of celery - chopped into finger-length sticks

250g raw shelled king prawns (frozen and defrosted are fine)

½ tsp celery salt (or substitute with ¼ tsp table salt)

½ tsp chilli flakes

2 tsp butter

Freshly ground black pepper

In Susannah's family, prawn cocktail is a Christmas celebratory favourite. While the traditional recipe of sweet prawns in Marie Rose sauce has stood the test of time, our version of this elegant starter is enhanced with the addition of alcohol. Here, we're frying the prawns in spices and serving them hot alongside a Bloody Mary sauce. This creates a delicious contrast of texture and temperature - and with the addition of tabasco, black pepper, horseradish and vodka, there's a definite kick to it! It's the perfect way to begin a festive meal.

There's only a small amount of vodka in the sauce, but the spiciness makes the flavour more noticeable than you'd think - make sure to taste it before you add any extra vodka!

- Combine the vodka, mayonnaise, tabasco, horseradish, tomato paste, 1 tsp worcestershire sauce and a good grinding of black pepper in a small bowl. Mix well, then stir in the lemon juice and the finely chopped cherry tomatoes
- Divide the celery sticks and halved tomatoes between 4 small bowls or ramekins. Add a large dollop of the sauce and a wedge of lemon alongside
- Pat the prawns dry with kitchen roll, then sprinkle them with the celery salt, chilli flakes, ½ tsp Worcestershire sauce and a good grind of black pepper
- Heat a frying pan over a high heat and melt the butter until sizzling. Add the prawns and fry for around 3 minutes, turning once or twice, until the prawns are cooked through and browning
- Remove the pan from the heat, divide the prawns between the bowls, then serve immediately

Equipment

Small mixing bowl

4 small serving bowls or ramekins

Kitchen roll

Frying pan

STARTERS AND LIGHT MEALS

Chicken and Brandy Pâté

Serves 4 as a starter — Prep time 10 minutes — Cook time 30 minutes + chilling time
Difficulty ❸

Ingredients

50ml + 1 tbsp brandy

170g + 2 tbsp salted butter

½ a white onion - finely chopped

1 tsp dried thyme

½ tsp dried sage

400g chicken liver - chopped into bite size pieces

1 tsp dijon mustard

A small bunch of fresh chives (approx. 5g) - finely chopped

Salt and freshly ground black pepper

Sourdough toast or seeded crackers, and cornichon pickles to serve

Equipment

Frying pan

Large bowl

Immersion blender or food processor

Small saucepan

4 small bowls or ramekins

Chicken liver pâté is a low-cost starter that's perfect for a celebratory meal or when entertaining. The inclusion of alcohol in pâté is traditional, and is one of the reasons that pâté can be so flavourful - the volatile compounds of alcohol help to carry flavours to the tastebuds. It's rich, luxurious, and ideal for having guests over because it has to be made in advance.

In fact, pâté is better made at least a day ahead of time. When aromatic ingredients like onion and brandy are heated they release flavourful aromas and compounds, and these compounds interact with the proteins in the meat. Over time, the dish develops a deeper, richer and more rounded flavour profile - mellow, lightly fruity flavours from the brandy with a warming hint of mustard and pepper. Once prepared and topped with butter, the pâté will last for 3 to 4 days in the fridge.

It's surprisingly easy to make pâté - simply fry the ingredients and blend them together. It's not very attractive while you're making it, but the smooth, creamy texture and brandy butter topping looks great in the end! Serve as a starter with crackers or buttered toast, or with a leafy salad for a light supper.

- Melt 1 tbsp butter in a frying pan and fry the onion, thyme and sage over a low heat for 5-10 minutes until the onion is soft. Tip the onion out of the frying pan into a large bowl

- In the same pan, melt a further 1 tbsp butter. Turn the heat up and fry the chicken liver on high for 5 minutes, stirring occasionally, until brown on the outside but still pink in the middle (you may need to do this in batches). Tip the liver out into the bowl with the onions

- Pour 50ml brandy into the empty frying pan and stir for a minute, scraping the bottom to de-glaze the pan. Add this all to the liver and onions along with 120g butter, the mustard, most of the chives (reserving a few to use as a garnish), and a pinch each of salt and pepper

- With an immersion blender or food processor, blend the liver and onion mixture to a smooth texture. Scoop it into small bowls or ramekins, smoothing down the top with the back of a spoon, and leave to cool for at least 10 minutes

- Melt the remaining 50g butter in a small saucepan and stir in 1 tbsp brandy. Spoon this over the pâté and sprinkle with the remaining chopped chives, then cover the ramekins and place in the fridge to chill for at least 3 hours or overnight

- Serve the pâté with sourdough toast or crackers, and cornichon pickles

COOKING WITH ALCOHOL

STARTERS AND LIGHT MEALS

Mussels in Stout, Bacon and Whisky

Serves 4 as a starter or 2 as a main — Prep time 20 minutes — Cook time 15 minutes
Difficulty ❷

Ingredients

150ml stout

40ml whisky

750g fresh mussels

2 tbsp butter

1 white onion - finely chopped

150g smoked bacon or lardons - finely chopped

1 clove of garlic - peeled, and crushed or finely chopped

150ml single (light) cream

A small bunch of fresh parsley (approx. 10g) - leaves picked and finely chopped

Salt

Crusty bread and lemon wedges to serve

Mussels always look elegant and sophisticated, so it's easy to forget that they are really very simple to cook. It takes less than 5 minutes for them to steam open, and they are one of the most affordable and environmentally friendly seafoods available.

Creamy, briny mussels hold their own amongst other bold flavours, so the malty bitterness of stout is a great partner. Swirled together with rich cream, lots of smoky bacon, fresh parsley and a hint of warming whisky, these mussels are visually impressive and truly delicious. Serve with lots of crusty bread for dipping in the sauce - and if you're serving these as a main, some skinny fries wouldn't go astray.

- To prepare the mussels, empty them into a large bowl and rinse well under cold water. Check for any mussels that aren't quite closed - give them a squeeze or a sharp tap, and if they don't close up discard them. You should also discard any with broken shells

- Pull off any beards from the mussels (fibrous hairy bits), and use a small knife to scrape off any large barnacles. Rinse the mussels again and you're ready to cook!

- Melt the butter in a large lidded pan, then add the onion, bacon and garlic. Cook over a medium heat for 5 minutes, stirring frequently, until the onion has softened

- Add the stout and ½ tsp salt and bring the mixture to a boil

- Add the mussels to the pan, stir well then put the lid on and turn the heat up high. Once the pan starts steaming, lower the heat to medium and cook for 4-5 minutes, shaking the pan occasionally, until the mussel shells have opened. If any remain closed, discard them

- Remove the pan from the heat and stir in the cream, whisky and chopped parsley, then divide between bowls. Top with a squeeze of lemon and serve with plenty of crusty bread for dipping

Equipment

Large bowl

Large lidded pan

STARTERS AND LIGHT MEALS

RED WINE FOCACCIA, PAGE 220

CHORIZO IN RED WINE AND HONEY, PAGE 18

SHALLOTS GLAZED IN WHITE WINE, PAGE 124

CHICKEN WITH BRANDY AND APRICOTS, PAGE 54

MAINS

Slow Cooked

Beef and Ale Stew with Ale Dumplings	50
Bourbon Brined Beef Short Ribs	52
Chicken with Brandy and Apricots	54
Coq au Cidre	56
Dark Beer and Aubergine Chilli	58
Lamb, Gin and Juniper Stew	60

Roasted and Grilled

Mojito Chicken	64
Rickard Family Jägermeister Chicken	66
Sweet and Spicy Tequila Lime Pork	68
Trout with Dill and Ouzo	70
Sangria Chicken	72

Pan Fried

Philly Cheese Steak with Beer Sauce	78
Salmon with Cava Sauce and Crushed Lemon Potatoes	80
Sticky Cider Sausages with Mustard Mash	82
Tequila and Habanero Salmon with Salsa Fresca and Black Beans	84
Dark Rum and Orange Pork Chops	86

Pasta and Rice

Port Pesto with Rigatoni	92
Fennel and White Wine Tagliatelle	94
Mushroom and Sherry Pasta	96
Tomato, Gin and Rosemary Pasta	98
Cheddar and Stout Risotto	100
Chicken, Amaretto and Saffron Biryani	102
Red Wine Risotto with Roasted Aubergine	104

Pies and Pastry

Mushroom and Stout Pasties	108
Parsnip and Cider Tarte Tatin	110
White Wine Chicken Pot Pie	112

The recipes in this chapter are very much the kinds of food we enjoy cooking at home. There are simple and elegant dishes, perfect for weeknight dinners or low-effort guests, that use simple cooking techniques to elevate the flavours and textures - our velvety rich **Cava Sauce** will make a simple dinner of salmon or chicken feel instantly fancier.

Some dishes in this chapter are classics, reinvented here with deliciously enhanced flavours from the inclusion of alcohol - the **Dark Beer and Aubergine Chilli** has a richness and umami flavour rarely found in a vegetarian chilli, while a sticky cider onion gravy in the **Sticky Cider Sausages with Mustard Mash** gets the very best from sausages.

There are amazing slow-cooked centrepieces for Sunday lunch or a family gathering, like the **White Wine Chicken Pot Pie**. Finally, there are casual meals, to feed an informal crowd, like the **Rickard Family Jägermeister Chicken**. There are a mix of vegetarian and non-vegetarian recipes, and we give veggie substitutions where suitable.

Many of the techniques in this chapter will be familiar, such as roasting a chicken or making a stew, and in every recipe alcohol is a key flavour component. However, the way that we incorporate alcohol into the dish varies depending on how it is cooked. In this chapter we have organised the recipes by their technique, split into five short sections.

Slow Cooked
Slow cooked meals are a natural place to introduce alcohol, where gentle simmering allows the liquid to impart rich, deep flavour into meat and vegetables. In this way, we can use alcohol to introduce deeper and more complex flavours into a dish - whether that's the herbal gin notes in the **Lamb, Gin and Juniper Stew** or the fragrant and tangy sauce of the **Coq au Cidre**, chicken in cider. During slow cooking, the aromatic compounds from the ingredients and the alcohol will mingle for a truly spectacular result. The flavours will continue to develop over time, which makes these dishes ideal for preparing in advance.

Roasted and Grilled
The added sugar in a glaze - sugar, honey or citrus juice - will caramelise in these roasted and grilled recipes, creating delicious sticky sauces that coat the meat in flavour. We love to add a splash of stronger alcohol like a spirit, in smaller quantities, to add maximum flavour impact here!

Fragrance is a big part of how our brains perceive flavour, so a dipping sauce or drizzle added after cooking are great finishing touches for a roasted or grilled dish - like the rum and lime drizzle on the herb-roasted

Mojito Chicken. The volatile alcohols and essential oils from fresh herbs can begin to evaporate with the warmth, and this evaporation carries the vibrant, fresh aromas of the dish to your nose, increasing the perception of the flavour.

Pan Fried

Much like roasted or grilled recipes, pan fried recipes involve a fast and direct transfer of heat from the pan to the food. Pan frying is best when not too much liquid is present, as the presence of water can prevent the Maillard reaction happening (when the surface of meat caramelises and turns deliciously golden brown). For the best results it helps to have a fairly dry surface, giving a more efficient sear for greater depth of flavour. So, as with roasted or grilled recipes, a marinade, glaze or sauce will coat the freshly cooked food in flavour - this is where we introduce alcohol.

These delicious dishes are quick to cook and are best prepared fresh, although saucy elements like the sticky glaze for the **Dark Rum and Orange Pork Chops** can be prepared ahead of time.

Pasta and Rice

It was fascinating creating these pasta and rice recipes because of the amazing flavours that can be added from one carefully matched alcoholic ingredient - they are a perfect example of how a dish can be so much more than the sum of its parts. The zestiness of Sauvignon Blanc adds a wonderful freshness to the **Fennel and White Wine Tagliatelle**, while the malty, hoppy sweetness of stout is the perfect partner for sharp cheese in a warming **Cheddar and Stout Risotto**.

Rice and pasta absorb liquid as they cook, so in the risotto dishes in particular we have chosen to use alcohol with a lower proof, and added a little water as well, to prevent overwhelming the flavour of everything else.

Pies and Pastry

We've put together a selection of our favourite recipes for hearty and warming pie fillings. In the **Parsnip and Cider Tarte Tatin**, the caramelisation of the sugars from the cider and parsnips creates a deep, rich and earthy flavour that's perfect for an autumnal feast. Meanwhile, the potato and barley in the hearty **Mushroom and Stout Pasties** absorb the dark stout as they cook, resulting in rich and savoury pastries that will tempt vegetarians and meat-eaters alike. All of these dishes can be made ahead of time, then reheated in the oven for crisp and perfect pastry.

MAINS
SLOW COOKED

Beef & Ale Stew with Ale Dumplings

Serves 4 — Prep time 20 minutes for stew + 10 minutes for dumplings
Cook time 2 hours 30 minutes — Difficulty ❷

Ingredients

380ml ale or dark beer

Salt and freshly ground black pepper

For the stew

400g stewing beef - chopped into bite size pieces

2 medium white onions - chopped into bite size pieces

3 medium carrots - trimmed, peeled and thickly sliced

100g white or chestnut mushrooms - roughly chopped

1 x 400g can of chopped tomatoes

2 tbsp tomato paste

1 tbsp worcester sauce

2 tsp marmite, vegemite or bovril (or a beef stock cube)

1 tsp dried tarragon (or mixed herbs)

1 tsp dried thyme

For the dumplings

100g cold salted butter

200g self-raising flour (or 200g plain flour + 2 tsp baking powder)

Equipment

Large lidded ovenproof dish (e.g. a dutch oven)

Large mixing bowl

This is a well-loved dish in our house, cooked more than once a month. It takes just minutes to put the stew together and requires very little attention while it cooks in the oven. The long cooking time softens the beef until it's ready to fall apart, and the end result is so delicious that it's not only a Wednesday evening favourite but also a dinner-for-friends staple.

We suggest using a full-flavoured ale here - nothing too citrusy or bitter but with plenty of hearty flavour, such as an amber ale, as this forms a large part of the gravy around the meat and vegetables. The dumplings are really worth it, and they also help to thicken up the stew, but if you don't have time you could serve the stew with mash, peas or crusty bread.

For the stew

- Preheat the oven to 170C / Gas Mark 4 / 350F
- Place all the stew ingredients in a large ovenproof dish together with 1 tsp salt, ½ tsp ground black pepper and 300ml of the ale (saving 80ml of ale for later). Mix it roughly together - don't worry about being thorough, as it'll be easier to stir once it has cooked for a while
- Put the lid on and place the stew in the oven for an hour and a half, stirring once after 30 minutes
- Remove the lid, stir, and cook uncovered for a further 20 minutes, allowing the stew to reduce

For the dumplings

- Once the lid has been removed from the stew, put the flour in a bowl along with a large pinch each of salt and pepper, then rub in the cold butter until roughly the texture of breadcrumbs
- Add the remaining 80ml ale a splash at a time, mixing together gently by hand until it just comes together into a soft dough. If it's too sticky add a little more flour, or if it's too dry add a little more ale or water. Try not to overmix it, as this will make the dumplings tough
- Take small pieces of dough and roll them by hand into balls about 3cm (1 inch) in diameter - you'll have approximately 15-20 dumplings in total
- Place the dumplings on top of the stew and put the lid back on. Cook covered for 20 minutes then uncovered for a further 15-20 minutes until the dumplings are rich golden brown on top and the stew is bubbling up around the edges
- Allow the stew to cool for at least 5 minutes before serving

TIP: We love using beef cheek in this recipe, if you can find it at the butcher! The tendons in beef cheek melt deliciously when cooked slowly in the oven, resulting in a rich and tender stew

COOKING WITH ALCOHOL

MAINS — SLOW COOKED

Bourbon Brined Beef Short Ribs

Serves 6 — Prep time 30 minutes + 3-12 hours brining — Cook time 4 hours — Difficulty ❸

Ingredients

50ml + 1 tbsp bourbon

2 tsp smoked paprika

2 tbsp Worcestershire sauce

3 garlic cloves - peeled, and crushed or finely chopped

2-3 beef short ribs (approx. 2kg total) - chopped into large pieces

3 white onions - thinly sliced

2 tbsp dark brown sugar

3 tbsp ketchup

1 tsp dijon mustard

1 tsp cider vinegar

Salt and freshly ground black pepper

Equipment

Large resealable food bag (or a very large bowl)

Large lidded ovenproof dish (e.g. a dutch oven)

2 x small bowls

Beef ribs have an intense savoury flavour that most beef dishes only dream of achieving, though they take some time to cook. The more a muscle has worked, the more flavourful it will be, and ribs do a lot of work! The meat around ribs has a lot of tough connective tissues, and during a long slow cook these break down for a rich, melt in the mouth texture.

Beef short ribs are a cut of meat most often seen in a Texan BBQ smokehouse, but at home it's easier to braise them in the oven. In this recipe, we are brining the ribs in a salty bourbon mixture for a few hours to tenderise and relax some of the muscle proteins, which helps to season the meat throughout while also creating juicier meat when cooked. The meat is then braised on a bed of onions, which caramelise in the bourbon and beef drippings to make a soft and sweet sauce.

Serve with buttery mash and lemony green beans to offset the richness, and with a hearty dollop of the caramelised onions.

- To make the brine, combine 50ml bourbon with the smoked paprika, Worcestershire sauce, garlic, plenty of fresh ground black pepper and 1 tsp salt per kg of beef ribs

- Put the beef ribs into a large resealable food bag and pour in all the brine. Remove as much air as possible then seal the bag and place in the fridge for at least 3 hours or overnight, turning every few hours to ensure the ribs are well coated in the brine

- When nearly ready to cook, preheat the oven to 160C / Gas Mark 3 / 325F

- In a small bowl, mix together the chopped onions with the brown sugar and 2 tbsp of the ketchup, and spread this mixture across the bottom of your ovenproof dish. Lay the beef ribs bone side down on top of the onions, pour the brine over the top and add a generous grinding of fresh black pepper

- Put the lid on then cook in the oven for 4 hours, or until the meat is tender throughout and falling off the bone, basting the ribs every 30 minutes with the liquid. If it starts to look dry, add a splash of water or bourbon. After a few hours, most of the fat should have rendered out of the beef and the meat will be soft enough to pull apart with a fork

- Transfer the ribs to a serving dish. Use a ladle to remove a bit of the excess fat from the onions - the amount of fat will vary depending on the short ribs

- Scoop the caramelised onions out of the pan and into a bowl. Stir in the mustard, vinegar, 1 tbsp bourbon and 1 tbsp ketchup

- Serve the beef ribs with a dollop of the caramelised onions on the side, and greens and creamy mash

TIP: Beef ribs can be tricky to find in the store but you can usually get them from a butcher

TIP: The more a muscle works, the more intense flavour it will have and the better it is when slow cooked. This applies to most meats, for example chicken legs have more intense flavour compared to chicken breasts, and lend themselves to longer cooking

MAINS — SLOW COOKED

Chicken with Brandy and Apricots

Serves 4 — Prep time 20 minutes — Cook time 1 hour — Difficulty ❷

Ingredients

100ml brandy

150g dried apricots - roughly chopped

2 tbsp cider or white wine vinegar

4 skin-on, bone-in chicken legs or 6-8 large chicken thighs

2 tbsp plain flour

1 white onion - thinly sliced

2 cloves of garlic - peeled, and crushed or finely chopped

250ml chicken stock

Salt and freshly ground black pepper

Oil

Mashed potato, rice or grains to serve

This is real crowd-pleasing comfort food, ideally suited to cooler weather. It's quick to put together, too, and can easily be scaled up to feed more people.

Warming, oaky brandy is in its element in a thick and sticky sauce of dried apricots, balanced out with a little tangy vinegar. We used to flambé the brandy in this dish, until we decided that risking a house fire doesn't do anything for the flavour!

Searing the chicken before cooking enhances the flavour, as the proteins and sugars in the meat begin to caramelise in the pan. We suggest using chicken legs or thighs here, as dark meat has a deeper flavour and stands up well to slow cooking without getting dry. Serve on pillowy mashed potato, or a bed of rice or grains.

- Combine ¾ of the chopped apricots with the vinegar and 1 tsp salt in a blender. Blend to a coarse paste so that there's still some texture (add a splash of the chicken stock if needed to help it blend)
- Pat the chicken legs dry with kitchen roll, then put them in a large bowl and sprinkle with the flour and a large pinch each of salt and pepper, turning to coat evenly
- Heat a splash of oil in a large lidded pan until very hot and just beginning to smoke, then carefully place the floured chicken in the pan. Cook on a high heat for 8-10 minutes, turning occasionally, until the chicken is well browned all over
- Turn the heat down low, then stir in the sliced onion and cook for a few minutes to soften. Pour in the brandy and simmer for a few more minutes to de-glaze the pan, scraping the bottom to get up any crispy bits
- Stir in the garlic, chicken stock, the blended apricots and the rest of the chopped apricots. Put the lid on and cook over a low heat for 20 minutes, then remove the lid, turn the chicken pieces over and simmer for a further 20 minutes to allow the sauce to thicken
- Cook your potatoes or rice now
- Serve the chicken with mashed potato or rice, and a generous dollop of the sticky apricot sauce from the pan

Equipment

Blender

Kitchen roll

Large bowl

Large lidded pan

MAINS — SLOW COOKED

Coq au Cidre

Serves 4 — Prep time 30 minutes — Cook time 1 hour 30 minutes — Difficulty ❷

Ingredients

400ml apple cider

2 tbsp plain flour

2 tbsp butter

800g bone-in, skin-on chicken thighs

150g smoked bacon - roughly chopped

1 tbsp dijon mustard

1 chicken stock cube

2 white onions - sliced into 6 or 8 wedges

2 leeks - cleaned, trimmed and thickly sliced

3 garlic cloves - peeled, and crushed or finely chopped

2 carrots - scrubbed, trimmed and thickly sliced

1 large cooking apple - peeled, cored and chopped into bite size pieces

Salt and freshly ground black pepper

Mashed potato or crusty bread to serve

Equipment

Large bowl

Large lidded ovenproof dish

Heavy bottomed frying pan (if your ovenproof dish can also be used on the stovetop, you can skip the frying pan and cook this all in one pot)

Kitchen roll

This dish began its life as our Somerset rendition of coq au vin, the classic French dish of chicken cooked in red wine. Swapping the red wine for cider and apples, traditional ingredients of South West England, produces a sauce with a gentle, mellow sweetness which pairs beautifully with the slow-cooked chicken and smoky bacon. It's a hearty, rustic dish, requiring minimal effort for maximum reward.

After searing the meat the coq au cidre is transferred to the oven. Here the sugars in the cider begin to caramelise together with the other ingredients, softening the leeks and carrots in the most meltingly delicious way. Cooking in the oven provides a consistent temperature for this, and means that you don't need to pay constant attention to it!

- Preheat the oven to 170C / Gas Mark 3 ½ / 350F
- Pat the chicken pieces dry with kitchen roll, then put them in a large bowl and sprinkle with salt, pepper and flour. Turn to coat evenly in the flour
- Heat a heavy bottomed frying pan (or large ovenproof dish) on the stove and, when very hot, add the butter in the pan to melt. Carefully place the floured chicken in the pan, skin side down, and cook over a high heat for 5 minutes, turning once or twice
- Stir in the bacon and cook for a further 5 minutes until the chicken and bacon are well-browned all over
- Turn off the heat and pour in the cider, scraping the bottom as you stir to capture any crispy bits, and then stir in the dijon mustard, a crumbled chicken stock cube and ½ tsp salt
- If the pan you're using is not ovenproof, transfer the stew into a large lidded ovenproof dish, together with the chopped onions, leeks, garlic, carrots and apple. Place in the oven to cook for 1 hour, stirring halfway through
- After 1 hour, turn the oven down to 160C / Gas Mark 3 / 325F. Remove the lid and give the stew a stir. Scoop the chicken pieces up on the top of the vegetables, skin side up - this will help the skin get crisp. Return to the oven without a lid, and cook for a final 25 minutes to allow the chicken skin to brown and the sauce to thicken
- If you're serving the coq au cidre with mashed potato, put the potatoes on to boil now
- Once the sauce has reduced and the chicken is brown and crisp, remove the pan from the oven and let it stand for five minutes before serving
- Serve with mashed potato or crusty bread to mop up the sauce

COOKING WITH ALCOHOL

MAINS — SLOW COOKED

Dark Beer and Aubergine Chilli

Serves 4 — Prep time 15 minutes — Cook time 1 hour 45 minutes — Difficulty ❶

Ingredients

400ml dark beer (e.g. ale, porter or stout)

1 medium aubergine (approx. 350g) - de-stalked and chopped into 1cm cubes

2 white onions - finely chopped

2 cloves of garlic - peeled, and crushed or finely chopped

1 tsp chilli powder

1 tsp dried oregano

1 tsp ground cumin

1 tsp ground cinnamon

2 tsp smoked paprika

1 x 400g can of kidney beans - drained and rinsed

1 x 400g can of black beans - drained and rinsed

2 tbsp tomato paste

1 x 400g jar of tomato passata (or a can of chopped tomatoes, blended until smooth)

1 medium sweet potato (approx. 300g) - peeled and chopped into 1cm cubes

2 tbsp dark brown sugar

1 lime - ½ juiced, ½ sliced into wedges to serve

Salt

Oil

Grated cheese, sour cream, fresh coriander and tortilla chips, taco shells or rice to serve

Equipment

Large deep heavy-bottomed pan

Aaron had a firm belief that a vegetarian chilli wouldn't be tasty - but this one convinced him otherwise. A great chilli should be thick and hearty, with a rich texture and well-balanced flavours and spices. Here, aubergine is first browned to develop smoky charred flavour, then slow-cooked until it absolutely melts in the mouth. Dark beer adds a deep rich flavour with hints of chocolate, while sweet potato and a little brown sugar helps to round out the hoppy notes.

It can seem like Mexican food contains a huge quantity of spices, but each spice balances out the others so that no one flavour overwhelms. Serve this delicious one-pot dish with your favourite chilli toppings, and alongside tortilla chips, taco shells or rice.

- Heat 1 tbsp oil in a large deep heavy bottomed pan until very hot and the oil is beginning to smoke. Add the chopped aubergine and cook on a high heat, stirring occasionally, for 10 minutes until the aubergines are browned all over and beginning to soften. Remove them from the pan and set to one side

- Turn the heat down to medium, add another splash of oil to the pan and fry the chopped onions for 5 minutes until beginning to soften. Stir in the garlic, chilli powder, oregano, cumin, cinnamon and smoked paprika, and cook for another 2 minutes until the spices are fragrant

- Stir in the kidney beans, black beans, tomato paste, tomato passata, chopped sweet potato, brown sugar, the beer, 1 tsp of salt and the cooked aubergine

- Bring the mixture to the boil, then turn the heat down low and simmer uncovered for about 1 ½ hours, stirring occasionally, until the sweet potato is soft and the sauce is rich and thick. If it starts to get too dry, add a splash of water or beer

- Stir in the juice of ½ a lime, then taste the chilli and add more salt or lime juice to your preference

- Serve with your favourite chilli toppings and sides, with a wedge of lime

MAINS — SLOW COOKED

Lamb, Gin and Juniper Stew

Serves 4 — Prep time 30 minutes — Cook time 1 hour 30 minutes — Difficulty ❷

Ingredients

80ml gin

500g stewing lamb (e.g. leg or shoulder) - chopped into bite size pieces

3 tbsp plain flour

500ml lamb or beef stock

2 large white onions - each sliced into 8 wedges

250g button or chestnut mushrooms - halved or quartered

2 cloves of garlic - peeled, and crushed or finely chopped

1 tbsp juniper berries - crushed in a pestle and mortar, or with the flat of a chef's knife

1 tbsp tomato paste

2 bay leaves

1 tsp dried rosemary (or a sprig of fresh rosemary)

150g blackberries (fresh or frozen)

2 tsp balsamic vinegar

Salt and freshly ground black pepper

Oil

Crusty bread to serve and parsley to garnish

Lamb is an excellent stewing meat, and in this recipe we've paired it with gin, juniper and blackberries. The sharp, clear notes from the gin and juniper balance the rich fats of the lamb for a warming meal with a hint of fruity fragrance.

Juniper berries are best known as the predominant flavouring in gin, but they can also be used in cooking. These purple-blue berries have been used for centuries in Scandinavian and German cuisine, where their sharp, piney fragrance is often used with strong flavours like gamey meats. A glass of chilled sloe gin would be a delightful accompaniment to this meal.

- Sprinkle the lamb pieces with a large pinch each of salt and pepper and 1 tbsp of the flour, turning to coat in the flour
- Heat a large splash of oil in a large lidded pan until very hot and, when just beginning to smoke, add the floured lamb. Sear on a high heat for 5 minutes, stirring occasionally until the lamb is well browned
- Turn the heat down then slowly pour the stock into the pan, scraping the bottom to de-glaze the pan and get up any crispy bits. Stir in 40ml of the gin, the onions, mushrooms, garlic, crushed juniper berries, tomato paste, bay leaves, rosemary and 1 tsp salt. Put the lid on and cook over a low heat for 1 hour, stirring halfway through
- After an hour has passed, mix the remaining 2 tbsp flour with a splash of the stewing liquid in a small bowl, adding a little more stewing liquid to make a smooth and runny paste. Stir the paste into the stew, followed by the blackberries, balsamic vinegar and the remaining 40ml gin
- Cook without the lid on for a further 30 minutes, stirring occasionally, until the meat is tender, the stew has thickened and the blackberries have begun to break down into the sauce
- Remove the bay leaves and sprinkle with parsley to serve, with crusty bread on the side

Equipment

Large lidded pan

Small bowl

MAINS — SLOW COOKED

MAINS
ROASTED AND GRILLED

Mojito Chicken

Serves 4-6 — Prep time 35 minutes — Cook time 1 hour + 15 minutes resting
Difficulty ❷

Ingredients

100ml white rum

1 large whole chicken (approx. 2kg)

2 tbsp butter

2 cloves of garlic - peeled, and crushed or finely chopped

A small bunch of mint (approx. 10g) - leaves picked

2 tsp white sugar

3 limes - zested and juiced

Salt

Green salad and crusty bread to serve

There's nothing like a roast chicken for feeding a crowd. Crispy golden skin with plenty of herbs and garlic make this dish enduringly popular - and in this recipe, classic roast chicken is raised to a new level with lots of fresh mint, lime and white rum. White rum is distilled from sugarcane, and this gives it a subtle sweet flavour which pairs well with the zestiness of the other ingredients.

Butterflying (or spatchcocking) a chicken is easier than it looks, and flattening it like this helps the chicken to cook quicker, more evenly, and with more crispy golden skin. It's also easier to carve and serve for a crowd. Serve simply with a large salad, and some crusty bread to mop up the juices.

For the chicken

- Remove the chicken from the fridge 30 minutes ahead of time to bring it to room temperature - this helps it cook more evenly
- Preheat your oven to 200C / Gas Mark 6 / 400F
- Put the chicken breast side down on a large chopping board with the legs towards you. Use a sharp pair of kitchen scissors to cut along both sides of the backbone and remove it, then check the chicken over, removing any small bone fragments
- Turn the chicken breast side up, then press down hard in the middle of the breastbone to flatten the chicken to the same thickness all over. Place the chicken into a roasting tray

For the mojito mix

- Melt the butter in a small saucepan or in the microwave. In a blender, combine the melted butter with the garlic, half the mint leaves, the sugar, 50ml white rum, 1 tsp salt and the lime zest (reserving the lime juice for later). Blend to a rough paste, then smear the paste all over the chicken
- Roast in the oven for 45-55 minutes until the chicken is cooked through to the bone and the juices run clear when you cut into it, or until the thickest part of the leg registers 75C (170F) on a digital food thermometer. The skin should be really crispy all over
- Remove from the oven, cover with foil and allow to rest for at least 15 minutes - use this time to prepare your green salad and bread

Equipment

Sharp kitchen scissors

Roasting tray

Small saucepan or microwave

Blender

Foil

Serving dish or platter

Small bowl

Bringing it together

- Lift the rested chicken onto a chopping board and use a sharp knife to joint the chicken into pieces. Place on a serving dish or platter
- In a small bowl, mix together the juice of the 3 limes with 50ml white rum. Stir in any juices from the chicken roasting dish. Drizzle the mixture over the chicken and sprinkle with the remaining mint leaves, then serve with salad and crusty bread

TIP: For extra crispy skin and the moistest chicken, spatchcock your chicken a day ahead of time and season the skin generously with salt, then leave it uncovered in the fridge overnight. This allows the salt to absorb into the meat, seasoning it and drying out the surface for a crispier skin. If you opt to do this, halve the amount of salt in the mojito mix

MAINS — ROASTED AND GRILLED

Rickard Family Jägermeister Chicken

Serves 4 — Prep time 20 minutes — Cook time 30 minutes — Difficulty ❶

Ingredients

50ml Jägermeister

8-12 chicken drumsticks (approx. 1.2kg total)

100ml tomato ketchup

20g light or dark brown sugar

40g runny honey

¼ tsp cayenne pepper (or ¼ tsp chilli flakes)

½ tsp garlic granules

Salt and freshly ground black pepper

This recipe is a twist on a forty-year-old classic BBQ sauce in the Rickard household, one that's been cooked at dozens of family gatherings. While it's great when roasted in the oven, it's phenomenal when cooked over an open flame. We suggest cooking a double batch of this chicken so you can eat twice as much!

Jägermeister is a word that tends to strike fear into the heart of many - a side effect of one too many Jäger-bombs, perhaps? Don't be put off, as this herbal liquor is incredible to cook with. Added in small quantities to the sweet and spicy barbecue sauce, the warming, citrusy, herbal flavours of Jäger are enhanced alongside the sweet caramelising sugars. Don't worry about the chicken blackening - it's all part of the flavour. Serve with a baked potato and some Gin Slaw from page 132.

- Preheat your oven to 220C / Gas Mark 7 / 425F
- Lay the chicken drumsticks on a large roasting tray and season generously with salt and pepper
- In a small bowl, mix together the Jägermeister, ketchup, brown sugar, honey, cayenne pepper, garlic granules, ½ tsp salt and a good grind of black pepper. Scoop about a third of the sauce into a separate small bowl and set to one side - this will be the dipping sauce to serve with the chicken
- Spoon about half the remaining sauce liberally on top of the chicken and rub it all over so that the chicken is fully coated. Put the tray in the oven and cook for 15 minutes
- After 15 minutes, remove the tray from the oven and brush or drizzle on half of the remaining sauce. Put the chicken back in the oven and cook for a further 10 minutes
- After 10 minutes, brush the remaining sauce on top of the chicken, and then cook for a final 5 minutes or until the chicken is cooked through
- Serve the chicken drumsticks alongside the dipping sauce, and with kitchen roll to clean up messy fingers!

Equipment

Large roasting tray

2 x small bowls

Kitchen roll

MAINS — ROASTED AND GRILLED

COOKING WITH ALCOHOL

Sweet and Spicy Tequila Lime Pork

Serves 4 — Prep time 15 minutes — Cook time 30 minutes — Difficulty ❷

Mexican food is a go-to midweek meal in our house, in a large part due to Aaron's Texan heritage. Texas shares a border with Mexico, so Mexican food is a big part of Texan culture and cooking. In this dish, the zesty, spicy flavours add flavour and depth to ordinary ingredients like pork, peppers and sweet potatoes, making the meal incredibly moreish. It's also a great way to eat more vegetables - and to love every moment of it!

Tequila has a bright, slightly sweet flavour which goes beautifully with the honey on the pork, caramelising together as it cooks. For a deliciously flame-kissed flavour, try searing the pork on a barbecue instead.

Ingredients

- 2 tbsp + 2 tsp tequila
- 2 tbsp runny honey
- 4 tsp smoked paprika
- 1 tsp chipotle chilli powder
- 1 lime - juiced (approx. 2 tbsp lime juice)
- A small bunch of fresh coriander (cilantro) (approx. 10g) - leaves picked and finely chopped
- 2 medium sweet potatoes (approx. 600g total) - peeled and diced
- 2 red or yellow peppers - thinly sliced
- 2 white onions - thinly sliced
- 1 clove of garlic - peeled, and crushed or finely chopped
- 600g boneless pork chops or loin - sliced into strips 2cm wide
- Salt and freshly ground black pepper
- Oil
- Rice and hot sauce to serve

Equipment

- 2 x large bowl
- Heavy bottomed frying pan or sauté pan

Method

- Mix together 2 tbsp tequila, 1 tbsp honey, 2 tsp of paprika, ½ tsp chipotle powder, 1 tsp salt, the lime juice and half of the chopped coriander in a large bowl
- Add the pork, stirring everything together well, then cover and set to one side to marinate
- In a separate bowl, mix together the sweet potatoes, peppers, onions, garlic, 2 tsp paprika, ½ tsp chipotle powder and a large pinch each of salt and pepper
- Heat a large splash of oil in a heavy bottomed frying pan. Fry the vegetables for 15-20 minutes on a high heat, stirring every few minutes, until they are soft and browning around the edges. Add a dash of water or lime juice if they start sticking to the bottom of the pan
- Cook the rice now according to pack instructions
- Once the vegetables are soft, remove them from the pan and set to one side
- Return the pan to the stove, and heat a splash of oil until just beginning to smoke. Place the pork in the pan and pour over the marinade. Cook on a high heat for 3-4 minutes on each side until the pork is cooked through
- Remove the pan from the heat, then stir in an extra 1 tbsp honey and 2 tsp tequila. Cover with a lid or foil for 5 minutes to allow the pork to rest
- Divide the pork between plates and pour over the sweet and spicy glaze. Sprinkle the rest of the chopped coriander over the vegetables, then serve the pork and vegetables with the rice and your favourite hot sauce

Trout with Dill and Ouzo

Serves 2 — Prep time 25 minutes — Cook time 25 minutes — Difficulty ❷

Ingredients

40ml + 2 tsp ouzo

½ a lemon - ¼ very thinly sliced, ¼ juiced

½ a white onion - very thinly sliced

A small bunch of fresh dill (approx. 15g) - finely chopped

2 trout - scaled, gutted and cleaned

2 tbsp olive oil, plus extra for drizzling

150g tender stem broccoli

300g new potatoes - scrubbed

1 tbsp butter

2 tbsp capers

1 tsp dijon mustard

Salt

Equipment

2 x small bowls

Kitchen roll

Deep roasting tray

Medium saucepan

Whole fish are surprisingly easy to cook, and make a beautiful and fragrant supper. Here, we've stuffed fresh trout with lemon, ouzo and herbs, and simply roasted them in the oven with tenderstem broccoli. The addition of ouzo - a clear spirit flavoured with anise - heightens the sweet, herbaceous notes of the dill, while the dressing of zesty lemon and capers cuts through the richness.

Sea bass or sea bream also work well in this recipe. Serve simply with a side dish of buttery new potatoes.

For the trout

- Preheat your oven to 200C / Gas Mark 6 / 400F
- In a small bowl, mix together the thinly sliced lemon, onion, 40ml ouzo and the chopped dill. Set to one side while you prepare the trout
- Rinse the fish and pat dry with kitchen roll, then use a sharp knife to cut off the head just below the gills, and to score a few deep slashes in each side of the trout
- Place the trout side by side in a deep roasting tray, then sprinkle liberally with salt and drizzle with olive oil. Rub the salt and oil all over the inside and outside of the fish. Spoon half of the dill mixture into the cavity of each trout
- Put the tenderstem broccoli into the roasting tray surrounding the trout, and drizzle a little more olive oil on the broccoli. Roast in the oven for 20 minutes, turning the tray halfway through to ensure that the fish cook evenly
- Once the fish are cooked, remove the tray from the oven and cover with a lid or foil to keep warm

For the new potatoes

- While the trout are cooking, put the new potatoes into a medium saucepan and cover with cold salted water. Bring the potatoes to the boil then simmer for 12-15 minutes until tender
- Drain the potatoes and allow them to steam for a minute in the pan, then add the butter to the saucepan together with a large pinch of salt and shake the pan around to mix it all together

For the dressing

- In a small bowl, whisk together 2 tbsp olive oil, 2 tsp ouzo, the dijon mustard, the juice of the remaining ¼ lemon and a pinch of salt. Stir in the capers

Bringing it together

- Divide the fish between two dinner plates and spoon over the caper dressing. Serve with the buttery new potatoes

MAINS — ROASTED AND GRILLED

Sangria Chicken

Serves 4-6 — Prep time 25 minutes — Cook time 1 hour + 20 minutes resting
Difficulty ❷

Sangria requires very few ingredients, but the taste can transport you to Spain in a moment - sweet and deliciously tangy, it's perfect for hot weather. This recipe combines the key sangria ingredients of red wine, brandy and oranges together with chicken, spices and herbs, creating deep rich flavours with a sweet citrus lift. The result is both eye-catching and mouth-watering.

Butterflying (or spatchcocking) a chicken is easier than it looks. Flattening it like this ensures that the chicken cooks evenly, and that a large area is bathed in wine to absorb the dark, fruity flavours. We suggest using a dry, fruity Spanish wine such as Rioja or Tempranillo, but you can use whatever you have to hand.

We're serving this chicken with roasted sweet potato and chorizo on the side, and lemony kale. It also pairs well with a selection of tapas dishes or a leafy salad.

Ingredients

- 300ml red wine
- 40ml brandy
- 1 large whole chicken (approx. 2kg)
- 2 large red onions - finely chopped
- 4 tsp smoked paprika
- ½ tsp ground cinnamon
- 3 cloves
- ½ tsp dried rosemary
- ½ tsp dried thyme
- 2 tsp balsamic vinegar
- 2 oranges - ½ juiced, 1 ½ cut into thick slices
- 3 large sweet potatoes (approx. 1kg total) - scrubbed and chopped into bite size pieces
- 150g chorizo - thickly sliced
- 1 tbsp light soft brown sugar
- 1 tsp cornflour (cornstarch)
- 200g curly kale - roughly chopped
- 2 cloves of garlic - peeled, and crushed or finely chopped
- ½ a lemon - juiced (or 1 tbsp bottled lemon juice)
- Salt and freshly ground black pepper
- Oil

Equipment

- Sharp kitchen scissors
- Deep roasting tray
- 2 x shallow roasting trays
- 2 x large bowls
- Small saucepan
- Wide deep frying pan
- Large plate or serving dish

Preparing the chicken

- Remove the chicken from the fridge 30 minutes ahead of time to bring it to room temperature - this helps it cook more evenly
- Preheat your oven to 220C / Gas Mark 7 / 425F
- Put the chicken breast side down on a large chopping board with the legs towards you. Use a sharp pair of kitchen scissors to cut along both sides of the backbone and remove it, then check the chicken over, removing any small bone fragments
- Turn the chicken breast side up, then press down hard in the middle of the breastbone to flatten the chicken to the same thickness all over. Place the chicken into a deep roasting tray, then use a sharp knife to cut a few slashes in the skin of the breast and legs

For the chicken

- In a large bowl, mix together 1 of the chopped onions together with 2 tsp of the smoked paprika, the cinnamon, cloves, rosemary, thyme, some freshly ground black pepper and 1 tsp salt. Stir in 2 tsp oil, 2 tsp balsamic vinegar and the juice of ½ an orange
- Rub the mixture all over the chicken until it is fully coated in the onion and spice mixture. Pour any remaining liquid into the tray with the chicken, then place the sliced orange pieces all around and on top of the chicken
- Pour the wine and brandy into the tray around the chicken, then place it in the oven. Roast for 20 minutes, then spoon some of the sangria liquid over the chicken before returning it to the oven. Repeat this every 10 minutes until the chicken is cooked through to the bone and the juices run clear when you cut into it, or until the thickest part of the leg registers 75C (170F) on a digital food thermometer - it should take 40-45 minutes in total

COOKING WITH ALCOHOL

For the roasted vegetables and chorizo
- In a large bowl, stir together the sweet potato, chorizo, remaining chopped onion, the remaining 2 tsp paprika, 1 tbsp oil, ½ tsp salt and a good grinding of black pepper
- When the chicken has been in the oven for about 30 minutes, divide the vegetable mixture between 2 shallow roasting trays and spread out into an even layer. Place in the oven and roast for 25-35 minutes, stirring once or twice, until the sweet potatoes are deep golden brown at the edges

For the chicken
- Once the chicken is cooked, remove it from the oven and carefully lift the chicken onto a large chopping board. Cover with foil and allow it to rest for at least 20 minutes while you make the sangria sauce
- Pour the remaining liquid from the chicken roasting pan into a small saucepan. Add the brown sugar and cornflour and cook over a low heat for 10-15 minutes, stirring occasionally, until the sugar has dissolved and the sauce has thickened slightly

For the kale
- Heat a splash of oil in a wide deep frying pan over a medium heat. Add the kale and garlic and cook for 5-10 minutes, stirring occasionally, until the kale is wilted. Add a large squeeze of lemon juice and a generous sprinkle of salt, and give it a final stir

Bringing it together
- Use a sharp knife to joint the chicken into pieces. Lift the pieces onto a serving platter and pour the sangria sauce over the top
- Serve the sangria chicken with the roasted sweet potato and chorizo, and with the lemony kale on the side

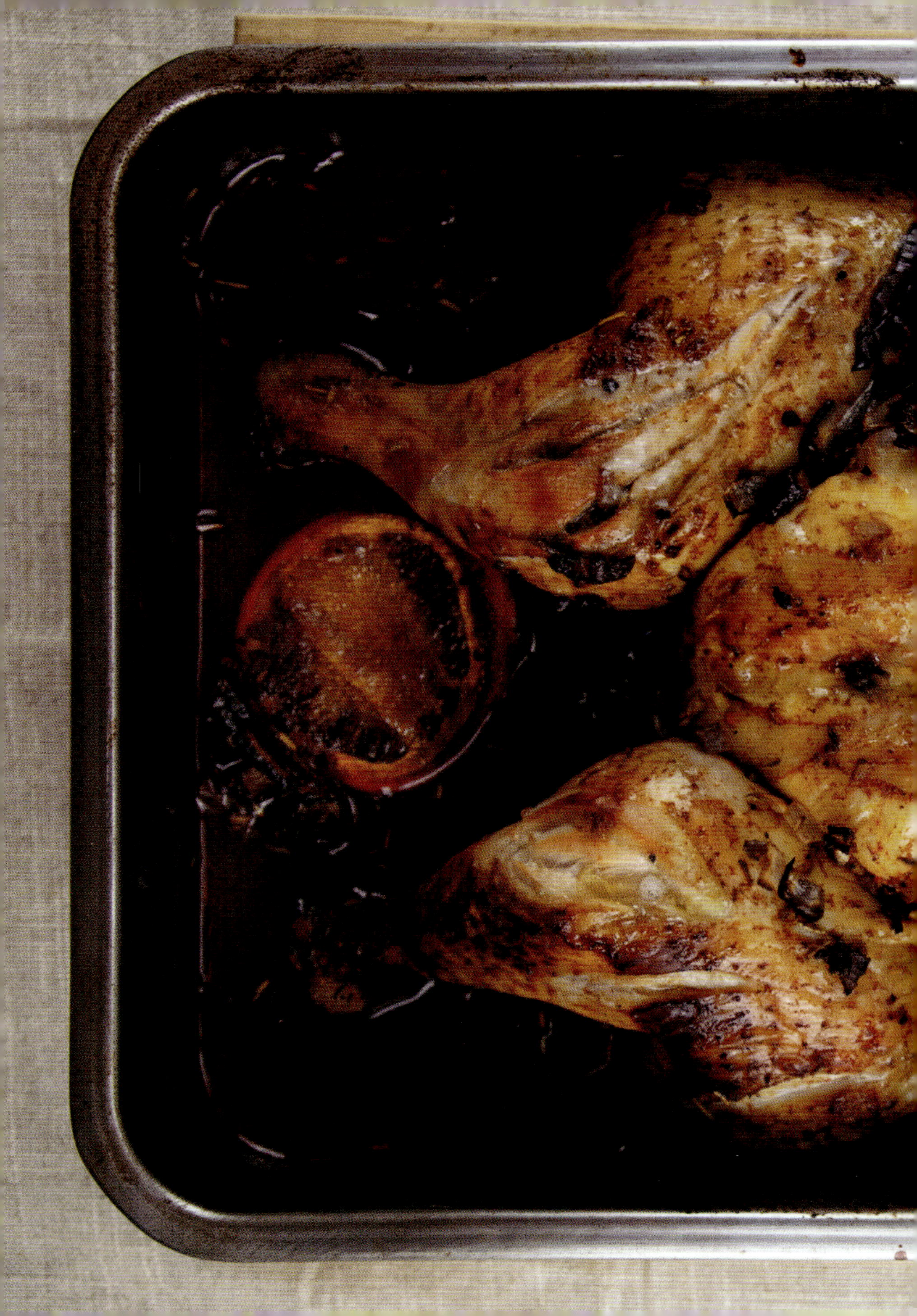

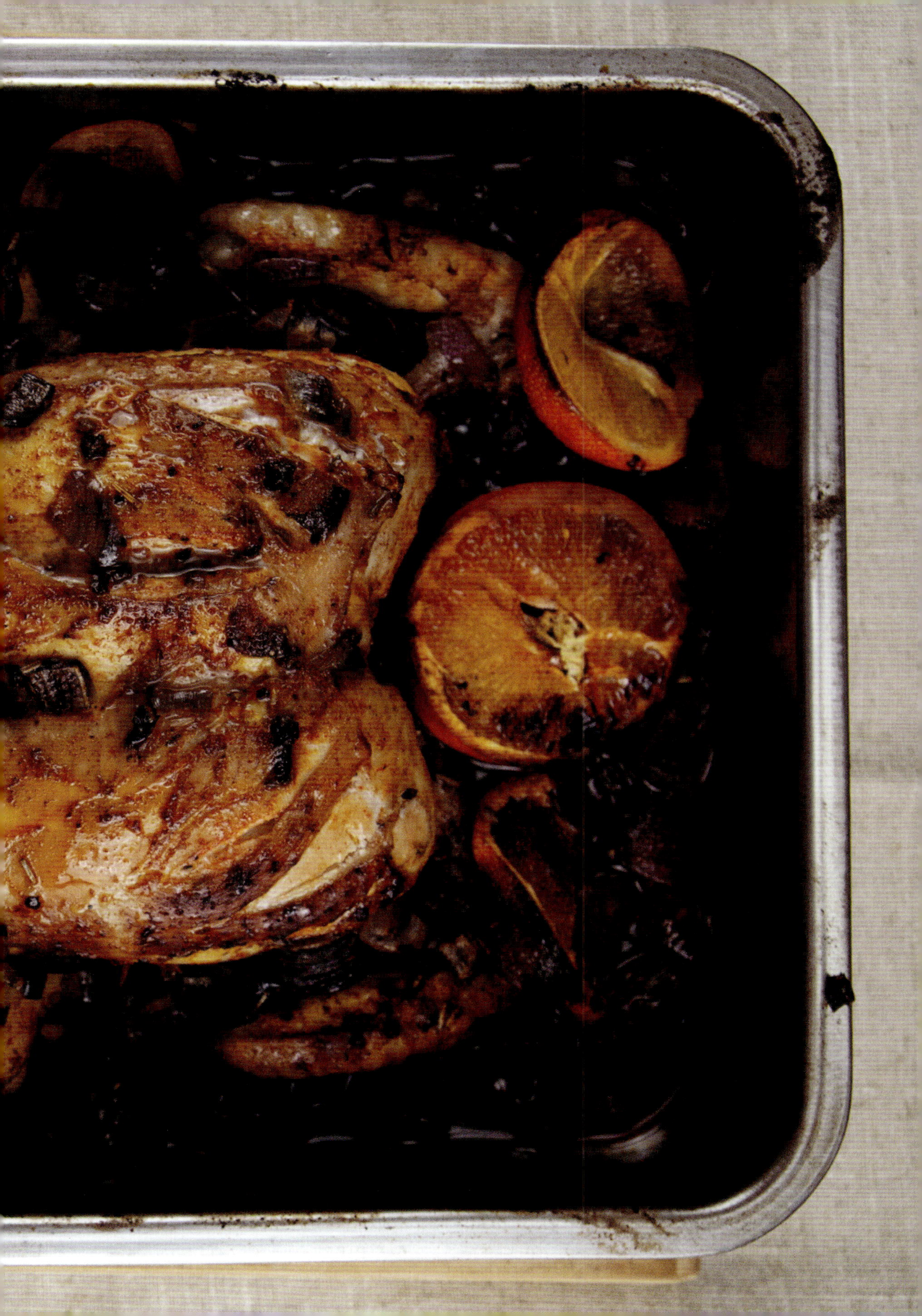

MAINS
PAN FRIED

Philly Cheese Steak with Beer Sauce

Serves 4 — Prep time 15 minutes + chilling time — Cook time 30 minutes — Difficulty ❸

Ingredients

300ml lager

500g frying steak

1 tsp cornflour (cornstarch)

20g butter

1 tsp white sugar

1 tsp Worcestershire sauce

4 long soft white rolls (e.g. subway or ciabatta rolls)

Pickled jalapeño peppers

2 white onions - thinly sliced

2 green peppers - thinly sliced

100g mild cheese (e.g. mild cheddar, American cheese or Swiss cheese) - grated

Mayonnaise

Oil

Salt and freshly ground black pepper

Equipment

Small bowl

Heavy bottomed frying pan

Very sharp knife

Whisk

This sandwich is so good, once you've made it you'll wish you'd made five. There's seared steak, fried onions, lots of melted cheese, and a thick beer and pepper sauce to bring it all together in a hearty bread roll. It's fairly straightforward, easy to cook for a crowd, and absolutely delicious.

For maximum flavour it's important to slice the beef really thinly, as this creates a wider surface area of meat to be seared. The process of searing in a smoking hot pan bonds the protein and sugar molecules in the meat, (also known as the Maillard reaction), creating a deliciously deep flavour and a crisp caramelised crust. Make sure to open a window, as your kitchen will get smoky!

- Place the beef in the freezer for 30 minutes to firm up - this makes it easier to slice thinly
- In a small bowl or cup, mix together the cornflour with a large splash of the lager to make a paste, and set to one side
- Separately, combine the remaining lager with the butter, sugar and Worcestershire sauce, and add a generous grinding of black pepper and ½ tsp salt
- Slice the rolls in half and spread them with a little mayonnaise, and add a handful of sliced jalapeño peppers to each. Set to one side

For the steak and onions
- Heat a splash of oil in a heavy bottomed frying pan on a very high heat
- Once the pan is really hot add the sliced onions and peppers together with a pinch of salt, and cook for 5-10 minutes until charred at the edges but still retaining their texture. Remove from the pan and set to one side
- Remove the beef from the freezer and place on a chopping board. Use a very sharp knife to slice the beef very thinly against the grain
- Heat the same pan on high until just beginning to smoke, then add a splash of oil and sprinkle the beef evenly across the pan, followed by a few large pinches of salt. Cook for a few minutes without stirring - this allows the beef to get crispy and flavoursome. Then stir and cook for a few more minutes until the beef is browned all over

Bringing it together
- Once the beef is cooked, turn the heat down low and return the peppers and onions to the pan. Make 4 piles out of the cooked beef, peppers and onions, approximately the size of your prepared bread rolls, and sprinkle each pile liberally with grated cheese. Continue to cook gently for a few minutes until the cheese has melted
- Once the cheese has melted, use a spatula to scoop each pile of beef and onions into the prepared rolls

COOKING WITH ALCOHOL

- Turn the heat back up high and pour in the beer sauce to de-glaze the pan, stirring to scrape up any bits of crispy beef or cheese. Boil hard for 5-10 minutes until the liquid has reduced, then whisk in the cornflour paste until smooth. Cook for a further 1 minute on a low heat, then drizzle the beer sauce all over the sandwich fillings and serve

TIP: If the cheese isn't melting, place a steel bowl over the top of each pile to make a makeshift lid

TIP: Look closely at the fibres in the meat - you'll notice that they all run in one direction. Slicing across the fibres helps avoid it being chewy, as it keeps the fibres short

MAINS — PAN FRIED

Salmon with Cava Sauce and Crushed Lemon Potatoes

Serves 4 — Prep time 10 minutes — Cook time 30 minutes — Difficulty ❷

Ingredients

100ml cava brut (dry sparkling white wine)

600g new potatoes - scrubbed

3 tbsp butter

½ a lemon - juiced (approx. 1 tbsp lemon juice)

Salmon fillets for 4 (150g-200g per person)

1 tbsp plain flour

100ml single (light) cream

Salt and freshly ground black pepper

Steamed broccoli or kale to serve, and parsley to garnish

There's something magical about the combination of sparkling wine and cream - cava is mildly acidic so it reacts with the cream to gently thicken the sauce, while the bubbles keep it light and silky smooth. The resulting texture of this sauce is light and silky, dancing on the tongue. It's perfectly complemented with this simply-cooked salmon and zesty potatoes.

For a vegetarian option, spoon the velvety cava sauce over grilled asparagus or portobello mushrooms.

For the potatoes

- Put the potatoes into a medium saucepan and cover with cold salted water. Bring to the boil and simmer for 12 minutes or until tender
- Drain the potatoes. Put 1 tbsp butter, a large pinch of salt and the lemon juice in the pan with the potatoes, then put the lid back on and give it all a good hard shake so that the potatoes are lightly crushed and coated in the butter and lemon

For the salmon

- Heat 1 tbsp butter in a large heavy frying pan over a medium heat. Meanwhile, sprinkle the salmon fillets with salt and pepper on both sides. When the butter is foaming, add the salmon fillets skin side down and cook for 4 minutes
- Gently turn the salmon over, and cook for 1 more minute (or 2 minutes if your salmon fillets are quite thick)
- Once the salmon is tender, remove from the pan onto dinner plates, cover, and leave to rest while you make the sauce

For the sauce

- In the same frying pan, melt 1 tbsp butter over a very low heat. Stir in the flour and cook for a minute, then gradually whisk in the cava until smooth. Cook for a minute over a low heat until the mixture is bubbling, then remove from the heat and stir in the cream and a pinch of salt

Bringing it together

- If you're serving this with greens, cook them now
- Sprinkle the salmon with a little chopped parsley, then serve with the lemony potatoes and a large spoonful of the cava sauce, and greens of your choice

Equipment

Medium saucepan

Heavy frying pan

Whisk

COOKING WITH ALCOHOL

MAINS — PAN FRIED

Sticky Cider Sausages with Mustard Mash

Serves 4 — Prep time 15 minutes — Cook time 45 minutes — Difficulty ❷

Ingredients

500ml apple cider

4 white onions - thinly sliced

1 large or 2 small apples - peeled or scrubbed, cored and finely chopped

1 tbsp marmalade

2 tbsp wholegrain mustard (1 tbsp for the onions, 1 tbsp for the mash)

8-12 cumberland sausages (or vegetarian sausages)

1kg floury potatoes (e.g. Maris Piper or King Edward) - peeled or scrubbed, and chopped into large, even chunks

2 tbsp butter

50-100ml milk

White pepper

Salt

Oil

Peas or greens to serve

Equipment

Large heavy bottomed pan

Medium saucepan

Potato masher

Frying pan or grill (broiler)

Turn this classic dinner up a notch with a sticky cider and caramelised onion sauce. Many fruits and vegetables contain natural sugars which caramelise when cooked slowly and gently - you can see this here in the onions and the apple cider. As the cider slowly bubbles and evaporates, the sugars in the onions caramelise and turn dark brown, developing a sweet richness of flavour. We're also adding a little marmalade for a hint of tangy citrus, and white pepper for a bit of bright warmth.

Served together with mustardy mashed potatoes and greens, it's a perfect dinner for a cool day. This recipe works just as well with good quality vegetarian sausages.

For the caramelised onion sauce

- Heat a splash of oil in a large heavy bottomed pan. Add the sliced onions and cook over a medium heat for 10 minutes, stirring occasionally, until the onions are soft and beginning to brown

- Add a generous splash of cider to the pan together with the chopped apple, marmalade, 1 tbsp wholegrain mustard, ½ tsp salt and a generous grinding of white pepper. Turn the heat up a little and bubble until the cider has reduced and mostly evaporated

- Add another splash of cider and repeat, allowing the liquid to evaporate before adding more, until you have used all the cider and the sauce is rich and thick, then cover with a lid and turn the heat off. If the sauce gets a bit too thick, add a splash of water (or more cider)

For the mustard mash

- While the onions are cooking, put your chopped potatoes into a medium saucepan and cover with cold water and a generous pinch of salt. Bring to the boil, then simmer for 15 minutes or until tender

- Drain the potatoes in a colander, then tip them back into the saucepan and let them steam for a minute with the lid off

- Mash the potatoes with the butter, 1 tbsp wholegrain mustard, ½ tsp salt and a splash of milk. Mash until smooth, adding a splash more milk to loosen if needed, then taste and adjust the seasoning. Set to one side to keep warm in the pan

Bringing it together

- While the potatoes are cooking, heat a frying pan or grill to medium-high and cook the sausages for 10-12 minutes, turning every few minutes until cooked through

- Add the cooked sausages into the caramelised onion sauce and cook over a low heat for 5 minutes, stirring occasionally

- Cook the peas or greens now

- Serve the sausages with a big dollop of caramelised cider onions, mustard mash and the peas or greens

COOKING WITH ALCOHOL

MAINS — PAN FRIED

COOKING WITH ALCOHOL

Tequila and Habanero Salmon with Salsa Fresca and Black Beans

Serves 4 — Prep time 15 minutes — Cook time 25 minutes — Difficulty 2

The flavours in this colourful meal are inspired by the Yucatan peninsula, where bold Mexican spices are used together with seafood and citrus to create bright, vibrant dishes. Fruity and fragrant habanero chilli is an integral part of Yucatan cuisine, and here we've paired it with salmon, lime and tequila. Although only a small amount of tequila is used, anyone who has drunk a shot of tequila knows that a little of its bright agave flavour goes a long way!

The oiliness of salmon gives it a strong flavour, which means it pairs well with the bold flavours used here. We're serving the salmon with black beans, simply spiced with a little cumin and garlic. The addition of bicarbonate of soda helps to soften the beans and makes them easier on the digestion. There's also a tangy fresh salsa alongside to add a little bite and acidity.

Ingredients

- 2 tbsp + 2 tsp tequila
- 2 x 400g cans of black beans
- 3 cloves of garlic - peeled, and crushed or finely chopped (1 clove for the beans, 2 cloves for the salmon)
- 1 tsp dried cumin
- ¼ tsp bicarbonate of soda
- A small bunch of fresh coriander (cilantro) (approx. 25g) - leaves picked and roughly chopped
- 3 tomatoes - finely chopped
- 2 spring onions - cleaned, trimmed and thinly sliced
- 1 ½ limes - juiced (approx. 3 tbsp lime juice)
- ½ tsp chilli powder
- Salmon fillets for 4 (150g-200g per person)
- 2 tbsp habanero chilli sauce (or your favourite hot sauce)
- 1 tbsp butter
- Salt
- Rice, and extra lime wedges and hot sauce to serve

Equipment

- Small saucepan
- 2 x mixing bowl
- Large heavy bottomed frying pan

- Cook the rice according to pack instructions

For the black beans

- In a small saucepan, combine the beans (including the water from the cans), 1 clove of crushed garlic, the cumin, bicarbonate of soda and ½ tsp salt. Cook over a gentle heat for 10 minutes then turn off the heat, cover and leave to one side

For the salsa fresca

- In a mixing bowl, stir together the chopped coriander, tomatoes, spring onions, 2 tsp tequila, the juice of ½ a lime, ½ tsp chilli powder and ½ tsp salt. Set to one side

For the salmon

- Mix together the remaining 2 cloves of crushed garlic, the habanero sauce, juice of 1 lime, 2 tbsp tequila and a large pinch of salt in a bowl. Add the salmon and turn to coat in the sauce, then leave to marinade for 5 minutes

- Heat 1 tbsp butter in a large heavy frying pan over a medium heat. When it begins to foam, add the salmon fillets skin side down, pour the marinade over the top and cook for 4 minutes

- Gently turn the salmon over and cook for 1 more minute (or 2 minutes if your salmon fillets are quite thick)

Bringing it together

- Once the salmon is tender, drain the liquid from the black beans. Serve the salmon fillets with the salsa fresca, black beans and rice on the side

MAINS — PAN FRIED

COOKING WITH ALCOHOL

Dark Rum and Orange Pork Chops

Serves 4 — Prep time 15 minutes — Cook time 30 minutes — Difficulty ❷

Ingredients

4 tbsp dark rum

1 orange - zested and juiced

1 tbsp black treacle

1 tbsp dark soft brown sugar

1 tsp dried thyme

1 tsp ground allspice

1kg floury potatoes (e.g. Maris Piper or King Edward) - peeled or scrubbed, and chopped into large, even chunks

2 tbsp butter (1 tbsp for the potatoes, 1 tbsp for the corn)

50ml milk

4 large thick bone-in pork chops (approx. 700g total)

1 tsp smoked paprika

4 corn cobs - husks and fibres removed

Salt

Oil

Equipment

3 x medium saucepans

Small bowl

Frying pan

Kitchen roll

Foil

Rich, sticky and flavourful, the dark rum and orange glaze on these pork chops elevates them beyond the everyday. Yet it's a relatively straightforward dish to cook and therefore perfect for a midweek meal - pork chops are a lean meat and lend themselves to quick cooking over a high heat, leaving them juicy and tender.

In this Jamaican-inspired dinner the rum is combined with treacle and allspice to make a dark fruity glaze. Allspice has a unique flavour, warming and rich while also enhancing the woody, peppery notes of the rum. Serve with delicious buttery corn on the cob and mashed potato to mop up the sauce.

For the glaze

- In a medium saucepan, combine the orange zest and juice, treacle, brown sugar, thyme, allspice and a pinch of salt. Simmer over a medium heat for 5-10 minutes, stirring occasionally, until thick and syrupy. Pour into a small bowl and set to one side

- Put a medium saucepan of water on to boil, for the corn

For the mashed potato

- Meanwhile, put your chopped potatoes into another saucepan, and cover with cold water and a generous pinch of salt. Bring to the boil and simmer for 15 minutes or until tender

- Drain the potatoes in a colander, then tip them back into the saucepan and let them steam for a minute with the lid off

- Mash the potatoes with 1 tbsp butter, a splash of milk and a large pinch of salt. Mash until smooth, adding a splash more milk to loosen if needed, then taste and adjust the seasoning. Set to one side to keep warm in the pan

For the corn cobs

- Add the corn cobs to the boiling water and simmer for 10 minutes until tender, then drain and put them back in the pan, but off the heat

- Add the smoked paprika and remaining 1 tbsp butter to the corn, together with a good pinch of salt. Put the lid on the pan and give it a good shake to mix it all around. Set to one side to keep warm in the pan

For the pork chops

- While the potatoes and corn are cooking, pat the pork chops dry with kitchen roll then sprinkle with a pinch of salt

- Heat a frying pan over a high heat until just beginning to smoke. Add a splash of oil to the pan and fry the chops for 5-10 minutes, turning occasionally, until golden brown and cooked through. Transfer to a plate and cover with foil to keep warm

Continued on next page

MAINS — PAN FRIED

Bringing it together

- Return the frying pan to the stove and turn the heat down low. Pour the glaze into the frying pan together with the rum, and bubble it all together for a minute or two to deglaze the pan and reduce the liquid
- Turn the heat off. Return the pork chops to the pan, and turn them until evenly coated in the glaze. Serve the glazed pork chops with the corn cobs and mashed potato on the side

TIP: If you can't get hold of allspice, substitute for equal parts cinnamon, nutmeg and cloves

TIP: You can use a digital food thermometer to tell when your pork chops are cooked - they should register 63C / 145F inside

MAINS
PASTA AND RICE

Port Pesto with Rigatoni

Serves 4 — Prep time 5 minutes — Cook time 20 minutes — Difficulty ❶

Ingredients

100ml port

150g sun-dried tomatoes in oil (drained weight) or 80g 'dry' sun-dried tomatoes

1 clove of garlic - peeled, and crushed or finely chopped

500g rigatoni (or another chunky pasta shape)

75ml extra virgin olive oil

100g pine nuts

75g parmesan cheese, plus extra to serve - finely grated

Salt and freshly ground black pepper

Food doesn't have to be complicated to be delicious, and it's always helpful to have an easy pasta dish in your repertoire. This is one of those meals that truly says "I need to eat something tasty, but there's nothing in the fridge". You can blend up the rich, savoury port pesto while the pasta cooks, and it's all ready in about 25 minutes. Large pasta shapes like rigatoni are great for trapping pesto inside them, but you can use whatever pasta you've got in the cupboard.

If you're just cooking for one or two people, any leftover pesto can be scooped into a jar and topped with a layer of olive oil - this acts as a barrier to keep out bacteria and preserve it for longer. Serve leftover pesto dolloped on chicken or roasted root vegetables, or swirled into a soup.

- Put a large pan of salted water on to boil for the pasta
- Drain the oil from the sun-dried tomatoes, and scoop them into a small saucepan. Add the garlic and port, and simmer together over a low heat for 10 minutes or until the tomatoes are soft
- Meanwhile, cook your pasta according to pack instructions. Reserve a small cupful of the cooking water before draining
- When the tomatoes have softened, scoop the mixture into a food processor and add the olive oil, pine nuts, parmesan and lots of black pepper. Blend the mixture to a coarse paste - add a splash more olive oil if it's looking too dry
- Scoop the pesto into the drained pasta together with a small splash of the cooking water, and stir well to combine
- Sprinkle each bowl with extra black pepper and parmesan to serve

Equipment

Large saucepan

Small saucepan

Food processor or blender

COOKING WITH ALCOHOL

MAINS — PASTA AND RICE

Fennel and White Wine Tagliatelle

Serves 4 — Prep time 10 minutes — Cook time 20 minutes — Difficulty ❶

Ingredients

150ml white wine

1 tbsp butter

1 fennel bulb (approx. 300g) - trimmed, and very thinly sliced

1 unwaxed lemon - zested and juiced

1 clove of garlic - peeled, and crushed or finely chopped

350g tagliatelle (or spaghetti)

200ml single (light) cream

50g parmesan cheese, plus extra to serve - finely grated

Salt and freshly ground black pepper

Simple and flavoursome, this is a great dish for a weekday evening. It takes just a few minutes to make a sauce of softly cooked fennel, lemon and garlic, stirred through tagliatelle and cream, for a surprisingly complex and flavourful result.

The zestiness and sweet anise flavour of fresh fennel pairs beautifully with white wine, which lifts the flavour and keeps the creamy pasta from feeling too heavy. We recommend using something fresh and fruity like a Sauvignon Blanc or Pinot Grigio. It's a fantastic way to use up the last of a bottle of wine - or a good reason to open one!

- Put a large pan of salted water on to boil, for the tagliatelle
- Meanwhile, heat a wide deep pan over a medium heat and melt 1 tbsp butter. Add the sliced fennel, lemon zest and garlic and cook gently for 10 minutes, stirring occasionally, until the fennel is very soft and just beginning to brown
- Once the pan of water is at a rolling boil, add the tagliatelle and cook according to pack instructions. Reserve a small cupful of the cooking water before draining
- Stir the white wine, cream, parmesan and half the lemon juice into the fennel, along with a good pinch of salt and some freshly ground black pepper. Mix well, then add the drained tagliatelle. Stir gently until everything is coated in a smooth sauce, loosening with a splash or two of the pasta water if needed
- Divide the pasta between bowls, topping each with more parmesan, black pepper and an extra squeeze of lemon juice at the table

Equipment

Wide deep pan

Large saucepan

MAINS — PASTA AND RICE

COOKING WITH ALCOHOL

Mushroom and Sherry Pasta

Serves 4 — Prep time 10 minutes — Cook time 25 minutes — Difficulty ❷

Ingredients

100ml dry (fino) sherry

2 tbsp butter

200g mixed mushrooms (eg. chestnut, oyster, shiitake) - tougher stems removed, and thinly sliced

1 white onion - thinly sliced

A small handful of fresh sage (approx. 5g) - leaves picked

400g pasta shapes

2 tbsp plain flour

400ml milk

Salt

Eating a simple yet tasty homemade pasta dish is one of the delights of life. This is another low-effort recipe where the result is more than the sum of its parts, thanks to the depth of flavour provided by the dry sherry in the mushroom sauce.

Fino sherry is usually served chilled and goes particularly well with salty dishes or tapas. Here, its savoury, herbal notes are enhanced by the addition of fresh sage leaves and earthy mushrooms. Using a mix of different mushrooms will provide a deeper flavour, but you can use whatever you have to hand. We particularly love shiitake mushrooms for their complex umami flavour.

- Put a large pan of salted water on to boil, for the pasta
- Meanwhile, heat a frying pan over a high heat and melt 1 tbsp butter in it. Add the mushrooms and onion and cook for 10 minutes, stirring occasionally, until the onion is soft and the mushrooms are brown. Stir in the sage leaves and cook for a few minutes until they begin to crisp around the edges
- Once the pan of water is at a rolling boil, add the pasta and cook according to pack instructions. Drain the pasta
- Turn the frying pan down low, then stir the remaining 1 tbsp butter into the mushrooms along with the flour and ½ tsp salt. Mix well so that the flour is evenly distributed, then add a splash of milk and stir until it is absorbed. Add the rest of the milk a little at a time, stirring well to prevent any lumps forming, then add the sherry
- Cook the mushroom sauce on a low heat for 10 minutes, stirring often, until the sauce is thick and smooth
- Stir the cooked pasta into the sauce, adding a splash of sherry or milk to loosen the sauce if needed. Divide the pasta between bowls and serve

Equipment

Large saucepan

Deep frying pan or sauté pan

MAINS — PASTA AND RICE

Tomato, Gin and Rosemary Pasta

Serves 4 — Prep time 5 minutes — Cook time 35 minutes — Difficulty ❶

Ingredients

100ml gin

2 white onions - finely chopped

2 x 400g cans of chopped tomatoes (or 800g tomato passata)

2 cloves of garlic - peeled, and crushed or finely chopped

½ tsp chilli flakes

1 tsp dried rosemary

1 tsp dried thyme

350g pasta

40g parmesan cheese, plus extra to serve - finely grated

Olive oil

Salt and freshly ground black pepper

This simple pasta dish is full of flavour, and a great one to add to your repertoire. When alcohol is added to a tomato-based sauce, rather than dominating the dish, it actually enhances the other flavours in a rather magical way. Alcohol is volatile, meaning that it evaporates easily, carrying aroma compounds to our noses. This enhances our perception of the rich, herby and slightly spicy flavours of the dish without a long cooking time.

Make sure to use good quality canned tomatoes for the best possible results. We've added rosemary and thyme to accentuate the herbal notes from the gin - you could substitute these for soft herbs like basil or tarragon, adding them towards the end of cooking to retain the fresh flavour.

- Put a large pan of salted water on to boil, for the pasta
- Heat a good splash of olive oil in a medium saucepan over a medium heat. Add the onions and cook, stirring occasionally, for 10 minutes or until the onions are very soft and beginning to brown
- While the onions cook, pour the cans of chopped tomatoes into a blender together with the gin and ½ tsp salt. Blend for a few moments until fairly smooth but still with a bit of texture. Alternatively, if you're using tomato passata, combine it with the gin and ½ tsp salt in a large bowl
- When the onions are soft, stir in the garlic, chilli flakes, rosemary and thyme, and cook for a further 2 minutes. Stir in the blended tomato and gin mixture and then put the lid on. Turn the heat down and simmer for 20 minutes until slightly thickened
- Once the pan of water is at a rolling boil, add the pasta and cook according to pack instructions until al dente. Drain the pasta and return it to the pan
- When the tomato sauce has had its 20 minutes, stir it through the pasta along with the grated parmesan. Sprinkle with extra parmesan, freshly ground black pepper and flaked sea salt to serve

Equipment

Large saucepan

Medium saucepan

Blender

MAINS — PASTA AND RICE

Cheddar and Stout Risotto

Serves 4 — Prep time 15 minutes — Cook time 30 minutes — Difficulty ❶

The classic Italian dish of risotto doesn't always have to be made with classic ingredients, and the fact that the rice absorbs liquid makes it perfect for cooking with alcohol. In our British version of this dish, we're using rich malty stout instead of the traditional white wine, and cheddar cheese instead of parmesan.

Stout has an earthy bitterness which is rounded out here with savoury marmite and worcestershire sauce, while the richness of the rice, salty cheddar cheese and cream ties everything together. Hearty and filling, and using mainly store-cupboard ingredients, it's an ideal dinnertime staple.

Ingredients

350ml stout beer or dark ale
1 white onion - finely chopped
2 tsp worcestershire sauce
1 tbsp balsamic vinegar
1 clove of garlic - peeled, and crushed or finely chopped
2 tsp marmite, bovril or vegemite
300g risotto rice
200g strong cheddar cheese - grated
50ml single (light) cream
Salt and freshly ground black pepper
Oil

- Heat 1 tbsp oil in a wide, lidded pan over a medium heat and cook the onion for 10 minutes until it is browning around the edges
- While the onions are cooking, combine the stout, worcestershire sauce, balsamic vinegar, a large pinch of salt and 600ml warm water in a small saucepan to make a stock. Heat until steaming, then turn off the pan
- When the onion is soft and brown, stir in the garlic, marmite and risotto rice and cook for 2 minutes. Turn the heat down low and add your first ladle of the hot stock mixture, and keep stirring. Cook until the liquid has all been absorbed, stirring regularly, then pour in the rest of the liquid. Put the lid on and cook over a very low heat for around 20 minutes, continuing to stir regularly, until all the liquid is absorbed
- Taste the risotto to check if it's done - the rice should be soft with just a little bite to it. If it isn't done yet, add a splash more water, cover and cook for a few more minutes
- Remove the pan from the heat, stir in the grated cheese and cream, then cover with a lid and allow it to sit for 5 minutes before serving with a generous grinding of fresh black pepper

Equipment

Wide deep lidded pan
Small saucepan

MAINS — PASTA AND RICE

COOKING WITH ALCOHOL

Chicken, Amaretto and Saffron Biryani

Serves 4-6 — Prep time 50 minutes — Cook time 45 minutes — Difficulty ❸

Ingredients

140ml amaretto liqueur (100ml for the marinade, 40ml at the end)

200ml milk

50g butter

2 bay leaves

A pinch of saffron (10-15 threads)

50g flaked almonds

3 white onions - thinly sliced

300g basmati rice

400g natural yogurt (200g for the marinade, 200g for the raita)

600g skinless, boneless chicken thigh fillets - chopped into large pieces

100g raisins or sultanas

3 cloves of garlic - peeled, and crushed or finely chopped

A small piece of fresh ginger - peeled and finely chopped to make approx. 1 tbsp

2 tsp mild curry powder

1 ½ tsp garam masala

½ tsp ground cinnamon

5 cloves

5 cardamom pods - lightly crushed

½ cucumber - grated or finely chopped

A small bunch of fresh mint or coriander (cilantro) (approx. 10g) - leaves picked and finely chopped (or use 1 tsp mint sauce)

Oil

Salt

Sugar

Mango chutney to serve

Equipment

Small saucepan

Jug

Frying pan

Large bowl

Large lidded ovenproof dish

Small bowl

Biryani is an Indian dish traditionally made for celebratory meals, opened or unwrapped at the table to release the aroma of spices. In our version, marinated chicken is layered with rice, fried onions, fragrant amaretto and saffron liquid and flaked almonds, then covered and baked.

In a rice dish it's important to get flavour into every bite - adding amaretto to the liquid ensures that the rice steams in the sweet fragrance of almonds. Serve the biryani with your favourite Indian chutney and this quick cucumber raita.

For a vegetarian version of this dish, substitute the chicken for 250g paneer cheese and 350g potatoes, chopped into large pieces.

For the biryani

- In a small saucepan, heat together the milk, butter, bay leaves, saffron and 100ml amaretto until just below boiling point. Once the mixture is steaming, pour it into a jug and leave to infuse

- Toast the flaked almonds in a dry frying pan over a medium heat for a few minutes until lightly browned. Set to one side

- Heat a frying pan on a high heat until very hot. Add 1 tbsp oil then fry the sliced onions for 10 minutes until they are deep brown and a little crispy, stirring occasionally. Remove from the heat and sprinkle with a pinch of salt

- Preheat the oven to 190C / Gas Mark 5 / 375F

- Put the rice in a small saucepan with 450ml cold water and ¼ tsp salt. Put the lid on and bring it to the boil and simmer for 5 minutes, then remove from the heat and leave to sit for 5 minutes

- In a large bowl, mix 200g of the yogurt together with the chicken, raisins, garlic, ginger, curry powder, garam masala, cinnamon, cloves, crushed cardamom pods and ½ tsp salt

- Spread out half the rice in a large lidded ovenproof dish. Add the chicken and all its marinade in a layer on top of the rice, then sprinkle over half of the fried onions and half of the toasted almonds. Cover with the remaining rice, then sprinkle with the remaining onions and almonds

- Pour the infused milk mixture over the top of the rice, then put the lid on and place in the oven. Bake for 40 minutes until the chicken is cooked through. Sprinkle the remaining 40ml amaretto over the top of the rice, then put the lid back on and leave to sit for 5 minutes before serving

For the cucumber raita

- In a small bowl, combine the remaining 200g yogurt with the grated cucumber, chopped mint or coriander, a pinch of salt and a pinch of sugar. Mix well

- Serve the biryani with mango chutney and the cucumber raita

MAINS — PASTA AND RICE

Red Wine Risotto with Roasted Aubergine

Serves 4 — Prep time 20 minutes — Cook time 45 minutes — Difficulty ❷

Ingredients

300ml red wine

3 tbsp olive oil

2 medium aubergines (approx. 700g total) - de-stalked and chopped into bite size chunks

350g risotto rice

700ml lukewarm vegetable stock

1 white onion - finely chopped

2 cloves of garlic - peeled, and crushed or finely chopped

2 tbsp tomato paste

1 tsp paprika

½ tsp chilli flakes

1 tsp dried thyme

50g parmesan cheese - finely grated

20g butter

A small bunch of fresh basil (approx. 10g) - leaves picked

1 tbsp red wine vinegar

Salt

Equipment

Roasting tray

Large bowl

Sieve

Jug

Wide lidded pan

There's something really fun about using a rich, spicy red wine in risotto, rather than a traditional white, and you can find different versions of red wine risotto throughout Italy. As well as turning the dish a gorgeous hue, the red wine adds a deep, rich flavour to this vegetarian dish. Spicy red wines need bold flavour partners, and in this risotto the umami-rich tomato, parmesan and smoked paprika bring a rich and rounded flavour. Meanwhile, the crisp, roasted aubergine sprinkled on top adds a harmonising saltiness to the tannins of the wine. A bold, spicy wine like Cabernet Sauvignon would be a great choice here.

We're using a slightly unusual technique of stirring the rice into the wine before cooking. This releases the rice starch into the wine, and as the wine is added to the risotto the creamy texture of the starch comes with it. This ensures a silky, rich risotto without having to stir constantly while it cooks, so it's an easier way to a great result.

- Preheat the oven to 190C / Gas Mark 5 / 375F

- Drizzle 2 tbsp olive oil into a large roasting tray. Add the chopped aubergine and ½ tsp salt and toss together until the aubergine is coated in the oil

- Roast the aubergine in the oven for 25-30 minutes, stirring halfway through, until crisp and turning golden brown. Once it is ready, remove from the oven and set to one side

- Meanwhile, combine the rice, wine and lukewarm stock in a large bowl, and stir for a few minutes until the liquid is cloudy. Drain the cloudy liquid through a sieve into another bowl or jug to use later, and set the rice to one side

- Heat 1 tbsp olive oil in a wide lidded pan over a medium heat and cook the onion for 5 minutes until soft and beginning to brown

- Stir in the drained rice, garlic, tomato paste, chilli flakes, smoked paprika, thyme and a large pinch of salt, then cook for another 2 minutes until fragrant

- Pour in ¾ of the wine and stock mixture and stir well. Turn the heat right down, cover the pan and cook gently for 20 minutes, stirring every 5 minutes to ensure that it isn't sticking (if it is, add a little more of the liquid)

- After 20 minutes, remove the lid, stir in the rest of the wine and stock mixture and cook with the lid off for a further 5 minutes or until the rice is al dente - it should be soft, but with just a bit of bite left

- Remove the pan from the heat, and stir in the grated parmesan cheese, butter, half the basil leaves and the red wine vinegar. Let it sit for a few minutes, then divide between bowls or plates and top with the roasted aubergine mixture and the remaining fresh basil leaves

MAINS — PASTA AND RICE

MAINS
PIES AND PASTRY

Mushroom and Stout Pasties

Serves 4 — Prep time 1 hour + chilling time — Cook time 50 minutes — Difficulty ❸

Ingredients

- 350ml stout or dark beer
- 250g button or chestnut mushrooms - finely chopped
- 1 white onion - finely chopped
- 1 clove of garlic - peeled, and crushed or finely chopped
- 50g pearl barley
- 250g potatoes - scrubbed or peeled, and finely chopped
- ½ tsp dried tarragon
- ½ tsp dried sage
- 50g cheddar cheese - grated
- 250g butter, plus extra for greasing - chilled and cut into cubes
- 500g plain flour, plus extra to roll out the pastry
- 1 egg - lightly beaten
- 6 tbsp cold water
- Salt and freshly ground black pepper
- Oil
- Green peas and tomato ketchup to serve

Equipment

- Large saucepan
- Food processor (optional)
- Mixing bowl
- Baking tray
- Baking paper (optional)
- Rolling pin (or use an empty wine bottle)
- Pastry brush

The pasty is a quintessential British comfort food - where we live, in the Southwest of England, the love of the pasty borders on reverence! Making them takes a bit of effort, but the golden brown flaky pastry and hearty savoury filling are worth it.

These pasties are filled with mushrooms, potato and barley, which are all cooked together in stout. The depth and richness of stout adds a savoury umami flavour that can often be lacking in vegetarian food. Barley provides a welcome chewiness and makes them very filling - serve these delicious pasties by themselves or with a side of green peas.

For the filling

- Heat a splash of oil in a large saucepan, and add the mushrooms, onion and garlic. Fry over a medium heat for 10-15 minutes until the onion is soft and beginning to brown
- Stir in the stout, pearl barley, chopped potatoes, tarragon, sage, ½ tsp black pepper and ½ tsp salt. Cover, bring to the boil and simmer for 30 minutes, stirring occasionally
- After half an hour, the barley and vegetables should be nearly tender and most of the stout absorbed into the barley. Remove the lid and continue to cook for a further 20 minutes, stirring occasionally, until the liquid has reduced and the mixture is thick and sticky. Set aside to cool for at least 15 minutes

For the pastry

- If you have a food processor, put the flour, cubes of butter and a pinch of salt in the food processor, and blitz it until the mixture forms crumbs. Slowly add the cold water, bit by bit, until the mixture forms a ball of pastry (you may not need all the water)
- Alternatively, put the flour, cubes of butter and a pinch of salt into a mixing bowl. Use your fingers to rub the butter into the flour until it forms crumbs, then add the cold water bit by bit until it forms a ball of dough
- Cover the pastry and chill in the fridge for at least 30 minutes

Bringing it together

- Preheat the oven to 180C / Gas Mark 4 / 350F, and grease your baking tray with a little butter or line it with baking paper
- Stir the grated cheese into the cooled filling mixture
- Divide the pastry into 4 equal pieces, and shape each into a ball. Sprinkle a clean surface with flour, and roll each piece of pastry into a circle about 3mm (⅛ inch) thick
- Spoon a quarter of the filling onto each piece of pastry, then fold the pastry over, pressing the edges together with your fingers to seal

- Brush them all over with beaten egg, then bake for 45-50 minutes, rotating the tray half way through, until the pasties are deep golden brown all over
- Cook the peas now, if you're having them
- Serve the pasties warm, with a dollop of tomato ketchup and peas on the side

Parsnip and Cider Tarte Tatin

Serves 4 — Prep time 30 minutes — Cook time 25 minutes — Difficulty ❷

Ingredients

250ml dry apple cider

3 large parsnips (approx. 400-450g total) - scrubbed and trimmed

1 tbsp olive oil

2 red onions - peeled, and sliced into 6 wedges

1 clove of garlic - peeled, and crushed or finely chopped

1 tsp dried rosemary

1 large sheet of ready rolled puff pastry (approx. 320g)

Plain flour for rolling

Salt and freshly ground black pepper

Green salad and horseradish sauce to serve

Equipment

Wide ovenproof frying pan

Rolling pin (or use an empty wine bottle)

It's really fun to make a tarte tatin, and strangely satisfying - the filling is caramelised in the pan, then puff pastry goes on top and it's baked upside down before being turned out to reveal the beautiful design. Tarte tatin doesn't have to be sweet, as the natural sugars in root vegetables caramelise when cooked gently. Here, parsnips and onions are browned and softened in dry cider to release sweet caramel flavours, then gently seasoned with a little rosemary and garlic.

This recipe works equally well with other firm, slightly sweet root vegetables such as carrots or beetroot. Serve the tart with a green leafy salad and a dollop of horseradish sauce to cut through the richness of the pastry.

- Preheat your oven to 200C / Gas Mark 6 / 400F
- Slice the parsnips lengthwise into 4-6 wedges, depending on their size
- Heat 1 tbsp olive oil in a wide ovenproof frying pan over a medium heat. Add the parsnip wedges, and fry for 5 minutes or until the parsnips are browning
- Add a generous splash of the cider and bring the pan to a gentle simmer then cook for a few minutes, occasionally turning each parsnip wedge onto a different side
- Scatter the onion wedges, garlic and rosemary over the parsnips, along with a good grinding of black pepper and ½ tsp salt
- Add another splash of the cider and cook for a further 10-15 minutes until the parsnips are just tender, adding the cider a splash at a time and allowing it to evaporate in between each addition, turning the parsnips occasionally
- Meanwhile, lay out the puff pastry on a clean floured surface and using a rolling pin, roll it to around 3mm (⅛ inch) thick. Cut out a rough circle about 2 inches wider than the pan
- When all the cider has evaporated, turn off the heat and use tongs or a fork to arrange the parsnips into a pretty pattern in the pan
- Lay the pastry circle over the top, tucking it in at the edges. Make a small slit in the top with a knife then place the whole pan into the oven. Bake for 20 minutes, or until the pastry is puffy and deep golden brown
- Remove the pan from the oven and allow to cool for 5 minutes, then invert the whole dish onto a large plate so that the parsnips are now on top of the pastry
- Serve slices of the tarte alongside a green salad with a dollop of horseradish sauce

MAINS — PIES AND PASTRY

White Wine Chicken Pot Pie

Serves 4-6 — Prep time 55 minutes — Cook time 30 minutes — Difficulty ❸

Ingredients

250ml white wine

1 tbsp butter

2 white onions - finely chopped

1 large leek - cleaned, trimmed and thinly sliced

2 medium carrots - scrubbed, trimmed and finely chopped

500g skinless, boneless chicken thigh fillets - chopped into bite size pieces

2 tbsp plain flour, plus extra for rolling the pastry

1 tsp dried thyme

1 tbsp worcestershire sauce

1 chicken stock cube

250ml milk

1 large sheet of ready rolled puff pastry (approx. 320g)

1 egg - beaten

Salt and freshly ground black pepper

Oil

Peas or greens to serve

Equipment

Medium saucepan

A large ovenproof dish approx 8cm (3 inches) deep

Large heavy-bottomed frying pan

Rolling pin (or use an empty wine bottle)

Pastry brush

Homemade pie is the very essence of comfort food, and this one is sure to please a crowd. In our take on a traditional chicken pie, white wine is the secret ingredient for the sauce. In fact, we firmly believe that every white sauce should contain white wine (or even sherry) as a replacement for some of the milk or cream. The slight acidity of wine helps the sauce to thicken, but the true impact is in the flavour - fresh and gently zesty, while still rich and luxurious, this is a sauce to be eaten by the spoonful!

We've used puff pastry to top the pie, but if you prefer two pastry layers, shortcrust pastry on the bottom is a great choice. We suggest using chicken thighs rather than chicken breast for this pie, as thighs stay moister when cooked for a long period of time.

- Preheat the oven to 200C / Gas Mark 6 / 400F
- Melt the butter in a medium saucepan over a medium heat. Add the onions, leek and carrots and cook with the lid on, stirring occasionally, for 10 minutes until the vegetables have begun to soften. Remove from the heat and set to one side

For the chicken

- Heat a large heavy-bottomed frying pan on high for a few minutes until very hot. Add a splash of oil and the chicken and cook on a high heat for 8-10 minutes, stirring occasionally, until well browned all over
- Turn the heat down low and pour in 100ml of the white wine to deglaze the pan. Stir for a minute, scraping the bottom of the pan to get up any crispy bits
- Sprinkle the flour over the chicken together with the thyme, worcestershire sauce, 1 tsp salt and a good grind of black pepper. Stir well and cook for 2-3 minutes on a low heat - the sauce will begin to thicken
- Slowly add the rest of the wine, stirring as you go to ensure that the sauce stays smooth. Crumble the chicken stock cube into the sauce, stirring to dissolve, then add the milk and the cooked vegetables. Continue to cook on a low heat for a further 5 minutes, stirring occasionally, until the sauce is thick and smooth

Bringing it together

- Lay out the puff pastry on a clean floured surface and using a rolling pin, roll it to around 3mm (⅛ inch) thick
- Scoop the pie filling into a large ovenproof dish then lay the pastry on top. Use a sharp knife to trim the pastry to about 2cm wider than the filling all round. Crimp the pastry edges with your fingers to make a neat rolled edge, and cut a small hole in the top of the pie to release steam as it bakes

COOKING WITH ALCOHOL

- Brush the top of the pie with half of the beaten egg then place it in the oven. Bake for 20 minutes, then brush the pie with the remaining beaten egg and bake for a further 5-10 minutes or until the pastry is deep golden brown and puffed up all over
- Remove the pie from the oven and allow to cool for at least 10 minutes - use this time to cook your peas or greens to serve alongside

MAINS — PIES AND PASTRY

CIDER MUSTARD, PAGE 144

SIDE DISHES AND CONDIMENTS

Side Dishes

Potato and Beer Dauphinoise (Beerphinoise)	120
Cider Braised Leeks	122
Shallots Glazed in White Wine	124
Beer Basmati	126
Bourbon and Bacon Corn-on-the-Cob	128
Spiced Rum Barbecue Pineapple	130
Gin Slaw	132
Prosciutto, Melon and Sherry Salad	134
Port Marinated Olives	136
Bourbon Glazed Carrots	138
Sherry and Lemon Gravy	139

Condiments

Cider Mustard	144
Red Wine and Caramelised Onion Chutney	146
Red Wine Salt	148
Ale Pickled Eggs	150

In the same way that a nice meal might be served with a bottle of good wine, or a cold beer, side dishes and condiments should enhance your enjoyment of food. For us, it's best to keep things simple, so these side dishes are made with as few ingredients and saucepans as possible. The addition of alcohol adds a new dimension, and can push a neglected side dish onto centre stage.

We've started with side dishes to serve hot alongside meats or a roast dinner, which serve to enhance the main dish beautifully. These are followed by hot and cold recipes for summer barbecues or warmer weather, which are a great way to bring complementary textures and flavours to a spread of dishes. And finally, we include recipes for a selection of condiments that can add oomph to any dish.

In fact, more so than in any other chapter, these recipes demonstrate the versatility of alcohol, and the surprising ways that it can enhance the food we eat. In some of these recipes we include alcohol as part of a dressing, stirred through other ingredients, which allows some of the finer notes of the alcohol to contribute to the flavour - the zesty, herbal notes of gin add a delicious freshness to the **Gin Slaw**.

In other vegetable dishes, the natural sugars of cider and wine aid the caramelisation of the vegetables in the **Cider Braised Leeks** and **Shallots Glazed in White Wine**, while also lending a fruity, tangy flavour profile. The addition of fat, such as butter or mayonnaise, helps to mute any harsh alcohol notes while also carrying the other aroma compounds - butter heightens the sweetness of bourbon in the **Bourbon Glazed Carrots**, while cream enhances the malty aromas of our **Potato and Beer Dauphinoise**.

When choosing and cooking side dishes, it's important to think about the flavour profile of the whole meal. Side dishes should have a contrasting element to the main dish - sweet, buttery **Bourbon Glazed Carrots** will work well alongside a rich and savoury meat dish or cauliflower cheese.

With plain, grilled dishes, a little acidity can be a welcome addition, so a slice of sticky **Spiced Rum Barbecue Pineapple** would be a great choice alongside a burger.

The condiments in this chapter are very rewarding to make, and they keep very well thanks to the preserving activities of salt and vinegar. They do need to be prepared ahead of time, though, as this allows the flavour compounds from the alcohol, vinegar and other ingredients to mingle together for a more rounded flavour profile. However it's well worth the wait here - the smugness you'll feel from bringing your own delicious **Red Wine Salt** or **Cider Mustard** to the table is worth it!

SIDE DISHES

Potato and Beer Dauphinoise (Beerphinoise)

Serves 4 — Prep time 35 minutes — Cook time 40 minutes — Difficulty ❷

Ingredients

200ml blonde beer or craft lager

200ml double (heavy) cream

nutmeg

1kg potatoes - peeled and very thinly sliced

2 cloves of garlic - peeled and thinly sliced

50g cheddar cheese - grated

Salt and freshly ground black pepper

There's nothing better than crispy, creamy potato dauphinoise to accompany a roast dinner or pan-fried fish, and this decadent side dish is not hard to make - it just requires a little patience for slicing the potatoes! In our version, some of the cream is replaced with beer, and the flavour comes through beautifully in a luscious, subtly malty sauce around the tender potatoes - rich without being heavy. A blonde beer or craft lager will be the best choice here, as anything particularly bitter or hoppy can overwhelm the creamy potatoes. With added hints of nutmeg and garlic, this side dish can easily be the star of the show.

It can be difficult to cook potato dauphinoise just right, so in this recipe the potatoes are par-cooked in cream and beer and then layered in the dish. This ensures that they are tender throughout, and the starch from par-cooking helps to thicken the rich and creamy sauce. Try to keep the potato slices quite thin, around 1-2mm thick, as this will help the potatoes to cook evenly.

- Preheat the oven to 170C / Gas Mark 3 / 325F
- Pour the cream and beer into a wide saucepan. Stir in ¾ tsp salt, about 30 grates of the nutmeg, a good few grinds of black pepper, the sliced potatoes and the sliced garlic. Turn the heat on and bring the mixture to a gentle boil, then reduce the heat down very low and cook uncovered for 10-15 minutes, stirring occasionally, until the potatoes are slightly softened and the sauce has begun to thicken
- Scoop the mixture into an ovenproof dish and spread it out evenly, gently pressing down on the layers of potato. Sprinkle the top liberally with grated cheese and more black pepper
- Place the dish in the oven and bake for 35-40 minutes until the potatoes are golden on top, soft when poked with a fork, and the sauce is bubbling up around the edges. Allow to cool for 5 minutes before serving

Equipment

Wide saucepan

Grater

Deep wide ovenproof dish

SIDE DISHES

Cider Braised Leeks

Serves 4 — Prep time 10 minutes — Cook time 1 hour — Difficulty ❶

Ingredients

300ml dry cider

30g butter

4 leeks (approx. 800g total) - cleaned, trimmed, and sliced into 10cm (4 inch) lengths

2 tsp wholegrain mustard

1 tsp marmite, vegemite or bovril

¼ tsp white pepper

1 tsp cornflour (cornstarch)

Salt

Braising is a very simple cooking method that involves browning food in a pan, then adding liquid and slowly cooking it over a very low heat. It's a great way to cook leeks, which need to be cooked gently to soften their fibres to a melt-in-the-mouth texture. Leeks are often used to complement other ingredients, but here they are the star of the show - the addition of cider highlights their natural sweetness as they caramelise in a rich sauce, while mustard adds savoury warmth.

This side dish is a great accompaniment to grilled chops or a hearty winter pie - but we also love them as a topping for savoury pancakes or cheese on toast.

- Melt the butter in a wide heavy bottomed pan, then add the leeks and fry over a medium heat for 5 minutes until golden brown, stirring occasionally
- Add the cider, turn the heat down low and stir in the mustard, marmite, white pepper and ¼ tsp salt. Simmer uncovered for 30-45 minutes, stirring occasionally
- When the leeks are soft and the cider has reduced by about two thirds, scoop a small ladleful of the liquid into a small bowl. Mix the cornflour with this liquid to form a smooth runny paste, then stir the paste into the pan with the leeks
- Stir well and cook for a further 5 minutes until the sauce has thickened and coated the leeks

Equipment

Wide heavy bottomed pan

Small bowl

SIDE DISHES

Shallots Glazed in White Wine

Serves 4 — Prep time 20 minutes — Cook time 50 minutes — Difficulty ❶

Ingredients

200ml white wine

1 tbsp butter

400g shallots - peeled and left whole

1 tbsp white wine or cider vinegar

1 tbsp white sugar

Salt

Shallots have a mild and sweet flavour, without the 'bite' of onion, and although often found in supporting roles they are completely delicious in their own right when given a chance to shine. In this recipe, shallots are caramelised in butter and tangy vinegar, then braised in white wine until tender and full of flavour. The wine imbues the shallots with sweet, bright fruit flavours - we'd suggest an oaked white wine here, such as Chardonnay or Viognier.

We love to serve these glazed shallots alongside a roast dinner, or with a cheeseboard for a festive occasion, as the small size makes them perfect bite size morsels. They are also delightful as part of a tapas spread - pair with Chorizo in Red Wine and Honey on page 18, and the Port Marinated Olives on page 136.

- Melt the butter in a lidded frying pan over a medium heat, then add the shallots, vinegar, sugar and a large pinch of salt
- Cook uncovered for 5 minutes, stirring occasionally - the shallots should begin to caramelise
- Turn the heat down very low. Add the wine, then cover and cook for 25-35 minutes, stirring occasionally, until the shallots are very soft and starting to collapse
- Remove the lid and cook for a further 10 minutes or until the wine has reduced to a sticky sauce. If it gets a little too dry, just add a splash more wine

TIP: To peel the shallots, cover them in boiling water for a minute and then drain them - this helps the skins to come off more easily

Equipment

Lidded frying pan

COOKING WITH ALCOHOL

SIDE DISHES

COOKING WITH ALCOHOL

Beer Basmati

Serves 4 — Prep time 5 minutes — Cook time 20 minutes — Difficulty ❶

Ingredients

440ml can of lager
300g basmati rice
Salt

Curry and beer are a classic combination, as rich spices pair wonderfully with the crisp notes of malt and citrus. With this side dish, we're enjoying curry in the best possible way, by cooking rice in lager. After all, rice has the wonderful ability to absorb liquid, and what better to absorb than beer? The resulting rice is perfectly cooked and fragrant with the note of hops.

We'd suggest using an Indian lager here, or something fairly pale and mild-flavoured - darker beers, like IPA or brown ale, tend to overpower the flavour of the rice. Make sure that it's a lager you like to drink, as the flavour comes through strongly.

- Pour the beer into a large saucepan (you may need to use a larger pan than normal due to the bubbles in the beer). Stir the beer for a minute to allow the foam to disperse, then add the rice and a pinch of salt. Put the lid on the pan
- Turn the stove on to medium high heat and bring the rice to the boil. Boil for five minutes, then turn off the heat and let the rice sit with the lid on for another 10 minutes
- Fluff up the rice with a fork and serve alongside your favourite curry

Equipment

Large saucepan

Bourbon and Bacon Corn-on-the-Cob

Serves 4 — Prep time 15 minutes — Cook time 35 minutes — Difficulty ❶

Ingredients

25ml bourbon

25g butter, plus extra to serve

150g smoked bacon - finely chopped

1 tbsp golden syrup or light soft brown sugar

½ tsp smoked paprika

4 corn cobs - husks and fibres removed

Salt and freshly ground black pepper

Buttery corn on the cob is a delicious side for any summer meal, and it's made even better by the addition of bourbon and smoky caramelised bacon. The warm, spicy notes of bourbon pair perfectly with sweet summer corn, and in part that must be because bourbon is distilled from corn!

We cook these corn cobs in foil parcels, either in the oven or on the barbecue. This makes them easy to prepare ahead of time for a delicious salty-sweet side dish, as well as being very low-maintenance to cook. For a vegetarian version, substitute the bacon for a finely diced onion.

- Light the barbecue, or preheat your oven to 200C / Gas Mark 6 / 400F
- Prepare 4 pieces of foil each large enough to wrap a corn cob
- Melt 25g butter in the frying pan then fry the bacon over a high heat, stirring occasionally, for 5-10 minutes until brown and crisp
- Turn the heat down low and stir the bourbon and golden syrup or brown sugar into the bacon, and allow to bubble for a minute. Remove the pan from the heat and stir in the paprika and some black pepper
- Place each corn cob onto a foil piece, then scoop a spoonful of bacon onto each one. Drizzle them with the buttery bourbon from the pan, then seal the foil pouches by scrunching them around the edges to form a parcel
- Place the foil parcel into a tray in the oven or on the cooler side of your barbecue. Cook for 20-30 minutes or until the corn is steaming hot and juicy
- Unwrap the parcels carefully and enjoy with an extra knob of butter and a sprinkle of salt on top of the corn

TIP: If you're cooking these in the oven, pop the corn cobs under the grill for a few minutes at the end to blacken the corn for greater depth of flavour

Equipment

Barbecue (grill) or oven

Foil

Frying pan

SIDE DISHES

Spiced Rum Barbecue Pineapple

Serves 6 — Prep time 10 minutes + 30 minutes marinating — Cook time 10 minutes
Difficulty ❶

Ingredients

75ml dark spiced rum

1 ripe pineapple - peeled, cored and cut into rings 1-2 cm (½ inch) thick

3 tbsp light or dark soft brown sugar

1 lime - juiced (approx. 2 tbsp lime juice)

Cooking fruit on a barbecue allows the natural sugars to caramelise, creating deep and deliciously sticky flavour. With the addition of a little brown sugar and spiced rum, it's a taste of tropical heaven. You can prepare this dish up to 6 hours ahead of time - just mix everything together and pop it in the fridge until you're ready to cook. Serve as a side dish with spiced kebabs or barbecued chicken (try the Rickard Family Jägermeister Chicken on page 66), or with a scoop of vanilla ice cream for a mouth-watering dessert.

Pineapple is excellent when cooked until flame-kissed, and has a firm texture so that it won't fall apart as it cooks. You can use tinned pineapple, just be careful when turning the thin slices. We also love to use this marinade on ripe peaches and nectarines.

- Combine all the ingredients in a bowl or large container and allow to sit and marinate for at least 30 minutes, stirring or shaking occasionally to mix the liquid and dissolve the sugar
- When ready to cook, preheat the barbecue or grill to a medium heat
- Use tongs or a fork to transfer the slices of pineapple to a barbecue or grill tray. Cook on a medium heat for 8-10 minutes, turning occasionally and drizzling with the sugary rum liquid when you turn them. The pineapple is ready when it's golden, sticky and caramelised all over
- Remove from the heat and allow to cool for a minute before tucking in - be careful as the caramelised sugars get very hot!

Equipment

Mixing bowl

Barbecue (grill) or grill (broiler)

SIDE DISHES

Gin Slaw

Serves 4 — Prep time 15 minutes — Difficulty ❶

Ingredients

3 tbsp gin

¼ of a white cabbage (approx. 200g) - cleaned and very finely sliced

2 large carrots (approx. 200g total) - scrubbed and coarsely grated

4 tbsp mayonnaise (approx. 80g)

½ lemon - juiced (approx. 2 tbsp lemon juice)

Salt

Elevate your coleslaw game with this startlingly good side dish, inspired by friends Joe and Sophie who created a gin slaw for our first alcohol-food-themed dinner together.

A great coleslaw needs a little acidity to brighten the flavour, and salt to avoid blandness. Gin and lemon bring a bright zestiness to this dish, as well as heightening the spice of freshly ground pepper, providing a gentle warmth that balances the sweetness of the carrots. It's a perfect side dish for a summer's day.

- Mix together the cabbage and grated carrot in a large bowl, then add the rest of the ingredients, ½ tsp salt and a good grinding of fresh black pepper
- Stir very well until everything is coated in a smooth sauce, then taste. You may wish to add a little more mayonnaise or lemon according to your preference. Store in the fridge for up to 2 days

Equipment

Mixing bowl

SIDE DISHES

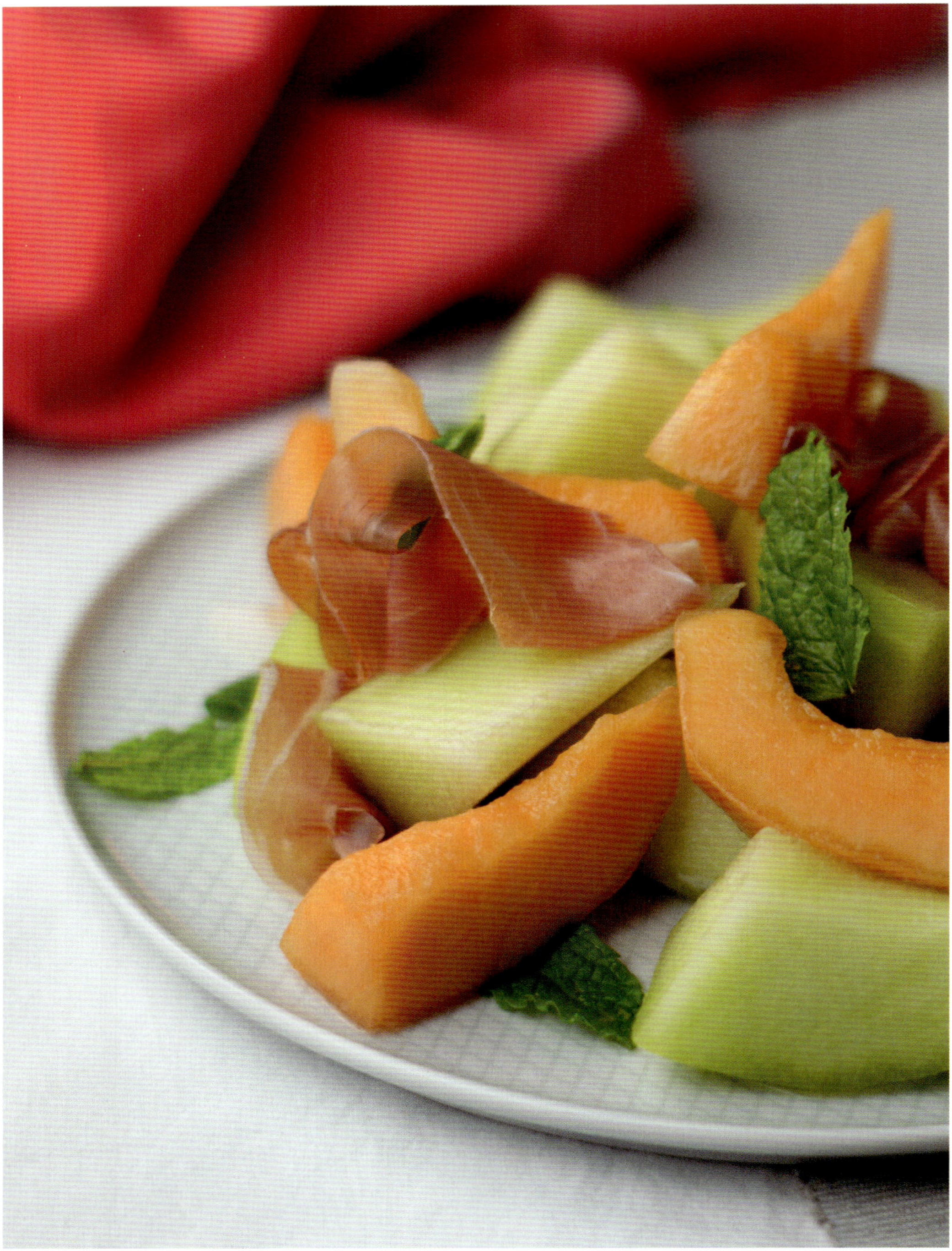

Prosciutto, Melon and Sherry Salad

Serves 6 — Prep time 15 minutes + 30 minutes resting — Difficulty ❶

Ingredients

60ml dry (fino) sherry

1 ripe melon approx. 900g (e.g. cantaloupe, honeydew, galia, or a mixture)

80g prosciutto, parma ham or jamón serrano - torn or sliced into long strips

A handful of fresh basil leaves (approx. 5g)

A handful of fresh mint leaves (approx. 5g)

Cool, dry fino sherry can be a great way to enhance flavour in savoury dishes without overpowering the flavour. The dryness is said to stimulate the taste buds, while its nutty almond notes make it a great match for savoury, salty flavours.

Here, sherry makes a perfect dressing for a fragrant summer salad of ripe melon, fresh herbs and dry-cured ham. This salad can be made anywhere from 30 minutes to 6 hours before serving. Serve alongside grilled vegetables or meats, or for lunch with good bread and a glass of chilled white wine.

- Halve the melon and scoop out the seeds, then slice off the skin with a sharp knife. Slice the melon into small wedges and put them in a large bowl
- Stir the parma ham together with the melon, along with the sherry, basil and mint leaves
- Cover the salad, place it in the fridge and allow it to sit for at least 30 minutes for the flavours to develop

Equipment

Large bowl

SIDE DISHES

Port Marinated Olives

Makes 1 large jar — Prep time 20 minutes + 2 days marinating — Difficulty ❶

Ingredients

80ml port

80ml extra virgin olive oil, plus extra to top up the jar

1 clove of garlic - peeled and thinly sliced

2 tsp smoked paprika

1 bay leaf

½ tsp chilli flakes

3 tbsp red wine vinegar

¼ tsp dijon mustard

250g mix of black, Kalamata and green olives (drained weight)

Salt and freshly ground black pepper

A good marinade can turn ordinary canned or jarred olives into something special. To flavour each olive, the marinade really needs to pack a punch - a thick marinade with strong flavours will cling to the olives and flavour them inside and out.

Here, we're marinating olives in Spanish-inspired flavours - port, smoked paprika, bay and garlic. The port provides a deep fruity note, and smoked paprika brings a rich warmth of flavour. We've also added a little mustard, as this helps the port and olive oil to emulsify. You can use any mix of black, green or Kalamata olives, but a good quality olive oil is essential.

- In a small saucepan combine 80ml olive oil with the sliced garlic, smoked paprika, bay leaf and chilli flakes. Cook over a very low heat for a few minutes, swirling the pan occasionally, until the paprika is fragrant and the oil is just beginning to bubble. Turn off the heat and allow to cool for 5 minutes on the stove

- Add the port and red wine vinegar to the saucepan together with the mustard, a large pinch of salt and good grinding of black pepper, then whisk it all together

- Drain any liquid from olives and give them a rinse - this helps to ensure that the black olives don't discolour the liquid

- Scoop the olives into a large jar and pour all the marinade on top, including the bay leaf and garlic slices. If the olives are not completely covered in marinade, top up the jar with olive oil. Seal the jar and give it a gentle shake around to ensure that the garlic is dispersed

- Place the jar in the fridge for at least 2 days to marinate, gently shaking the jar once or twice during this time. The olive oil may thicken and solidify in the fridge, so bring to room temperature before eating. The olives will keep for up to 2 weeks in the fridge

Equipment

Small saucepan

Whisk

Large jar

SIDE DISHES

Bourbon Glazed Carrots

Serves 4 — Prep time 10 minutes — Cook time 25 minutes — Difficulty ❶

Ingredients

2 tbsp bourbon

500g carrots - peeled and thickly sliced on the diagonal

2 tbsp butter

2 tbsp maple syrup

Salt

Chopped mint to garnish

Glazed carrots make a perfect accompaniment to a Sunday roast, where their sweet earthiness balances rich and hearty flavours. The trick to making glazed carrots is to use plenty of butter, which helps to carry other flavours. Then add ingredients that will complement the natural sweetness of the carrots - we love to use bourbon for this, with its sweet notes of vanilla and oak. Together with a splash of maple syrup, these are carrots like you've never tasted before.

- Place the carrots in a large saucepan and cover with cold salted water. Bring to the boil and simmer for 10-15 minutes until the carrots are tender but still with a little bite
- Remove from the heat and drain the water from the carrots, then add the butter and maple syrup into the hot saucepan with the carrots. Stir until the butter has melted, then add the bourbon and a pinch of salt
- Put the saucepan over a low heat and cook, stirring frequently, for 3-5 minutes to slightly thicken the sauce around the carrots
- Garnish with a sprinkle of mint, and serve warm

Equipment

Large saucepan

Sherry and Lemon Gravy

Serves 4-6 — Prep time 10 minutes — Cook time 20 minutes — Difficulty ①

Ingredients

100ml dry fino sherry
Chicken drippings and scrapings from the roasting pan
400ml chicken stock
1 tsp worcestershire sauce
2-3 bay leaves
2 tbsp plain flour
½ lemon - juiced (approx. 1 tbsp)
Salt

Dry, complex fino sherry is an excellent addition to your kitchen. Its light, herbal flavour is prominent enough to counter heavier meat or fat flavours, but mellow enough that it melts into the background of a dish leaving zesty aromas and a hint of creaminess. This makes it our favourite alcohol to use in a gravy for a roast dinner, where the crisp fat of roast potatoes or chicken skin needs a flavour partner that can shine without overwhelming.

This gravy recipe was created specifically to accompany a simple roast chicken, so we use the drippings from the roasting pan. However, if you haven't roasted a chicken, substitute the chicken drippings for 2 tbsp butter and 1 tsp soy sauce for extra savoury flavour. As well as roasted meats, this gravy goes well with a tray of roasted root vegetables and onions.

- Combine the sherry, chicken drippings, chicken stock, worcestershire sauce and bay leaves in a small saucepan. Turn the heat on and bring to the boil, then simmer over a low heat for around 15 minutes. This cooks off some of the harsher alcohol notes from the sherry, creating a more rounded flavour
- After 15 minutes, mix the flour with a splash of the gravy in a small bowl, adding a little more gravy to make a smooth runny paste. Whisk the flour paste into the gravy then simmer for a further 5 minutes, stirring occasionally, until the gravy has thickened
- Add a generous squeeze of lemon juice and ½ tsp salt and stir well. Taste the gravy, then add more salt or lemon if needed

Equipment

Small saucepan
Small bowl
Whisk

SHERRY AND LEMON GRAVY

BOURBON GLAZED CARROTS

COOKING WITH ALCOHOL

SIDE DISHES

CONDIMENTS

COOKING WITH ALCOHOL

Cider Mustard

Makes 3 small jars — Prep time 25 minutes + 24 hours soaking — Waiting time 1 week Difficulty ❶

Ingredients

250ml dry apple cider
80g yellow mustard seeds
80g black mustard seeds
100ml apple cider vinegar
3 tbsp runny honey
½ tsp dried turmeric
Salt

Homemade mustard is a very rewarding thing to make, yet surprisingly uncommon. Simply soaking mustard seeds in cider and blending with a few other ingredients produces a condiment to be proud of (although you need to wait a week before eating it, to allow the flavour to develop). Crushing or blending mustard seeds releases the mustard oil inside, and this is what makes mustard spicy - so the smoother you blend it, the more spicy it will be!

We love the slight sweetness of cider in this mustard, but you can customise this recipe to your taste - try adding horseradish, chilli or even using your favourite ale rather than cider. Mustard seeds have antimicrobial properties, so it keeps for a long time in the fridge.

- Combine all the mustard seeds and cider in a small bowl. Stir well, then cover and leave for around 24 hours. You'll notice that the mustard seeds absorb almost all the liquid

- The next day, heat your oven to 120C / Gas Mark ½ / 250F. Wash three jars and lids in very hot soapy water and rinse well, then place the jars on a tray in the oven for 20 minutes to sterilise them while you make the mustard

- Pour the soaked seeds and any liquid into a blender, together with the vinegar, honey, turmeric and 1 ½ tsp salt. Blend for a short time until the mustard is thickened and yellow, but with some seeds still remaining - it's up to you how smooth you make it. Bear in mind that a smoother mustard will end up spicier!

- Carefully scoop the mustard into the hot jars. Wipe the edges of each jar carefully with a damp cloth or paper towel, then close the lids tightly. Label the jars and store in the fridge for a week before using

Equipment

Small bowl
Blender or food processor
3 jam jars with lids
Baking tray

Red Wine and Caramelised Onion Chutney

Makes 2 jars — Prep time 20 minutes — Cook time 2 hours — Difficulty ❸

Ingredients

300ml red wine

2 white onions - thinly sliced in half or quarter moons

100g light or dark soft brown sugar

2 medium apples (cooking or eating apples are fine) - peeled, cored and finely chopped

75ml balsamic vinegar

2 tsp pickling spices

Salt

Oil

Red wine gives this rich, thick chutney a glorious hue and deep fruity flavour, ideal with strong cheese and crackers. It keeps well and is fairly simple to make - onions are cooked until soft and golden brown, then simmered together with wine, apples and spices. Red wine is both sweet and acidic, so this chutney requires a bit less sharp vinegar than many recipes. You can use any wine here, as the spices and vinegar overpower any fine nuances of flavour.

Serve this chutney with sharp cheese, on a sandwich, or alongside a roast dinner. Alternatively, this chutney is truly scrumptious inside a homemade sausage roll. For a festive twist, try adding the zest of an orange.

- Heat 1 tbsp oil in a large wide saucepan over a low heat. Add the onions and cook for 15 minutes, stirring occasionally, until the onions are soft and golden brown

- Stir in the brown sugar and cook for a further 10 minutes until the mixture is glossy and bubbling. Add the chopped apples, red wine, balsamic vinegar, spices and 1 tsp salt and stir well

- Bring the mixture to a boil, then simmer the mixture over a very low heat for 1 to 1 ½ hours, stirring occasionally, until most of the liquid has evaporated and the mixture is rich and thick. The chutney is ready when a spoon leaves a clear wide trail across the bottom of the saucepan for a moment when you stir it

- Meanwhile, heat your oven to 120C / Gas Mark ½ / 250F. Wash the jars and lids in very hot soapy water and rinse well, then place the jars in the oven for 20 minutes to sterilise them

- Carefully ladle the chutney into the hot jars. Wipe the edge of each jar carefully with a damp cloth or paper towel then close the lids tightly and leave to cool completely

- Label the jars then store in the fridge for up to 3 months

TIP: If you don't have pickling spices, use a lightly ground mixture of at least two of the following spices: mustard seed, fennel seed, black pepper, ginger, allspice

Equipment

Large wide saucepan

2 small jars with lids (or 1 very large jar)

CONDIMENTS

Red Wine Salt

Makes 1 jar — Prep time 1 hour + 3 days drying time — Difficulty ❷

Ingredients
300ml red wine
150g coarse sea salt

Flavoured salts are a great way to refresh your everyday recipes, adding nuances of flavour without much extra effort. And what better than a salt flavoured with red wine? Red wine salt adds a rich, dark and deeply fruity flavour dimension to your cooking, and it looks beautiful on the table. You'll often find red wine salt in tourist shops in parts of Italy, but those pale creations are nothing compared to the extraordinary seasoning that you can make at home.

Try using your red wine salt as a dry rub on meats before roasting, sprinkled over fresh baked goods (like the Peanut Butter and Bourbon Cookies on page 250), or to dress ripe sliced tomatoes. It also makes a wonderful gift.

This recipe is also a great way to use up leftover red wine - just use one part salt to two parts of wine. The flavour of the wine comes through very strongly, so use one you like!

- Pour the wine into a small saucepan and simmer over a very low heat for 45 mins to 1 hour, checking and swirling the pan fairly often, until the wine has reduced to just a few tablespoons of liquid
- Remove the pan from the heat and stir the sea salt into the wine. Mix well, then spread the mixture in a thin layer over a large plate or ceramic dish - don't use a metal tray, as the salt can cause rust to form
- Cover carefully with a tea towel and leave for at least 3 days, shaking and stirring each day, until all the moisture has evaporated and the salt is completely dry
- Break up any large lumps in the salt, either with a wooden spoon or by giving it a quick pulse in a blender, then transfer to an airtight jar or salt grinder
- The salt should last indefinitely, as salt is a preservative

Equipment
Small saucepan
Ceramic dish or large plate
Tea towel
Empty jar or salt grinder

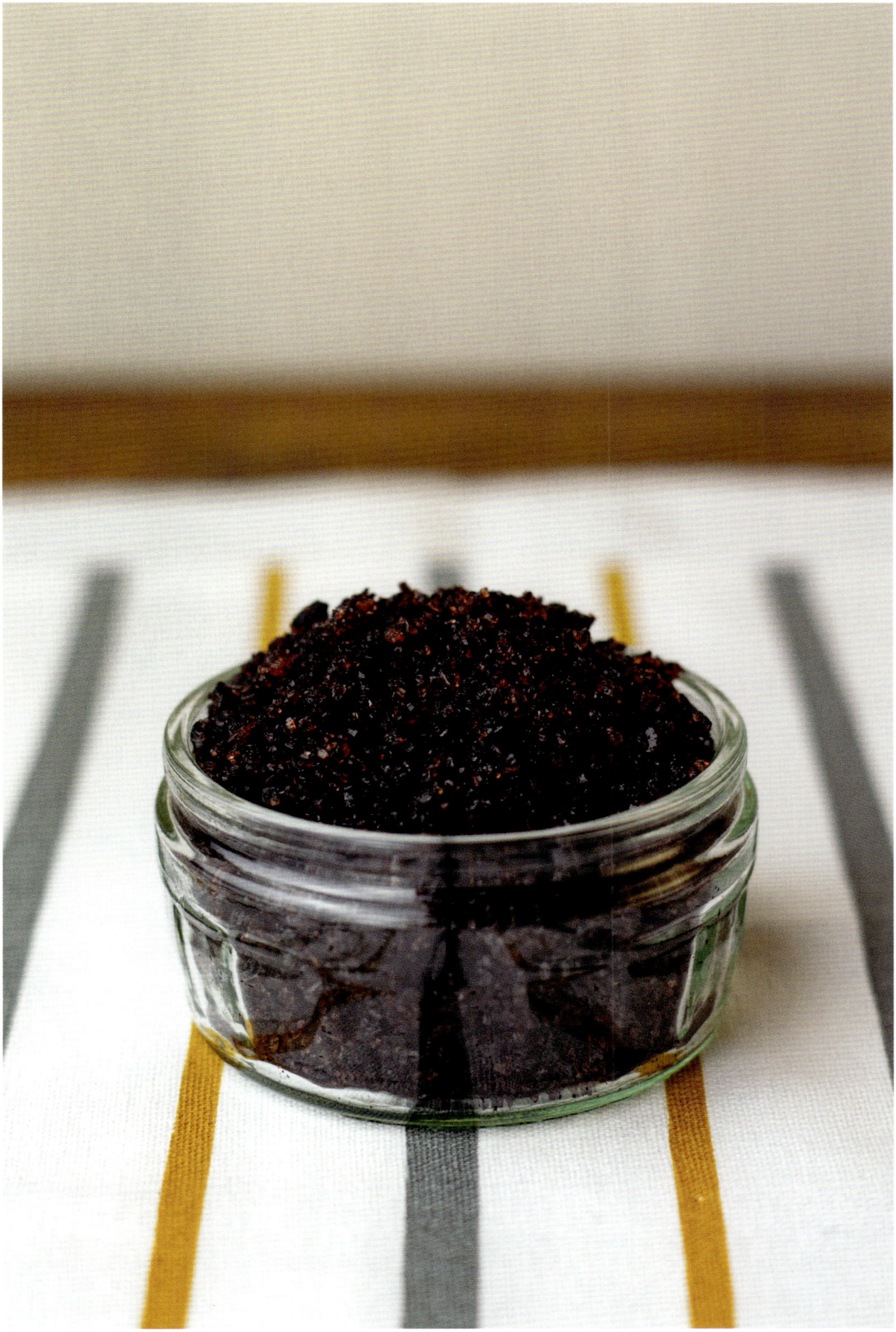

Ale Pickled Eggs

Makes 1 very large jar — Prep time 30 minutes + cooling time — Pickling time 2 weeks
Difficulty ❶

Ingredients

100ml ale or dark beer (approx. - see below)

12 eggs

300ml cider vinegar (approx. - see below)

1 tsp white sugar

3 tsp salt

Equipment

Large saucepan
Small saucepan
Large wide jar
Scales or measuring jug

We first made these delicious eggs as a gift for a friend who calls pickled eggs 'Irish cupcakes', because they are served in cupcake wrappers at many British pubs. While versions found in pubs can be rubbery and vinegary, these homemade pickled eggs are savoury and tangy - perfect with a pint and a packet of crisps. Aside from making an unusual gift, they are a long-lasting and versatile ingredient that are great added to a cheeseboard, noodle soup, or even a sandwich. We recommend using a flavourful ale that you really enjoy drinking, as the flavour will come through in the eggs.

These pickled eggs will keep indefinitely in a cool dark place, but are best enjoyed within 6 months.

For the eggs

- Place the eggs gently into a large saucepan and cover with cold water. Bring to the boil, then start a timer and keep the eggs at a boil for 10 minutes
- Remove the saucepan from the heat and place it into the sink, then run cold water into the pan for a few minutes to cool the eggs. Set the eggs to one side and allow them to cool completely (this will make them easier to peel)
- Wash a large wide jar in hot soapy water, then rinse and dry it
- Once the eggs are cool, peel and place into your jar

For the pickling liquid

- To figure out how much pickling liquid you need, put the jar of eggs on your scales and zero the scales. Pour cold water into the jar over the eggs until it covers the eggs completely - the weight of water you have added is the amount of pickling liquid that you will need to make. (In the jar pictured, we needed 400g/400ml pickling liquid). If you don't have scales, you can measure the amount of water with a jug
- To make the pickling liquid, combine 1 part beer and 3 parts vinegar in a small saucepan (to make 400ml pickling liquid this would be 100ml beer and 300ml vinegar)
- Add the sugar and salt to the beer mixture, then bring the liquid to the boil and simmer for 5 minutes. Remove from the heat and leave to cool for 15 minutes
- Once cool, pour the beer mixture over the eggs, then seal the lid and label the jar
- Now for the hard part! Put the jar into a cool dark place and wait at least 2 weeks before tasting the eggs

TIP: Our favourite way to peel eggs is to roll them firmly along a kitchen surface to crack the shell all over. Then simply remove the cracked shell using a teaspoon

CONDIMENTS

WHISKY STICKY TOFFEE PUDDING, PAGE 168

HOT DESSERTS

Sloe Gin and Blackberry Cobbler	156
Roasted Apricots in Madeira	158
Rhubarb and Gin Crumble	160
Pear and Amaretto Frangipane Tart	162
Chocolate and Rum Fondants with Raspberry Sauce	164
Red Wine Chocolate Fudge Pudding	166
Whisky Sticky Toffee Pudding	168

As we turn our attention towards sweet dishes, a whole new world of flavour pairings opens up! Hot desserts tend towards deeper flavours and stodgier textures than their cold counterparts, and in this short chapter we've created recipes that are perfect for a cold day or dark evening.

The first four recipes of this chapter are fruit-based - the fruit is either surrounded in alcohol as it bakes, poached in alcohol, or roasted in the oven with a sticky alcohol glaze. In these recipes, we can consider the addition of alcohol much like using a spice: the aim is to enhance the beautiful fruit flavour and fragrance, not to overpower it. In our **Pear and Amaretto Frangipane Tart**, amaretto adds extra moisture and fragrance, while Madeira wine brings the incredible warmth of caramelised honey and sunshine to **Roasted Apricots**.

We've found that the key to making these fruit desserts with alcohol is recognising flavour combinations, and observing how those flavours work together. It's also something that you do more often than you think - when you garnish a drink or make a cocktail. We might garnish a sloe gin cocktail with a blackberry, so a **Blackberry Cobbler** is a great place for a splash of sloe gin. In the same way, tart fruits like lemon or rhubarb are naturals in a gin and tonic, so we've used gin in our **Rhubarb and Ginger Crumble**.

If you wanted to choose an alcohol for an apple recipe, you might start by thinking, where would we use apple as a garnish? Apple is a classic garnish for bourbon cocktails, or for mulled wine or cider, so a splash of any of these ingredients could be what your next apple crumble is looking for.

The next three recipes in this chapter are recipes with rich sauces: **Red Wine Chocolate Fudge Pudding**, **Whisky Sticky Toffee Pudding**, and **Chocolate and Rum Fondants with Raspberry Sauce**. The use of cocoa or brown sugar in these desserts gives them deeper, bolder flavours than the fruitier recipes and, as a result, the alcohols that we choose to match with them need to be stronger in flavour. With a rich chocolate sauce we like to add a hint of other dark flavours like red wine, spiced rum or even a fruity liqueur like sloe gin. Meanwhile, a caramel sauce with toffee and molasses aromas is a great place to add alcohol with similar flavour accents, like a peated whisky, bourbon, or even a pear liqueur.

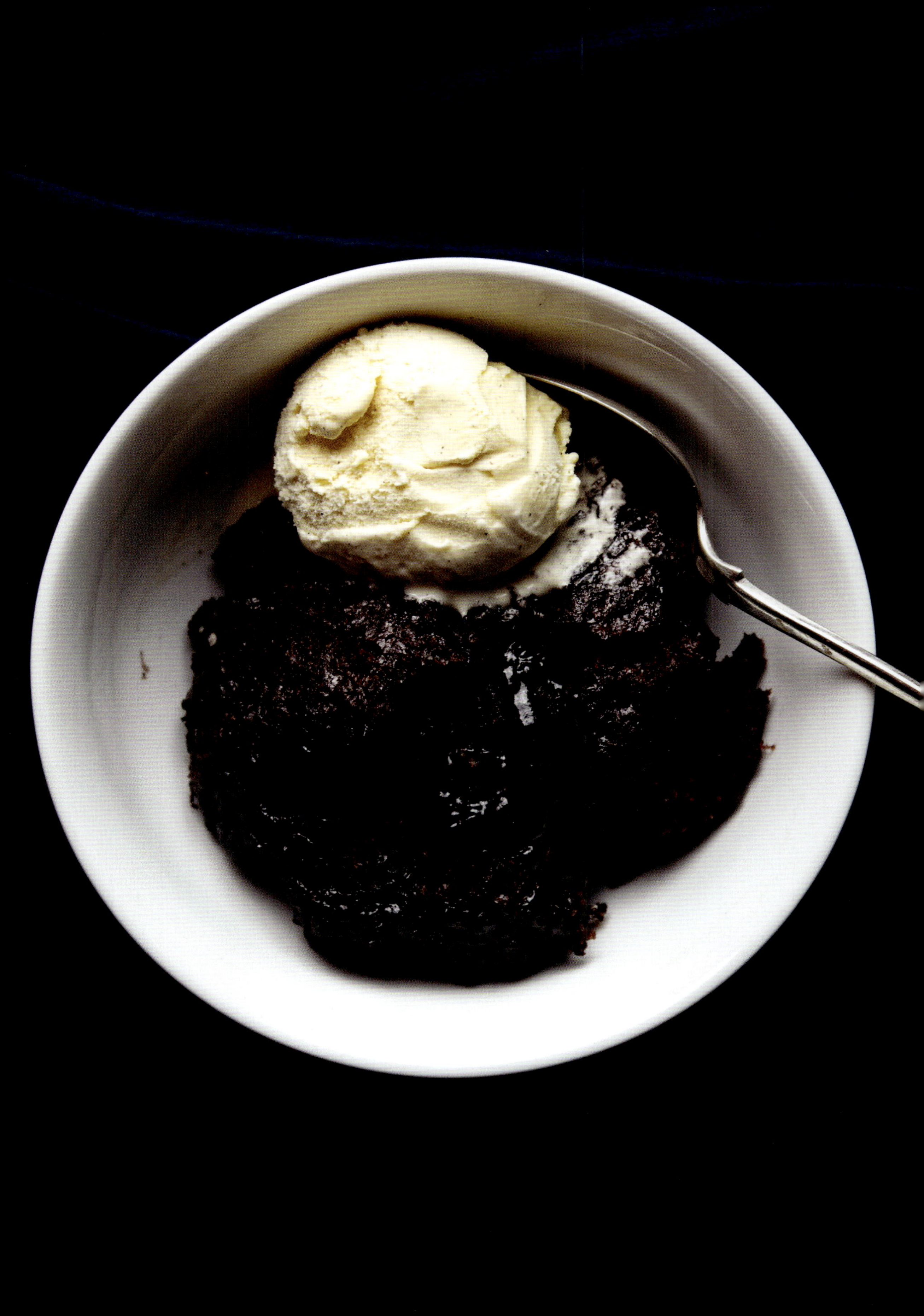

Sloe Gin and Blackberry Cobbler

Serves 4-6 — Prep time 25 minutes — Cook time 35 minutes — Difficulty ❷

Ingredients

60ml + 1 tbsp sloe gin

600g blackberries or a mix of summer berries (fresh or frozen)

100g granulated sugar + 2 tbsp for sprinkling (60g for the fruit, 40g for the topping)

2 tbsp cornflour (cornstarch)

60g butter

120g self-raising flour (or use 110g plain flour mixed with 2 level tsp baking powder)

2 tbsp milk

1 tsp vanilla extract

Ice cream, cream or natural yogurt to serve

Cobbler is a classic American baked dessert, and provides a fluffier alternative to its crunchy cousin, the crumble. It's fairly quick to make the scone-like mixture, which tops sweet, bubbling fruit for a fragrant and wholesome dessert - what's not to love?

Into the cobbler and the berries we introduce sloe gin - rich and plummy, the fragrance of sloe gin accentuates the same complex aromas within the berries, and will fill your kitchen with a wonderful aroma. If you can't find sloe gin, substitute for another fruit liqueur or use 40ml of your favourite gin.

Ice cream makes a delicious accompaniment, but for a lighter option we love to serve this cobbler with a dollop of natural yogurt.

- Preheat the oven to 170C / Gas Mark 3 ½ / 350F
- In a wide ovenproof dish, combine the berries, 60g sugar, 60ml sloe gin and 2 tbsp cornflour. Mix everything together in the dish until roughly combined
- To make the cobbler topping, measure the butter and flour in a large mixing bowl. Use your fingers to rub the butter into the flour until the mixture resembles breadcrumbs
- Stir the remaining 40g sugar into the butter and flour mixture, then sprinkle over the milk, vanilla extract and remaining 1 tbsp sloe gin. Mix it gently until you have a soft dough
- Take small spoonfuls of the dough and roll them gently in your hands to make little balls - they don't need to be perfect! Place the dough balls on the top of the berry mixture, then sprinkle the top of the cobbler with the remaining 2 tbsp sugar
- Put the dish in the oven and bake for 30-35 minutes, or until the cobbler mixture is well risen and deep golden brown on top and the berries are bubbling up around the edges. Remove from the oven and let it sit for 5 minutes, then serve with ice cream, cream or a dollop of natural yogurt

Equipment

Ovenproof dish approx 23cm (9 inch) round, or 20cm (8 inch) square

Large mixing bowl

HOT DESSERTS

Roasted Apricots in Madeira

Serves 4 — Prep time 10 minutes — Cook time 25 minutes — Difficulty ❶

Ingredients

100ml Madeira, sweet Marsala or other dessert wine (80ml for the apricots, 20ml for the mascarpone)

6-8 apricots - halved and stoned

1 tbsp + 1 tsp light soft brown sugar

150g mascarpone cheese

Roasting seems to transform the humble apricot. The heat of the oven ripens and sweetens the apricot in the way that summer sun does, concentrating and caramelising the natural fruit sugars. To encourage this process we need to add a little sugar and moisture, and a sweet dessert wine is an excellent choice here. The aroma of dried dark fruits and subtle molasses in Madeira accentuates the sweet honey flavour of the apricots, and brings a complex caramel note to the dish.

If your apricots aren't quite ripe, we'd suggest increasing the sugar to 2 tbsp. This recipe also works wonderfully with other summer stone fruits like peaches or nectarines (they just take a little longer to cook). Serve with a dollop of sweetened Madeira mascarpone.

- Preheat the oven to 200C / Gas Mark 6 / 400F
- Place the halved apricots cut-side up into an ovenproof dish where they all fit in one layer. Sprinkle the apricots with 1 tbsp of the brown sugar and 80ml of the Madeira wine
- Put the dish in the oven and cook for 20-25 minutes until the apricots are soft but not completely collapsed. Half way through, shake the dish and spoon some of the liquid on top of the apricots to baste them
- Once the apricots have softened, remove the tray from the oven and spoon some of the liquid over the apricots again
- Separately, scoop the mascarpone into a small bowl and stir until soft and smooth. Add the remaining 1 tsp brown sugar and 20ml Madeira and stir well
- Dollop the sweetened mascarpone on top of the roasted apricots, swirl it slightly, then take the dish to the table to serve

TIP: If you can't get the stones out of the apricots, don't worry - just roast them with the stones in, and remove them afterwards

Equipment

Ovenproof dish

Small bowl

HOT DESSERTS

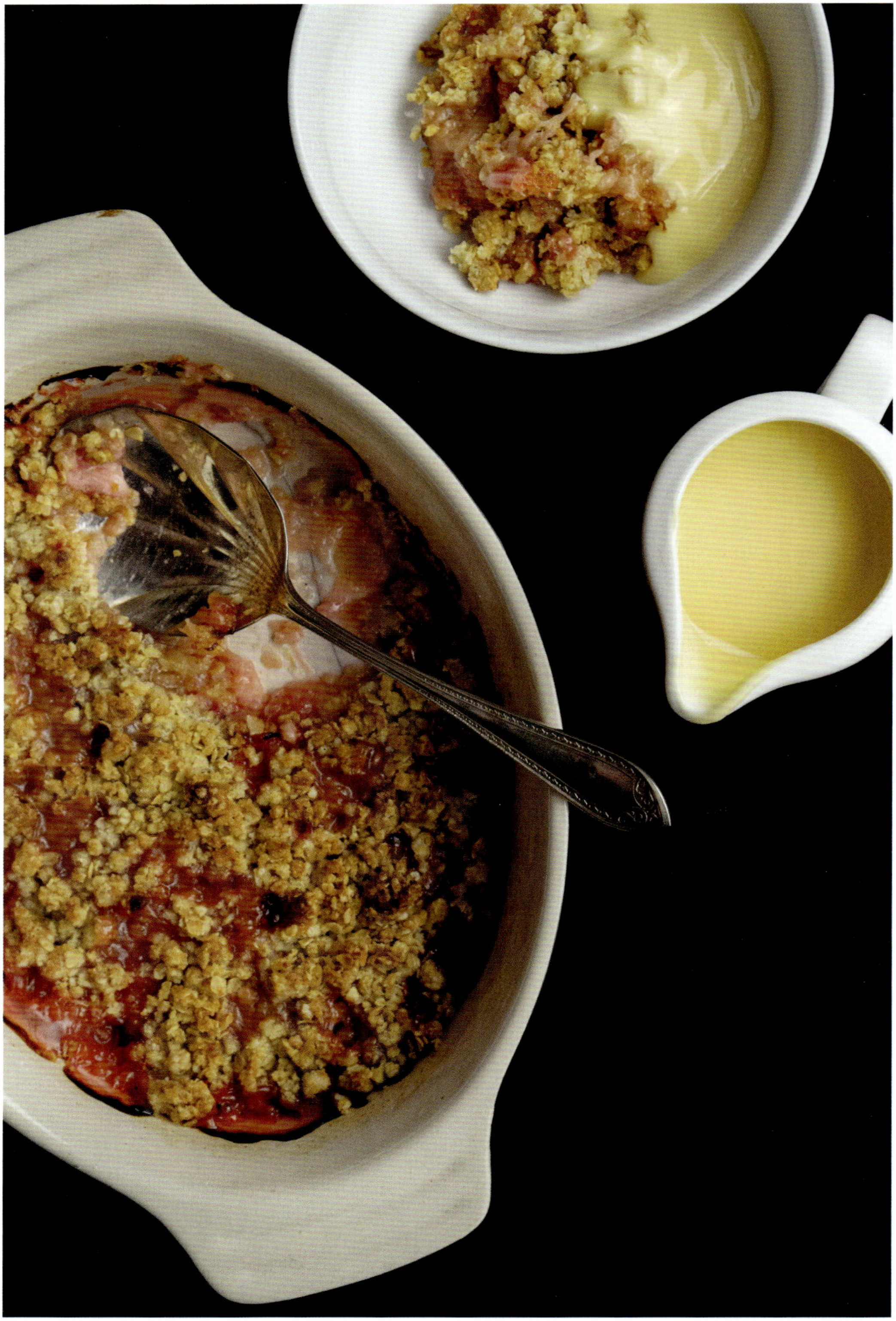

Rhubarb and Gin Crumble

Serves 4 — Prep time 25 minutes — Cook time 35 minutes — Difficulty ❶

Ingredients

4 tbsp gin

6 rhubarb stalks (approx. 600g total) - trimmed and sliced into 1 inch lengths

2 tsp cornflour (cornstarch)

100g + 2 tbsp white sugar

70g butter

70g rolled oats

70g plain flour

½ tsp ground ginger

¼ tsp freshly ground cardamom

Custard or cream to serve

This comforting, seasonal crumble is easy to make and goes down a treat after Sunday lunch. The flavours of gin are a great match for sour fruits like rhubarb - think of the lemon, lime or grapefruit that might be used to garnish a gin and tonic. Our crumble is spiced with ginger and cardamom for a warming, aromatic feel, but you could experiment by adding other gin botanicals - a few crushed juniper berries, a little lemon zest or even a sprinkle of crushed coriander seeds work wonderfully.

To achieve a truly crumbly, craggy texture, we use melted butter in the topping. This helps the mixture to clump together, and the addition of oats ensures a crisp textural contrast. Serve with a generous dollop of cream or custard.

- Preheat the oven to 180C / Gas Mark 4 / 350F
- Put the sliced rhubarb, gin, cornflour and 2 tbsp sugar into the baking dish. Mix them together then spread out the rhubarb into an even layer
- Separately, mix together the oats, flour, ginger, cardamon and 100g sugar in a large mixing bowl
- Melt the butter in a small saucepan or the microwave, then stir this into the dry mixture until the mixture forms large crumbs
- Sprinkle the crumble mixture over the top of the rhubarb - don't press it down - then bake for 30-35 minutes until the crumble is golden brown on top and bubbling around the edges. Allow to cool for 5 minutes then serve with custard or cream

TIP: To get the seeds out of the cardamom pods, use the flat of a knife to crush them on a chopping board, then extract the seeds. Crush the seeds in a pestle and mortar, or in a clean pepper grinder

Equipment

Medium sized ovenproof dish

Mixing bowl

Small saucepan or microwave

Pear and Amaretto Frangipane Tart

Serves 8-10 — Prep time 1 hour 30 minutes — Cook time 45 minutes — Difficulty ❸

Ingredients

100ml amaretto liqueur

3 or 4 pears (approx. 400g total unprepared weight) - peeled, cored and sliced into 4-6 wedges

175g + 1 tbsp plain flour

25g icing sugar (powdered sugar)

225g butter - 100g chilled, 125g softened (remove from the fridge for 30 mins)

2 eggs + 1 egg yolk

200g caster sugar

1 tbsp cornflour (cornstarch)

120g ground almonds

2 tbsp apricot or plum jam

Salt

Equipment

Small saucepan

Food processor (optional)

23cm (9 inch) tart tin, preferably with a removable base

Flat baking tray

Rolling pin (or empty wine bottle)

2 x large mixing bowls

Electric beater or wooden spoon

Pastry brush

This tart might well be Aaron's favourite dessert in the whole book. Each bite is a marriage of juicy poached pears and rich, decadent frangipane, brought together with amaretto liqueur and a sticky glaze.

It can be hard to find perfectly ripe pears, so gentle cooking on the stove is ideal, and ensures that the almond-scented amaretto infuses each slice. The tender pears are then baked on a bed of fluffy, buttery frangipane and crisp pastry for a truly delightful result.

When baking the tart, we suggest putting a hot baking tray underneath it in the oven. This helps to ensure an even transfer of heat so that the pastry cooks well throughout.

For the poached pears

- Place the sliced pears and amaretto liqueur in a small saucepan. Cover and cook over a medium heat for 10 minutes until the pears are tender but still holding their shape. Remove from the heat and allow to cool in the pan

For the pastry

- If you have a food processor, put 175g plain flour in a food processor together with the icing sugar and 100g chilled butter. Blitz it until the mixture forms crumbs, then add the egg yolk and 3 tbsp water and pulse until the mixture forms a ball of pastry (if it doesn't stick together, add an extra 1-2 tbsp of water)

- Alternatively, grate 100g chilled butter into a mixing bowl. Add the flour and icing sugar and use your fingers to rub the butter into the flour until it forms crumbs. Then add the egg yolk and 3 tbsp water and mix together gently until you have a soft ball of dough, adding extra water to bring it together if necessary

- Cover the pastry and chill in the fridge for at least 15 minutes

- Grease the tart tin with plenty of butter, and sprinkle with flour

- Roll out the chilled pastry on a clean floured surface into a circle approximately 3mm (⅛ inch) thick and 30cm (11 inches) in diameter, a bit wider than your tart tin. Gently transfer the pastry to the tin and press it to the sides, making sure that you don't stretch the dough. Chill in the fridge for a further 30 minutes

- Preheat the oven to 180C / Gas Mark 4 / 350F, and place a flat baking tray inside the oven to heat up

For the frangipane

- In a large mixing bowl, combine 125g softened butter with the caster sugar and beat well for a few minutes until pale and light. Add the eggs, cornflour and remaining 1 tbsp plain flour and beat well for a few more minutes. Gently fold in the ground almonds, together with a pinch of salt and 2 tbsp of the amaretto poaching liquid

Bringing it together
- Remove the pastry from the fridge. Scoop the frangipane into the pastry case and spread it out with the back of a spoon. Remove the pears from their poaching liquid (saving the liquid for later) and arrange them on top of the frangipane. Place the tart into the oven, on top of the preheated baking tray. Bake for 40-45 minutes until the top is firm and deep golden brown, and the pastry is cooked through

For the amaretto glaze
- While the tart is baking, add 2 tbsp apricot or plum jam to the rest of the amaretto liquid from the pears. Simmer over a low heat for 10-15 minutes, stirring occasionally, until the liquid is thick and syrupy
- When the tart is out of the oven, leave it to cool for 10 minutes then brush the amaretto glaze liberally all over the tart. Serve warm

Chocolate and Rum Fondants with Raspberry Sauce

Serves 4 — Prep time 30 minutes — Cook time 15 minutes — Difficulty ❸

Ingredients

4 tbsp dark or spiced rum

1-2 tbsp cocoa

75g raspberries (fresh or frozen)

A squeeze of lemon juice (a dash of bottled juice is fine)

120g butter + extra for greasing

120g dark chocolate (min. 70% cocoa solids) - broken into pieces

120g + 2 tbsp white sugar

2 eggs

2 tbsp plain flour

Salt

Ice cream or cream to serve

Chocolate fondants, or lava cakes, are (arguably) the most romantic dessert to serve on a special occasion. With their firm, pert exterior and soft heart, they are truly a dish to love. Non-romantically, this recipe serves four.

Fondant means 'melting' in French, referring to the way the outside of the cake firms up while the centre stays silky soft and gooey. Here, rich dark chocolate is paired with the spicy caramel notes of dark rum for a hint of naughtiness. Amaretto liqueur or brandy also work beautifully here, lifted by a bright raspberry sauce.

You can prepare chocolate fondants a few hours ahead of time - just pop the ramekins in the fridge until you're ready to cook, then bake for 11-15 minutes from cold. If you only want to bake two of the fondants, cover the other two ramekins tightly and freeze for up to two weeks. Make sure to defrost fully before baking.

- Preheat the oven to 190C / Gas Mark 5 / 375F
- Grease the inside of the ramekins with butter. Place 1 tbsp of cocoa into the first ramekin and turn the ramekin until the inside is coated with cocoa, then tip the remaining cocoa into the second ramekin. Repeat until the insides of all four ramekins are coated with cocoa

For the sauce
- In a small saucepan, combine the raspberries with 2 tbsp sugar, 2 tbsp rum, and a squeeze of lemon juice
- Cook over a medium heat for 5 minutes, stirring frequently, until the sugar has dissolved and the raspberries have broken down into a sauce. Scoop the sauce into a bowl and set to one side

For the fondants
- Put an inch or two of water into a saucepan and heat over a medium heat until the water is barely simmering
- Combine the butter, broken chocolate pieces and the remaining 2 tbsp rum in a heatproof bowl and set this over the pan of simmering water, ensuring that the bowl isn't touching the hot water. Stir the mixture gently until the chocolate has melted and the mixture is smooth, then remove from the heat and allow to cool for a few minutes
- Meanwhile, in a separate mixing bowl, beat the remaining 120g sugar together with the eggs and a pinch of salt until light and fluffy
- Gently fold the cooled chocolate mixture into the egg mixture with a spatula, then fold in the flour until just combined

Equipment

4 ramekins or dariole moulds

Small saucepan

Heatproof bowl

Mixing bowl

Electric beater or whisk

- Divide the batter between the ramekins and bake for 10-14 minutes, checking after 10 minutes. The fondants are ready when the tops are firm and just starting to pull away from the edge of the ramekin, but there's still a slight wobble when you move the tray
- Rest the fondants for 2 minutes, then run a knife around the edge of each and invert onto a plate. Serve immediately with a dollop of raspberry sauce and some ice cream or cream

TIP: We find that 12 minutes is the optimum cooking time, but it will vary depending on your oven. If you really want them perfect, cook one ahead of time to get the timings right, eat it, and claim you only made three

HOT DESSERTS

Red Wine Chocolate Fudge Pudding

Serves 6 — Prep time 30 minutes — Cook time 35 minutes — Difficulty ❷

Ingredients

- 400ml red wine
- 200g self-raising flour (or use 190g plain flour mixed with 3 level tsp baking powder)
- 225g white sugar
- 6 tbsp cocoa (3 tbsp for the pudding, 3 tbsp for the sauce)
- 75g butter
- 2 tbsp golden syrup
- 175ml milk
- 100g light or dark soft brown sugar
- Cream or ice cream to serve

This recipe is a twist on Susannah's dad's favourite pudding, an Australian classic - rich, gooey chocolate pudding with a thick fudge sauce. It's a self-saucing pudding, a rather magical dish where hot wine is poured on top of the batter before baking. As it bakes, the heavy sauce drops to the bottom of the dish and bubbles up around the sides. It might seem strange to pour liquid on top of cake batter, but don't worry - you haven't ruined it!

Red wine goes beautifully with cocoa, and it adds a dark fruitiness to the rich fudge sauce. Enjoy this pudding in plentiful quantities with a generous drizzle of cream or a scoop of vanilla ice cream.

- Preheat the oven to 180C / Gas Mark 4 / 350F

For the pudding

- Mix together the self-raising flour, white sugar and 3 tbsp cocoa in a large mixing bowl
- Separately, melt together the butter and golden syrup in a small saucepan or the microwave. Stir this into the dry ingredients, followed by the milk, then beat well with a wooden spoon until smooth. Pour the mixture into a large ovenproof dish and smooth the top with a spoon

For the fudge sauce

- Pour the red wine into a small saucepan and heat until nearly boiling
- Meanwhile, mix together the brown sugar and remaining 3 tbsp cocoa in a small bowl. Sprinkle the mixture all over the top of the chocolate pudding batter
- Gently pour the hot wine all over the top of the sugared pudding until you have a layer of hot wine sitting on top of the batter. Place the dish in the oven and bake for 30-35 minutes until brown and crisp on top, with fudge sauce bubbling up around the sides. The pudding is done when a sharp knife poked into the cakey centre comes out clean
- Allow to rest for 5 minutes, then serve with cream or ice cream

Equipment

- Large mixing bowl
- Large ovenproof dish
- 2 x small saucepans
- Small bowl

HOT DESSERTS

Whisky Sticky Toffee Pudding

Serves 6 — Prep time 40 minutes — Cooking time 40 minutes — Difficulty ❸

Ingredients

80ml + 2 tbsp whisky

175g dates - stoned and chopped into large pieces

200ml boiling water

170g butter (120g for the sauce, 50g for the pudding)

270g light or dark soft brown sugar (120g for the sauce, 150g for the pudding)

150ml double (heavy) cream

2 eggs

175g plain flour

1 tsp baking powder

½ tsp mixed spice or pumpkin spice

Salt

Ice cream or custard to serve

Treacly and luxurious, sticky toffee pudding is an easy-to-make dessert, certain to please a crowd. Traditionally, dates are soaked in boiling water before being added to the mixture, which creates the pudding's famous stickiness and wonderful sweetness. We love to go a step further, and soak the dates in whisky. This adds a warm, slightly spicy flavour that permeates throughout the dish as it steams in the oven. Pair it with our simple whisky toffee sauce, and lashings of ice cream or custard.

If you can bear to use a smoky, peaty scotch here, it's worth it. During cooking, the sweetness and smokiness are enhanced, adding a delicious bite to this classic pudding. But if your single malt is too precious to cook with, a cheap one will work beautifully here too.

- Cover the dates in 200ml boiling water and 80ml whisky and allow to soak for at least half an hour

For the toffee sauce

- In a small saucepan, combine 120g butter, 120g brown sugar, the double cream, 2 tbsp whisky and a pinch of salt. Cook over a low heat, stirring occasionally, until the butter has melted and the sugar has dissolved
- Spoon about a third of the toffee sauce into the bottom of a large ovenproof dish and place the dish in the freezer while you make the pudding. Leave the rest of the toffee sauce to one side

For the pudding

- Preheat the oven to 180C / Gas Mark 4 / 350F
- In a large mixing bowl, beat together the remaining 50g butter and 150g brown sugar until pale and creamy. Add the eggs one at a time, beating well with each addition
- Fold in the flour, baking powder, a pinch of salt and the mixed spice until just combined, then stir in the dates along with all of the soaking liquid
- Take the baking dish out of the freezer and pour the pudding mixture on top of the chilled toffee sauce. Place in the oven and bake for 35 minutes, or until the top is firm and golden brown and a knife comes out dry when poked into the pudding
- Warm the remaining toffee sauce over a low heat, then serve the pudding with a generous helping of warm toffee sauce and lashings of ice cream or custard

Equipment

Small bowl

Small saucepan

Ovenproof dish approx 25cm (10 inches) square and at least 8cm (3 inches) deep

Large mixing bowl

Electric beater or wooden spoon

HOT DESSERTS

ROASTED PLUM AND PORT RIPPLE ICE CREAM,
PAGE 200

COLD DESSERTS

Alcoholic Chocolate Mousse	174
Tequila Key Lime Pie	178
Crema Catalana con Madeira	180
Amaretto and Ginger Cheesecake	182
Rum, Raisin and Pistachio Posset	184
Chocolate and Amaretto Ganache Pots	186
Gin, Lime and Elderflower Cheesecake	188
Prosecco Panna Cotta	190
Aperol Spritz Jellies	192
Rosé and Raspberry Trifles	194
Orange and Tequila Sorbet	196
Piña Colada Sorbet	198
Roasted Plum and Port Ripple Ice Cream	200

Whether it's the crisp crack of the surface of a **Crema Catalana** against your spoon, or a generous scoop of **Piña Colada Sorbet** that you're after, you'll find something in this chapter that will truly delight.

The recipes in this chapter can be roughly divided into mousses, custards, dairy, jelly, and frozen desserts. Each of these sections uses slightly different techniques for cooking with alcohol, which we'll talk through below. An understanding of these principles isn't essential, but it will make adapting these desserts to your own preferences, or choice of ingredients, easier.

It's worth bearing in mind that all these desserts need to be made a little ahead of time in order to cool or chill. It makes them ideal for stress-free entertaining, or for those days when you want to look like a domestic divinity ("here's one I made earlier...").

The first recipe in this chapter, the **Alcoholic Chocolate Mousse**, is one of our favourites in this book, purely because it is so very science-based. It seems crazy to make a two ingredient chocolate mousse, and even more so when one of those ingredients is alcohol. That being said, it is possible, and this very possibility brings us joy - we've given nineteen different flavour combinations here, but the variations are endless, as long as you stick to the right ratio of alcohol to chocolate.

After this is a group of recipes we called 'custards'. These desserts offer the perfect base for the flavours of alcohol, and use egg to set a cream mixture. There are three in this chapter: **Tequila Key Lime Pie**, **Crema Catalana con Madeira**, and **Amaretto and Ginger Cheesecake**. These desserts truly show the adaptability of alcohol in adding incredible depth of flavour to classic recipes.

We've then included four dairy-based recipes without eggs. Instead, the dessert is set to the perfect texture either simply through the thickening action of alcohol on cream (such as in the **Rum, Raisin and Pistachio Posset**), or with the addition of gelatine or chocolate (as in the **Chocolate and Amaretto Ganache Pots**).

There are two recipes here including jelly. For the most delicious alcoholic jelly, we've found that it's vital to use a fruity alcohol as the base - Aperol and rosé wine are our stars here, both very drinkable in their own right. Then, we add a bright and tangy fruit to the jelly mixture to create a beautiful, fresh flavour profile - here, fresh orange is the perfect partner to sunny and bitter Aperol, while raspberries add a delicious tartness to a summer fruit **Rosé Trifle**.

And finally, we've included three frozen dessert recipes in this chapter: two sorbets, and an ice cream. It's a cheat ice cream, actually, that uses shop bought ice cream, which we swirl with rich, jammy **Roasted Plums and Port**. These are recipes written for people who, like us, don't have an ice cream maker - with just a freezer and a blender, you can produce a frozen dessert to be proud of!

We actually made our **Orange and Tequila Sorbet** long before we considered writing a cookbook - then, it was a palate cleanser served as part of a university student five course meal! We like to think that we've grown up a bit since then… but truthfully, this sorbet is still best served with a shot of tequila on the side.

With an understanding of the techniques here, we hope that you feel confident enough to experiment with these recipes - just note that the amount and type of alcohol used are carefully selected to achieve the perfect consistency. So, if you are adapting these recipes then be sure to use a similar alcohol! Prosecco could be substituted for another sparkling wine, but switching it for a spirit or liqueur might create a rather disappointing result. If you prefer vodka and lemon over gin and lime, try that in the **Gin, Lime and Elderflower Cheesecake**. Retaining the proportions, and substituting similar alcohols for another, can create wonderful results - the fun is in the discovery.

Alcoholic Chocolate Mousse

Serves 4 — Prep time 10 minutes — Cook time 15 minutes — Difficulty ❷

Ingredients

Dark Chocolate Mousse with Port

200ml port

200g dark chocolate (min. 80% cocoa solids)

5g caster sugar

Dark Chocolate Mousse with Stout

200ml stout

200g dark chocolate (min. 80% cocoa solids)

10g caster sugar

Milk Chocolate Mousse with Cointreau

50ml cointreau

200g milk chocolate (min. 30% cocoa solids)

50ml water

Milk Chocolate Mousse with Irish Cream

150ml Irish cream

200g milk chocolate (min. 30% cocoa solids)

White Chocolate Mousse with Coconut and Pineapple

100ml coconut rum

200g white chocolate

100g fresh pineapple to decorate - chopped into small pieces

White Chocolate Mousse with Tequila and Lime

75ml tequila

200g white chocolate

1 unwaxed lime - zested and juiced

Equipment

Medium saucepan

Large bowl

Metal heatproof bowl

Whisk

Ice

This rich and silky chocolate mousse is surprisingly easy to make, despite the novel technique used. The French molecular gastronomist Hervé This devised a little-known method for combining chocolate and water to create a smooth and light mousse - simply melting the ingredients together, then beating the mixture while chilling, allows the chocolate and liquid to emulsify. Of course, we're using alcohol instead of water!

This mousse doesn't require any added eggs or dairy, as the thickening comes entirely from the emulsification of cocoa solids and alcohol. The cocoa content of the chocolate dictates just how much alcohol should be added for the perfect texture - a high quality, dark chocolate can take more alcohol, while a milk or white chocolate mousse uses a smaller amount.

We've included the ingredients for six mousses here, but they all follow the same method.

- Prepare a medium saucepan of barely simmering water, and alongside it a large bowl of cold water with a few generous handfuls of ice

- Break the chocolate into a metal heatproof bowl and add the alcohol, along with any other ingredients in your chosen recipe

- Place the metal bowl over the saucepan of hot water, ensuring that the bowl isn't touching the hot water, and stir gently until the chocolate has melted and the mixture is smooth

- Take the bowl out of the saucepan and place it into the bowl of iced water, which will begin to chill it from the outside. Immediately begin whisking the mixture and continue for a few minutes as the chocolate cools and begins to thicken. This will take about 5 minutes in total

- Stop whisking when the chocolate has reached the texture of whipped cream, being careful not to overmix (it will firm up a little more after you have stopped whisking)

- Pipe or scoop the mousse into bowls, and serve. If you aren't eating it immediately, store in the fridge, but allow it to come to room temperature before serving

TIP: If the mixture is overbeaten it can become grainy or stiff instead of light and smooth. This can easily be fixed by heating the mixture to re-melt it, then cooling & beating again

TIP: Using a metal mixing bowl for the mousse mixture will help it to cool more quickly when placed in the ice water. This rapid cooling helps the mousse to emulsify and thicken. If you don't have a metal bowl, you could use a small metal saucepan instead

Other flavour suggestions:

Dark Chocolate Mousse with:

- 200ml mulled wine
- 100ml coffee liqueur, 100ml water
- 75ml chilli vodka, 125ml water
- 75ml whisky, 125ml water
- 50ml mint liqueur, 150ml water

Milk Chocolate Mousse with:

- 75ml banana liqueur, 25ml water
- 75ml sloe gin, 25ml water
- 75ml amaretto liqueur, 25ml water
- 75ml vodka, 25ml water and topped with a handful of fresh raspberries

White Chocolate Mousse with:

- 50ml brandy, 25ml mint liqueur, 25ml water
- 40ml amaretto liqueur, 40ml kirsch, 20ml water
- 70ml coffee liqueur, 30ml vodka
- 50ml whisky, 50ml water

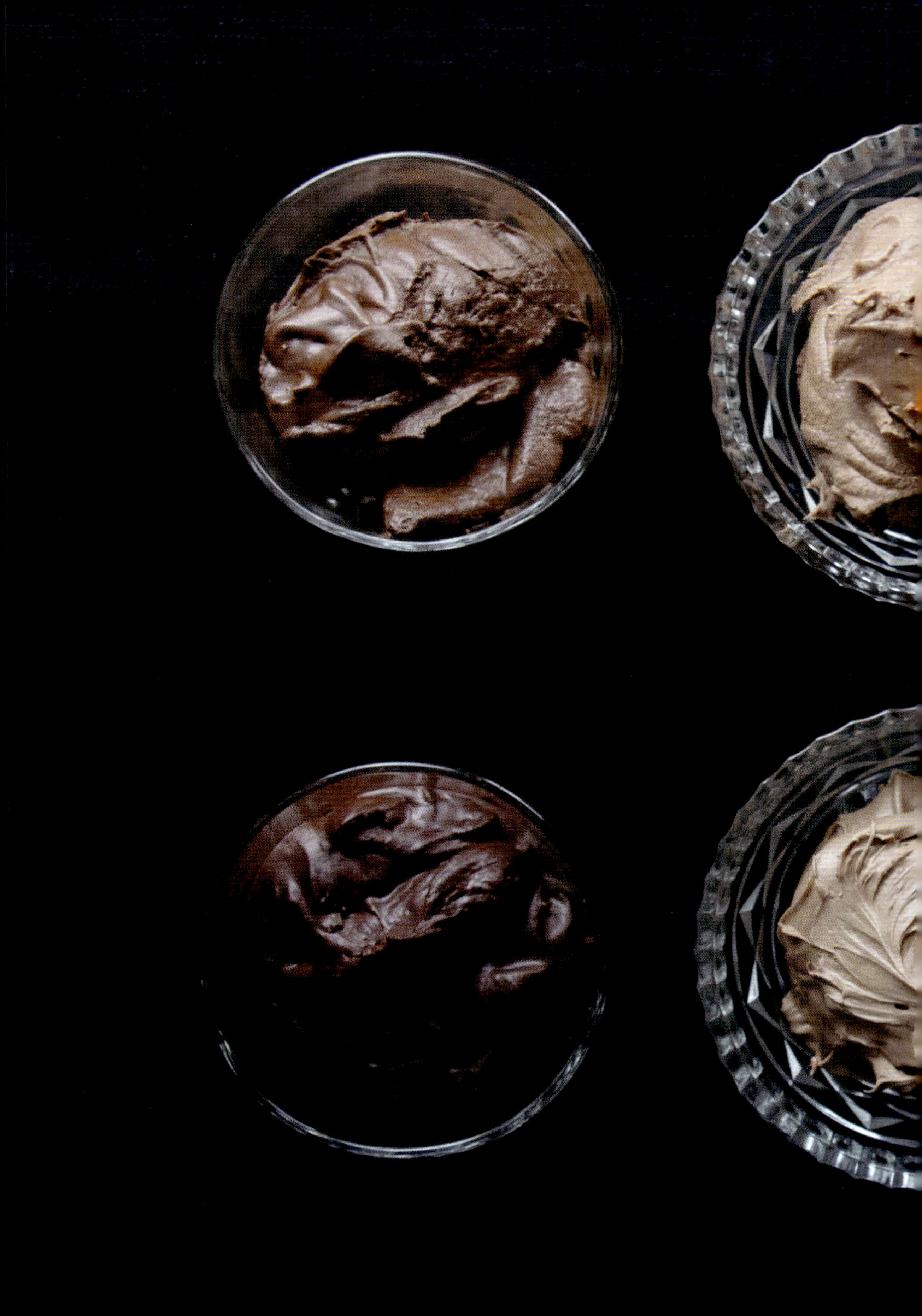

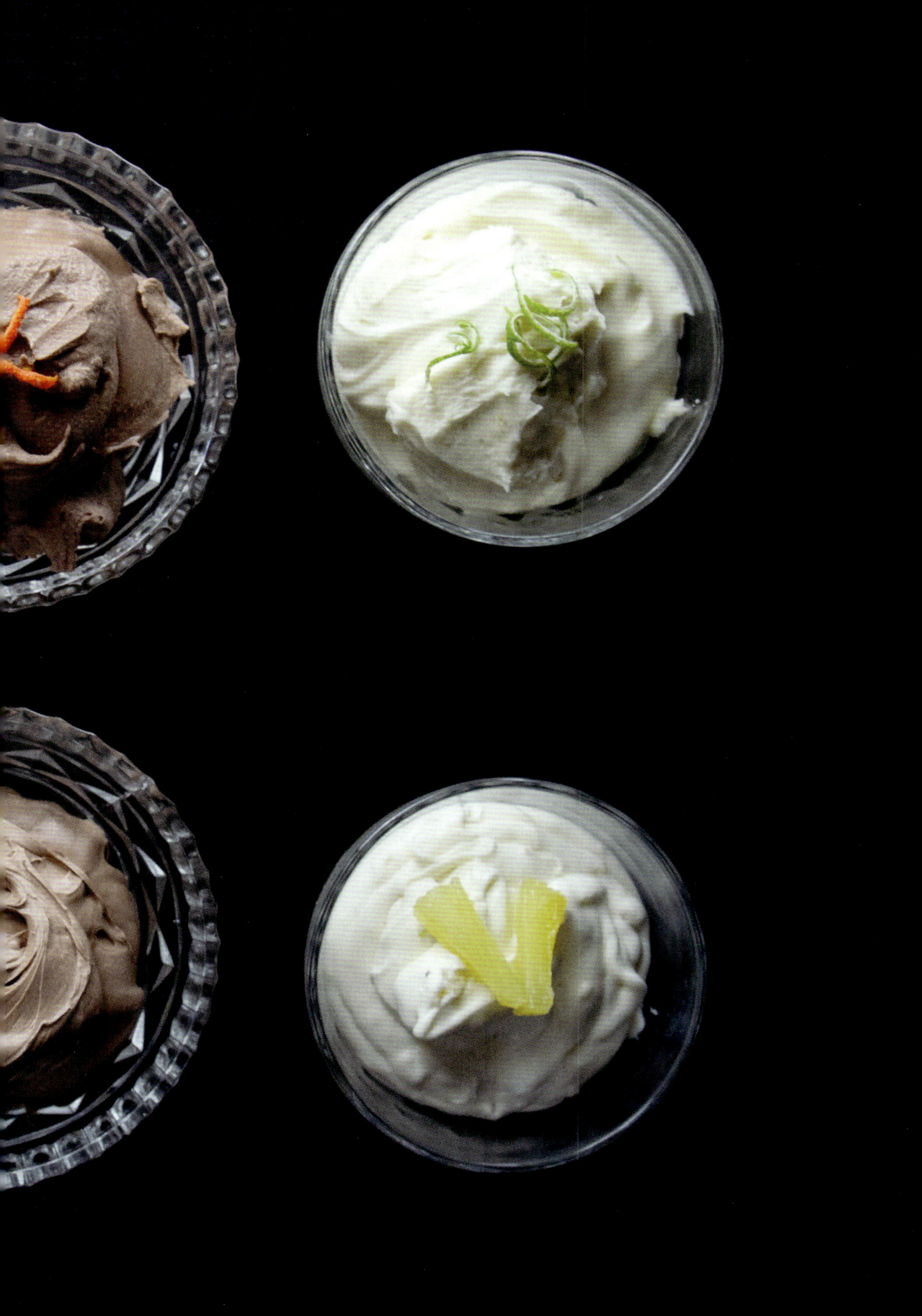

COOKING WITH ALCOHOL

Tequila Key Lime Pie

Serves 8 — Prep time 45 minutes — Cook time 20 minutes + 4 hours chilling
Difficulty ❸

Key lime pie is an American favourite, traditionally made with Key limes - a tart, aromatic variety of lime grown in tropical regions including the Florida Keys. Our recipe tastes just as good using regular limes, and with the addition of plenty of tequila! Tequila has a bright, tart flavour which is strong enough to stand up to the sweet citrus and cream.

The pie is only baked for a short time, and sets as it chills to produce a rich, tangy lime custard filling. This recipe fills a pie to about 3cm deep, so if you're using a deeper pie dish you may not need to press the crust all the way up the sides of the dish.

We don't use any green food colouring in our pie, but you could use a few drops if you want a brighter colour!

Ingredients

- 75ml + 1 tbsp tequila
- 300g digestive biscuits
- 80g butter, plus extra for greasing the tin
- 2 tbsp runny honey or agave nectar
- 6 unwaxed limes (5 for the pie filling, 1 to decorate)
- 1 x 400g can of condensed milk
- 3 egg yolks
- 150ml double (heavy) cream
- Green food colouring (optional)

- Preheat the oven to 160C / Gas Mark 3 / 325F and grease a 22cm pie or tart dish with butter

For the crust

- Put the digestive biscuits into a resealable freezer bag, push the air out and then crush the biscuits with a rolling pin - alternatively, blitz them in a food processor to fine crumbs. Tip into a mixing bowl
- Melt the butter in a small saucepan or in the microwave, then stir the melted butter into the biscuit crumbs together with 1 tbsp tequila and 1 tbsp honey or agave. Mix well
- Spread the mixture over the bottom and sides of the greased pie dish, pressing down firmly with the back of the spoon
- Place the pie dish in the oven and bake for 5 minutes to dry out the crust a bit, then remove from the oven and allow to cool for at least 10 minutes

For the filling

- While the pastry is cooling, zest and juice 5 of the limes. Put the zest and juice into a large bowl together with the condensed milk, egg yolks and 75ml tequila. Whisk it all together for a minute until combined and smooth, adding a few drops of green food colouring if you want a brighter colour
- Pour the filling into the pie crust then place the dish in the oven and bake for 20 minutes, turning the dish half way through if it looks like it's cooking unevenly. Remove from the oven and allow to cool to room temperature. Once cooled, place in the fridge and chill for at least 3 hours or overnight

Bringing it together

- To serve, beat the cream and remaining 1 tbsp honey together with a whisk until it holds soft peaks. Pipe or spread the whipped cream on top of the pie, and garnish with thin slices of the remaining lime or a sprinkle of lime zest. Slice and serve!

Equipment

- 22cm (9 inch) diameter pie or tart dish
- Food processor or a freezer bag and rolling pin
- Small saucepan or microwave
- 3 x mixing bowls
- Whisk

COLD DESSERTS

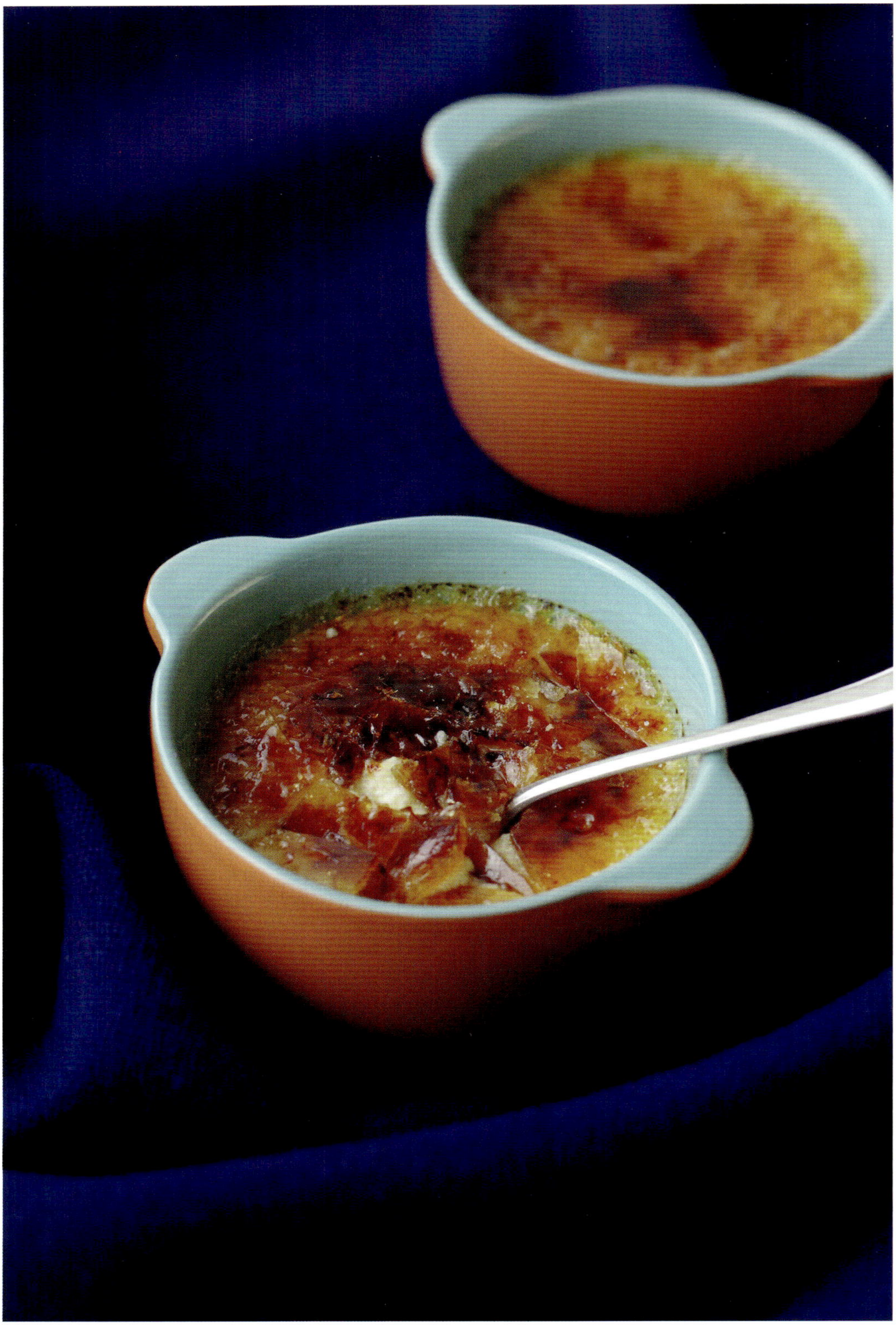

Crema Catalana con Madeira

Serves 6 — Prep time 30 minutes — Cook time 35 minutes + 2 hours chilling
Difficulty ❷

Crema Catalana originates in the Catalan region of Spain, and is similar to the French dessert crème brûlée, where luscious custard is topped with a crown of scalded, crisp caramel. It's an easy custard to make - simply infusing cream with orange, lemon and cinnamon, then whisking into egg yolks and placing in the oven.

In our version of this dish we add sweet Madeira wine, which contains aromas of caramel and burnt sugar, and a hint of citrus or spice. As a result it accentuates the similar flavours in the Crema Catalana, while also adding honeyed sweetness and sultry complexity of flavour. You can make these desserts ahead of time and chill in the fridge for a day or two, then simply caramelise the top under the grill or with a blowtorch before serving.

Ingredients

3 tbsp Madeira, sweet Marsala or other dessert wine

6 egg yolks

4 tbsp + 9 tsp caster sugar

600ml double (heavy) cream

½ an orange - zested

½ an unwaxed lemon - zested

1 cinnamon quill (or ¼ tsp ground cinnamon)

- Preheat the oven to 150C / Gas Mark 2 / 300F
- Place 6 ramekins into a deep ovenproof tray, then pour cold water into the tray to about halfway up the sides of the ramekins
- In a mixing bowl, whisk the egg yolks together with 4 tbsp caster sugar and 3 tbsp Madeira for a minute until combined
- In a small saucepan, combine the cream with the orange zest, lemon zest and the cinnamon quill. Cook over a very low heat for 5 minutes to allow the flavours to infuse
- Turn the heat up a bit and heat the cream until nearly boiling, then remove from the heat. Strain the cream into a jug, discarding the cinnamon quill
- Slowly pour the hot cream into the beaten egg mixture, whisking as you pour, until all the cream is added and you have a smooth textured custard
- Divide the custard between the ramekins then place the tray in the oven. Bake for 30-35 minutes or until the custards are just set, with a slight wobble when you move the tray. Cool at room temperature for an hour, then place in the fridge to chill for at least another hour or overnight
- When you are ready to serve, sprinkle each custard with 1 ½ tsp caster sugar, spreading the sugar out to an even layer using the back of a teaspoon. Place under a **very** hot preheated grill for a few minutes, or heat with a blowtorch, until the sugar on top has melted and turned golden brown
- Crack the melted sugar with the back of a spoon and enjoy!

Equipment

6 ramekins

Deep ovenproof tray, large enough to fit all the ramekins inside it

Mixing bowl

Whisk

Small saucepan

Sieve or tea strainer

Jug

Grill (broiler) or blowtorch

COLD DESSERTS

Amaretto and Ginger Cheesecake

Serves 8-10 — Prep time 30 minutes — Cook time 55 minutes + 4 hours chilling
Difficulty ❸

Ingredients

- 80ml amaretto liqueur
- 100g flaked almonds
- 300g ginger biscuits
- 160g butter, plus extra for greasing
- 600g full fat cream cheese
- 150g natural yogurt
- 150g caster sugar
- 3 tbsp plain flour
- 1 tsp ground ginger
- 1 tsp vanilla extract
- 3 eggs - lightly beaten

This baked cheesecake is bound to impress any guests - the creamy, dense filling is sweet and fragrant, laced with amaretto liqueur, vanilla extract and ginger. Heaped generously over a buttery, slightly crunchy base of ginger biscuits and toasted almonds, it's a slice of heaven.

Amaretto liqueur is usually made with apricot kernels and these kernels contain compounds which taste like almond, with underlying notes of sweet cherry, vanilla and marzipan. Amaretto can be a very sweet liqueur, so the addition of slightly sour natural yogurt in the creamy cheesecake helps to temper the sweetness.

Serve this cheesecake by itself, or with a handful of fresh raspberries.

- Preheat the oven to 170C / Gas Mark 3 ½ / 350F, and lightly grease a 22cm springform tin with butter

For the base

- Heat a small dry frying pan on the stove over a medium heat. Add the flaked almonds and toast them gently for around 5 minutes, stirring, until the almonds are golden brown and fragrant. Set ¼ of the toasted almonds to one side and allow to cool, then store them in an airtight container until ready to serve the cheesecake

- Tip the remaining toasted almonds into a food processor along with the ginger biscuits. Blitz to coarse powder then tip into a mixing bowl - you may need to do this in batches. (If you don't have a food processor, just pop the biscuits and almonds into a resealable freezer bag, push the air out and then crush the biscuits with a rolling pin)

- Melt the butter in a small saucepan or in the microwave, then stir the melted butter into the crushed biscuit and almond mixture until combined. Spread the mixture over the bottom and sides of the greased tin, pressing down firmly with the back of a spoon

- Place the tin in the oven and bake for 10 minutes, then remove from the oven

- Turn the oven temperature down to 160C / Gas Mark 3 / 325F

Equipment

- 22cm (9 inch) diameter springform tin
- Frying pan
- Food processor or a freezer bag and rolling pin
- Small saucepan or microwave
- 2 x mixing bowls
- Flat baking tray
- Electric beater or wooden spoon

For the filling

- In a large mixing bowl, beat together the cream cheese, yoghurt, sugar, flour, ginger, vanilla and amaretto for a minute until smooth. Stir in the beaten eggs gently until combined

- Pour the filling over the biscuit base and smooth it gently with a spoon, then set the tin on a flat baking tray (to catch any spills in case the springform tin leaks). Bake the cheesecake for 45-55 minutes, rotating the tin after 30 minutes, until it is just set with a slight wobble and beginning to brown on top

- Turn the oven off and prop the door ajar with a tea towel, then leave the cheesecake to cool in the oven for 30 minutes - this helps reduce cracks forming in the cheesecake
- Remove from the oven and allow to cool to room temperature, then chill in the fridge for at least 2 hours or overnight
- Sprinkle the rest of the toasted almonds on top before serving

COLD DESSERTS

Rum, Raisin and Pistachio Posset

Serves 4 — Prep time 25 minutes + 2 hours chilling — Difficulty ❶

Ingredients

100ml dark spiced rum

50g raisins

50g unsalted pistachios - shelled and roughly chopped

125g white sugar

425ml double (heavy) cream

¼ tsp ground cinnamon

¼ tsp ground ginger

Nutmeg

Posset originated in medieval England, where alcohol was sometimes added to milk or cream to preserve it for longer. Over the centuries this dish has evolved into a chilled dessert, where the key ingredients are still cream and alcohol. The alcohol thickens the cream to a thick, smooth texture similar to custard or panna cotta.

Although wine is the most traditional alcohol in a posset, our version is enhanced with dark spiced rum. In this recipe, we make a spiced rum syrup with blended raisins and pistachios. This creates a slightly thicker textured dessert with fruitiness running all the way through, reminiscent of rum and raisin ice cream.

The possets are straightforward to make, and can be made up to 2 days ahead of time and kept in the fridge. Top with chopped pistachios shortly before serving so that the pistachios don't go soggy.

- Combine the rum, raisins and half the chopped pistachios in a blender. Blend for a minute to a fairly smooth consistency, then pour this into a small saucepan. Add the sugar and cook over a low heat for around 5 minutes, stirring, until the sugar has melted into a syrup, then turn the heat off

- In a separate saucepan, combine the cream, cinnamon, ginger and around 20 grates of the nutmeg. Cook over a medium heat until the cream is just coming to the boil, then turn the heat off

- Slowly pour the rum and raisin syrup into the still hot cream, whisking as you pour, until the mixture is combined

- Divide the posset mixture between 4 ramekins or small bowls, then transfer to the fridge to cool for at least 2 hours until set

- Before serving, sprinkle with the remaining chopped pistachios to decorate

Equipment

Blender

2 x small saucepans

Grater

Whisk

4 ramekins, small bowls or coffee cups

COLD DESSERTS

Chocolate and Amaretto Ganache Pots

Serves 4 — Prep time 20 minutes + cooling time — Difficulty ❶

Ingredients

50ml amaretto liqueur

150g dark chocolate (min. 70% cocoa solids) - broken into pieces

10g butter (or 2 tsp)

225ml single (light) cream

1 orange - zested and juiced

Flaky biscuits or fresh fruit to serve (e.g. strawberries, slices of apricot or clementine)

For a taste of dark indulgence, look no further than a chocolate ganache pot. Only a few ingredients are required for these individual desserts, and you can have them chilling within 20 minutes. The addition of alcohol ensures that the chocolate and cream mixture stays lusciously soft, while the sweetness of amaretto avoids the need for extra sugar.

Dark spirits tend to partner well with chocolate, as the flavours are bold enough to stand up to the high cocoa content. We've chosen to use amaretto liqueur in this recipe, but we've also enjoyed these ganache pots with dark rum and brandy. You can make the ganache pots up to 2 days ahead of time, as they keep well in the fridge - just bring to room temperature before serving with flaky biscuits, shortbread, or fresh fruit for dipping.

- Put an inch or two of water into a saucepan and heat over a medium heat until the water is barely simmering
- Break the chocolate into a heatproof bowl and add the butter, single cream, orange zest and orange juice
- Place the bowl over the saucepan of hot water, ensuring that the bowl isn't touching the hot water, and stir gently until the chocolate has melted and the mixture is smooth
- Remove the bowl from the hot water, and stir the amaretto into the mixture
- Divide between 4 small glasses or coffee cups, then set to one side and allow to cool for approximately 30 minutes. Serve at room temperature with flaky biscuits or fruit for dipping

Equipment

Small saucepan

Heatproof bowl

4 small glasses or coffee cups

COLD DESSERTS

Gin, Lime and Elderflower Cheesecake

Serves 8-10 — Prep time 30 minutes + 3 hours chilling — Difficulty ❷

Ingredients

75ml + 1 tbsp gin

300g digestive biscuits

70g butter, plus extra for greasing the tin

500g mascarpone cheese

125g icing sugar (powdered sugar)

125ml elderflower cordial

1 ½ unwaxed limes - zested and juiced

200ml double (heavy) cream

This fragrant, zesty no-bake cheesecake is quick to make and deliciously indulgent. In our house it's a go-to recipe for summer birthdays!

Elderflower cordial has an alluring fragrance with citrusy notes and, when it's not being used in cocktails, it goes particularly well with citrus and cream. While it seems like you're adding quite a lot of gin to the cream and mascarpone, the acidity of the lime juice and elderflower cordial helps to thicken the mixture in the fridge so that it sets to a rich, smooth texture - and with a definite flavour of gin!

You can make this cheesecake a day or two ahead of time. We love to serve it with a glass of prosecco, topped with elderflower cordial.

For the base

- Grease the base of a 22cm loose bottomed cake tin with a little butter
- Put the digestive biscuits into a resealable freezer bag, push the air out and then crush the biscuits with a rolling pin - or blitz them in a food processor to fine crumbs. Tip into a mixing bowl
- Melt the butter in a small saucepan or in the microwave, then stir the melted butter into the biscuit crumbs together with 1 tbsp gin. Mix well
- Spread the mixture across the bottom of the greased tin, pressing down firmly with the back of a spoon. Chill the base in the fridge while you make the filling

For the filling

- Beat together the mascarpone cheese, icing sugar, elderflower cordial, 75ml gin, the lime juice and almost all the lime zest (reserving a little lime zest for decoration)
- Pour in the double cream and beat the mixture gently until smooth and combined - it will still be a bit runny, as it firms up in the fridge
- Spoon the filling into the base and spread it out evenly, then sprinkle the remaining lime zest on the top to decorate
- Chill the cheesecake for at least 3 hours or overnight to set. When you're ready to serve, run a knife around the edge of the cheesecake then slide it out of the tin

Equipment

22cm (9 inch) diameter springform tin

Food processor or a freezer bag and a rolling pin

Small saucepan or microwave

2 x mixing bowls

Electric beater or whisk

COLD DESSERTS

COOKING WITH ALCOHOL

Prosecco Panna Cotta

Serves 4 — Prep time 20 minutes + 2 hours chilling — Difficulty ❷

Ingredients

100ml prosecco

300ml double (heavy) cream

100g caster sugar

5g gelatine powder

Vegetable or sunflower oil

Fresh raspberries to serve

This is a dessert for a special occasion, luxurious and with a hint of sparkle. Panna cotta contains very few ingredients, and this means that any flavourings really have the chance to shine. Prosecco has floral aromas of honeysuckle, peach and pear, which are delightfully softened in cream for a lightly fruity finish.

Despite its sweetness, prosecco is mildly acidic, and when acid is added to cream it thickens it. This means that the prosecco helps to set the panna cotta, so very little gelatine is needed to get the perfect panna cotta wobble. Serve with a glass of bubbly, and a few fresh raspberries to contrast with the rich cream.

- Put a few drops of vegetable or sunflower oil into 4 ramekins or small coffee cups, then wipe it around with a piece of kitchen roll to lightly grease the inside

- Heat the cream, sugar and prosecco together in a small saucepan, stirring occasionally, until the sugar has dissolved and the mixture is almost boiling

- Remove the pan from the heat and sprinkle the gelatine powder over the hot liquid. Whisk well for 2-3 minutes, ensuring that the gelatine is completely dissolved (if it hasn't dissolved, return the pan to the heat for a moment and keep whisking to make sure it dissolves completely, but making sure not to boil it as the gelatin won't set this way)

- Divide the mixture between the ramekins and chill for at least 2 hours or overnight to set

- Before serving, dip the base of each ramekin into hot water for a few minutes to loosen the panna cotta. Run a knife around the edge of each panna cotta and then invert onto a plate. Serve the panna cotta by itself, or with a handful of fresh raspberries

TIP: If you are using leaf gelatin, follow the pack instructions for preparation of the gelatine and use the quantity required to set 190ml (⅓ pint) of liquid

Equipment

4 ramekins, coffee cups or panna cotta moulds

Kitchen roll

Small saucepan

Whisk

Aperol Spritz Jellies

Serves 4 — Prep time 20 minutes — Chilling time 6 hours or overnight — Difficulty ❷

Ingredients

300ml prosecco

50g white sugar

1 x 12g sachet of gelatine powder

100ml Aperol

50ml vodka

1 orange - ½ juiced, ½ thinly sliced to garnish

Designed around the beautiful Italian Aperol Spritz cocktail, these elegant party desserts are a tongue-in-cheek nod to the vodka jelly - cornerstone of so many house parties!

In our grown-up version, the combination of sweet prosecco, bitter Aperol and fresh orange create a sophisticated refresher with a hint of fizz. Aperol and vodka are added after the mixture has been removed from the heat, which prevents the alcohol from evaporating. Topped with a slice of orange, these bright jellies are perfect for a celebration.

If you're serving a crowd, try making these mini cocktails in shot glasses instead.

- Heat the prosecco and sugar together in a small saucepan, stirring occasionally, until the sugar has dissolved and the mixture is almost boiling
- Remove the pan from the heat and sprinkle the gelatine powder over the hot liquid. Whisk well for 2-3 minutes, ensuring that the gelatine is completely dissolved (if it hasn't dissolved, return the pan to the heat for a moment and keep whisking to make sure it dissolves completely, but making sure not to boil it as the gelatin won't set this way)
- Stir in the Aperol, vodka and juice of half an orange, then leave the mixture to cool for 10-15 minutes until lukewarm
- Divide the mixture between 4 small glasses, then carefully place in the fridge for at least 4 hours or overnight to set
- Decorate the jellies with orange slices to serve

Equipment

Small saucepan

Whisk

4 small glasses

COLD DESSERTS

Rosé and Raspberry Trifles

Serves 4 — Prep time 1 hour + chilling — Difficulty ❸

Ingredients

150ml + 2 tbsp rosé wine

200g fresh raspberries (100g for the jelly, 100g for decoration)

50g caster sugar (30g for the jelly, 20g for the custard)

6g (1 tsp) gelatine powder

150g firm sponge cake (e.g. madeira cake) - sliced into pieces approx. 2cm (½ inch) thick

170ml double (heavy) cream (50ml for the custard, 120ml for the rosé cream)

150ml milk

1 egg yolk

1 tbsp cornflour (cornstarch)

A few drops of yellow food colouring (optional)

Mint leaves to decorate

This summery creation is an elegant dessert for a warm evening - it takes trifle above and beyond the more familiar sherry-laden Christmas varieties. Cake is soaked in tangy raspberry and rosé jelly, then layered with sweet rosé cream and velvety homemade custard for a sweet, sunshiney treat. You can prepare the layers ahead of time, then assemble when you're ready to serve.

Rosé is not often used in cooking, as its light flavour can easily be overwhelmed by other ingredients. But we love how the floral notes come through in the rosé-scented cream on top of the trifle, while its berry flavours are enhanced in the raspberry jelly. A fruity rosé works best here, such as Tempranillo or Grenache.

For the fruity jelly

- Combine 100g of the raspberries with 75ml rosé wine in a blender. Blend until smooth
- Heat the remaining 75ml rosé wine together with 30g sugar in a small saucepan, stirring occasionally, until the sugar has dissolved and the mixture is almost boiling
- Remove the pan from the heat and sprinkle the gelatine powder over the hot liquid. Whisk well for 2-3 minutes, ensuring that the gelatine is completely dissolved (if it hasn't dissolved, return the pan to the heat for a moment and keep whisking to make sure it dissolves completely, but making sure not to boil it as the gelatin won't set this way)
- Stir the blended raspberry liquid into the hot wine mixture
- Put the cake slices in a dish or container where they can all sit in one layer. Pour the raspberry liquid over the cake, turning the slices so that they soak in the jelly. Chill in the fridge for at least an hour to set

For the custard

- In a small saucepan, heat 50ml double cream with 150ml milk until just below boiling point
- Separately, whisk together the egg yolk, cornflour and 20g sugar
- Slowly pour the hot cream into the beaten egg mixture, whisking as you pour, until all the cream is added and you have a smooth textured custard
- Return the whole mixture to the saucepan and heat gently, stirring with a whisk, for 5-10 minutes until the custard has thickened to coat the back of a spoon. Add few drops of yellow food colouring, if wanted
- Pour the custard into a jug, cover with cling film to stop a skin forming, and chill in the fridge for at least 1 hour

Equipment

Blender

Small saucepan

Small dish or container

2 x mixing bowls

Whisk

Jug

4 dessert bowls or large wine glasses

For the rosé cream
- In a large mixing bowl, beat the remaining 120ml double cream with a whisk until it begins to thicken
- Add the remaining 2 tbsp rosé wine and continue to beat until the cream is thickened and holds its shape

Bringing it together
- When you're ready to serve, slice the jellied cake into cubes. Place a few around the edges of each dessert bowl together with a small handful of raspberries, pushing them to the edges so that you can see them through the glass
- Dollop in a few spoonfuls of the custard
- Spoon the whipped cream on top, then decorate with the remaining raspberries and a few mint leaves

Orange and Tequila Sorbet

Serves 4-6 — Prep time 15 minutes + 9 hours chilling time — Difficulty ❶

Ingredients

50ml tequila

50g white sugar

400ml good quality orange juice - chilled

½ lemon - juiced (approx. 1 tbsp lemon juice)

Homemade sorbet makes a delicious after dinner treat. The bright flavour of tequila pairs well with citrus fruits, and very few other ingredients are needed - just make sure to use good quality orange juice for the best results. Taste buds are less sensitive to very cold flavours, which is why we've added sugar and tangy lemon juice. This ensures a balance of sweet and tart flavours when the sorbet mixture is frozen.

Enjoy this bright sorbet as a refreshing dessert, or serve a small scoop in a shot glass as a palate cleanser between courses. The sorbet keeps well for a few weeks in the freezer.

- In a small saucepan, combine the sugar with 50ml of the orange juice. Heat over a low heat for a few minutes, stirring occasionally, until the sugar has dissolved, then remove the pan from the heat. Stir in the rest of the orange juice, lemon juice and tequila
- Pour the sorbet mixture into a wide freezer-proof container, then cover with a lid or cling film and freeze for 2-3 hours
- Remove the sorbet from the freezer and use a fork to break up the ice crystals, giving it a good stir. Put it back in the freezer for a further 2-3 hours or until the sorbet is quite firm
- Scoop the mixture out of the container and into the blender. Blend for a minute until the mixture is thick and smooth
- Scoop the sorbet back into the freezer container and freeze for a further 3 hours or overnight
- To serve, take the sorbet out of the freezer and allow to soften for a few minutes before scooping into bowls

Equipment

Small saucepan

Wide freezer-proof container

Blender

COLD DESSERTS

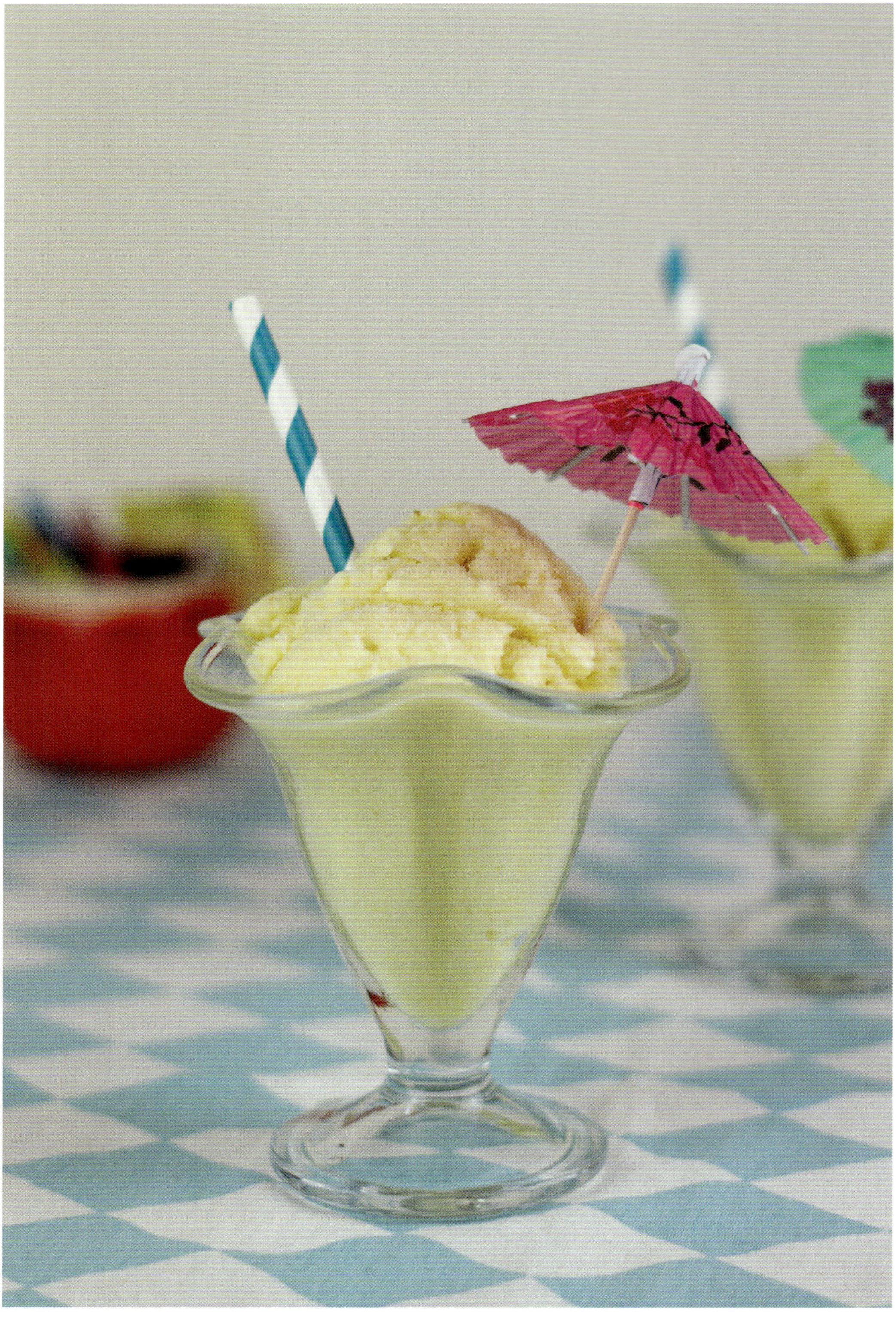

Piña Colada Sorbet

Serves 4-6 — Prep time 15 minutes + 8 hours chilling time — Difficulty ①

Ingredients

100ml white rum

½ a ripe pineapple - peeled, cored and roughly chopped (approx. 350g prepared weight)

200ml full fat coconut milk (½ a standard can)

100g white sugar

1 lime - juiced (approx. 2 tbsp lime juice)

Despite being labelled a "retro" cocktail, the piña colada is enduringly popular. Almost everyone loves a piña colada - sweet, refreshing pineapple stands up to the flavour of white rum, and the addition of creamy coconut makes it incredibly drinkable.

This creamy summer sorbet is the ultimate no-bake dessert. It's fairly easy to make, and you don't need an ice cream maker (just a blender and a freezer). Serve this sorbet in a cone - or scoop it into a tall glass, top with a cocktail umbrella and imagine that you're on a tropical beach.

- Combine all the ingredients in the blender, and blend on high speed for a few minutes until the mixture is smooth and the sugar has dissolved
- Pour the sorbet mixture into a wide freezer-proof container and spread it out with a spatula. Cover and freeze for 3-4 hours
- Scoop the mixture out of the container and back into the blender. Blend until smooth again, breaking up any large ice crystals
- Scoop the sorbet back into the freezer container and freeze for a further 3 hours or overnight
- To serve, take the sorbet out of the freezer and allow to soften for a few minutes before scooping into bowls or cones

Equipment

Blender

Wide freezer-proof container

Roasted Plum and Port Ripple Ice Cream

Makes 1.2L — Prep time 15 minutes — Cook time 35 minutes + 2 hours chilling
Difficulty ①

Ingredients

100ml port

250g plums - stoned and quartered

1 tbsp butter

1 tsp mixed spice or pumpkin spice

1L good quality vanilla or clotted cream ice cream

½ an orange - zested (optional)

In this dessert, sticky roasted plums and port are rippled through softened ice cream to create something both beautiful and delicious. We've cheated a bit here by using shop-bought ice cream. It's quicker than making your own, and not everyone has an ice cream maker - the texture is just as good.

Roasting stone fruits like peaches or plums in the oven caramelises the sugars in the fruit, releasing the juices and concentrating their natural sweetness. We've added port to these roasted plums, which provides complex notes of caramel, figs and spice, and helps to create a rich, jammy texture perfect for swirling into ice cream. The addition of a little orange zest gives a deliciously festive feel, but if you're serving this in summer you may prefer to skip the orange.

Enjoy a scoop of this ice cream on its own or alongside a hot dessert such as the Whisky Sticky Toffee Pudding on page 168.

- Preheat the oven to 170C / Gas Mark 3 ½ / 350F
- Combine the plums, butter and mixed spice in a roasting tray. Place the tray in the oven and roast for 20 minutes, stirring after 5 minutes to spread the melting butter around the plums
- After 20 minutes add the port and the orange zest, and return the tray to the oven for a further 15 minutes until the plums are sticky and jammy. Remove the tray from the oven, give it another stir then allow to cool completely
- Once the plums have cooled, take the ice cream out of the freezer and leave it at room temperature for 10-15 minutes or until the ice cream is just soft enough to spread
- In a small freezer-proof dish, spread about one third of the ice cream in a layer. Dollop half of the plum mixture across the ice cream. Add half the remaining ice cream, and then the rest of the roasted plums, and finally top with the rest of the ice cream
- Gently swirl through the mixture once or twice with a knife to create a few ripples, then cover with cling film or a lid and freeze for at least 2 hours
- To serve, take the ice cream out of the freezer and allow to soften for a minute before scooping into bowls

Equipment

Small roasting tray

Freezer-proof dish or loaf tin

COLD DESSERTS

CIDER SODA BREAD, PAGE 214

SAVOURY BAKING

Three Cheese and Onion Vodka Tarts   206
Cider Crust Pork Pie   208
Goat's Cheese and Port Canapés   212
Cider Soda Bread   214
Stout and Rye Bread   216
Red Wine Focaccia   220

Baking from scratch is incredibly satisfying, and the results far outweigh the effort required. These recipes are designed to give you an introduction to making bread and pastry, and the many benefits of including alcohol in these recipes for flavour and function. The techniques are not difficult, but an understanding of the basic science will help you to adapt these recipes to your own taste.

The previous chapters of this book have often included alcohol in a liquid form, such as a sauce, glaze or marinade. In this chapter, and its partner **Sweet Baking** on page 222, we require new techniques to incorporate alcohol in our cooking. Ultimately, the challenge - and fun - of baking with alcohol is incorporating a liquid into something that should become solid.

We begin with a shortcrust pastry recipe in our **Three Cheese and Onion Vodka Tarts**. Vodka is the trick to perfect pastry - alcohol isn't absorbed into flour in the same way as water, resulting in reduced gluten formation (gluten is the protein that makes bread and pastry chewy) and a crumblier, flakier pastry. This is an adaptable savoury cheese tart and, with the pastry mastered, you could swap the cheese and onions for your own favourite filling.

Next up is hot water crust pastry. A traditional baking technique that uses a large amount of water, we couldn't resist adapting this pastry technique to use apple cider in our **Cider Crust Pork Pie**. This adds a beautiful flavour, and the sugars in the cider also help the pie crust to caramelise to a rich golden brown.

This chapter also includes three different bread recipes: **Cider Soda Bread, Stout and Rye Bread** and **Red Wine Focaccia**. In each one, we've chosen an alcohol that adds a certain flavour profile, while also discussing how the alcohol itself impacts the recipe. In a soda bread, the acidity of cider helps to create the rise, and in a rye bread the natural yeasts from the stout contribute to the chewy texture and rich, malty flavour. On the other hand, the red wine in our focaccia recipe slows the yeast activity a little, but adds a beautiful depth of flavour and stunning colour.

Three Cheese and Onion Vodka Tarts

Makes 12-16 mini tarts — Prep time 1 hour — Cook time 30 minutes — Difficulty ❸

Ingredients

5 tbsp vodka

180g plain flour, plus extra for sprinkling

90g butter, plus extra for greasing - chilled

1 red onion - thinly sliced into half moons

75g cheddar cheese - grated

75g red leicester or colby cheese - grated

50g feta cheese - chopped into small cubes

Salt and freshly ground black pepper

Equipment

Food processor (optional)

2 x mixing bowls

Frying pan

Flat baking tray

12-hole mini tart tin

Rolling pin (or empty wine bottle)

Vodka is an incredibly useful ingredient in the kitchen - the neutral flavour makes it the secret ingredient for perfect shortcrust pastry.

Usually, pastry is made with water and if it's mixed too much the gluten develops, making it tough. Vodka has a high percentage of alcohol, and alcohol is not absorbed into flour in the same way as water. The result is tender, flaky pastry every time! We've filled this 'perfect pastry' with sweet caramelised onions and tangy cheddar, red leicester and feta cheeses. Serve these mini tarts for afternoon tea or in a lunchbox, or make one large tart for a weekend lunch.

For the pastry

- If you have a food processor, put the flour and cubes of the chilled butter in the food processor, and blitz it until the mixture forms crumbs. Add 4 tbsp of the vodka and a large pinch of salt. Pulse until the mixture forms a ball of pastry (if it doesn't stick together, add an extra 1 tbsp of vodka)
- Alternatively, grate the chilled butter into a mixing bowl. Add the flour and use your fingers to rub the butter into the flour until it forms crumbs. Then add 4 tbsp vodka and mix together gently until you have a soft ball of dough, adding extra vodka to bring it together if necessary
- Cover the pastry and chill in the fridge for at least 20 minutes

For the filling

- While the pastry is chilling, heat a splash of oil in a frying pan and fry the sliced onion over a medium heat for 10 minutes until soft and brown. Scoop into a mixing bowl and add a good grind of black pepper, and allow to cool for at least 10 minutes

For the pastry

- Preheat the oven to 190C / Gas Mark 5 / 375F, and place a flat baking tray inside the oven to heat up
- Grease the tart tins with plenty of butter, and sprinkle with flour
- Roll out the chilled pastry on a floured surface until approximately 3mm (⅛ inch) thick. Cut circles a little larger than your tart tins, using a mug as a guide, kneading and re-rolling any extra pastry. Gently transfer the pastry circles to the tart tins and press to the sides, making sure that you don't stretch the dough. Chill in the fridge for a further 15 minutes

Bringing it together

- Use a sharp knife to trim off any overhanging pastry at the edge of the tarts
- Stir the grated cheddar and red leicester cheeses into the cooled onion. Spoon cheese mixture into each tart, then add a few cubes of feta cheese on top

COOKING WITH ALCOHOL

- Place the tart tins on top of the preheated flat baking tray and bake for 15-20 minutes, or until the tarts are deep golden brown on top and cooked through

TIP: You can use this recipe to make one large 23cm (9 inch) tart instead, if you prefer

SAVOURY BAKING

Cider Crust Pork Pie

Makes 1 very large pork pie — Prep time 1 ½ hours + chilling — Cook time 1 hour
Difficulty ❸

We had a revelation late one night - and as usual, it was food related. Hot water crust pastry is an essential part of a pork pie, but what about hot cider pastry? In this recipe, the traditional pairing of pork and apple comes together in a beautiful homely pie with rich scrumpy pastry.

Classic hot water pastry combines lard, hot water and flour to make a firm pie crust that can withstand even the runniest gravy. In this recipe we use hot apple cider instead of water in the crust. The sugars in the cider caramelise as the pie bakes, providing a rich flavour and a lovely golden brown colour. Together with a pork filling spiced with fragrant apple, sage and nutmeg, and cider jelly for a little acidity, this pie is perfect for a picnic or lunch.

The recipe might look intimidating, but it's more lengthy than difficult! You need to slice the filling quite small, so make sure to sharpen your knife before you begin. Serve with a dollop of the Cider Mustard from page 144.

Ingredients

- 275ml dry still apple cider (175ml for the pastry, 100ml for the jelly)
- 1 white onion - finely chopped
- 1 medium cooking or eating apple - peeled, cored and finely chopped
- 200g smoked bacon
- 150g pork shoulder
- 400g pork mince (15-20% fat)
- 1 tsp dried sage
- ½ tsp dried thyme
- ½ tsp ground white pepper
- 175g lard
- 500g plain flour, plus extra for sprinkling
- 1 egg - beaten
- 6g gelatine powder (to set 250ml liquid)
- Nutmeg
- Salt
- Oil

Equipment

- Frying pan
- A very sharp knife
- Grater
- Small saucepan
- Large mixing bowl
- Measuring jug
- Deep, loose bottomed 15cm (6 inch) diameter tin
- Rolling pin (or empty wine bottle)
- Flat baking tray
- Whisk
- Funnel

For the filling

- Heat a splash of oil in a frying pan and cook the chopped onion and apple together over a medium heat for 10 minutes, stirring, until soft and starting to brown. Remove from the heat and allow to cool
- Meanwhile, use a very sharp knife to chop the bacon and pork shoulder into chunks around 5mm (¼ inch) thick
- When the onion and apple mixture has cooled, scoop it into a large mixing bowl. Stir in the pork mince, pork shoulder, bacon, sage, thyme, white pepper, about 30 grates of the nutmeg and 1 tsp salt

For the pastry

- Heat 175ml cider and the lard together in a small saucepan over a medium heat until the lard has melted
- Combine the flour and ¼ tsp salt in a large mixing bowl. Pour the hot lard mixture into the flour and beat well with a wooden spoon to form a dough
- Wait a few minutes until the mixture is cool enough to handle, then turn the dough out onto a clean surface and knead for a few minutes. Set to one side and allow to cool until just lukewarm
- Preheat the oven to 180C / Gas Mark 4 / 350F, and grease the pie tin and sprinkle the inside with flour
- Cut off about ¼ of the pastry dough and set to one side - this will be the pie lid. Roll out the rest of the warm pastry on a clean floured surface into a circle approx 30cm (12 inches) diameter - wide enough to cover the bottom and sides of the tin, overhanging the top by about an inch

- Transfer the pastry to the tin, pressing it up the sides with your hands. If the pastry slides down, leave it to cool a bit longer then try again. If there are any holes, patch them with a spare bit of pastry (hot water pastry doesn't suffer as much from overworking as other forms of pastry, so don't worry about bashing it around to get it to the shape you need)
- Spoon the pork filling into the pastry and press it down with the back of a spoon. It should come just to the top of the tin - if you have too much filling, put it to one side and bake separately in a muffin tin
- Roll the remaining pastry into a circle for the lid
- Brush beaten egg around the edges of the pie, then put on the lid and use your fingers to press the edges together. Use a sharp knife to trim the edges of the pie and cut a hole in the top to let out steam as it bakes. Brush the top of the pie with beaten egg
- Place the pie onto a baking tray (in case it leaks during baking) and bake for 30 minutes
- After 30 minutes, remove the pie from the oven and brush with beaten egg again. If any extra liquid has boiled out of the pie while cooking, brush off the liquid with a pastry brush to avoid the crust getting soggy, then return to the oven for a further 30 minutes until the pie is deep golden brown and cooked through
- Cool the pie to room temperature, then chill in the fridge for at least 4 hours or overnight

For the jelly
- Once the pie has chilled, heat 100ml of cider in a small saucepan until nearly boiling
- Remove the pan from the heat and sprinkle the gelatine powder over the cider. Whisk well for 2-3 minutes, ensuring that the gelatine is completely dissolved (if it hasn't dissolved, return the pan to the heat for a moment and keep whisking to make sure it dissolves completely, but making sure not to boil it as the gelatin won't set this way). Stir in the remaining 150ml cider and mix well
- Put the pie in a dish to avoid any spills, and make two small holes in the top of the pastry. Using a funnel, slowly pour the warm liquid into the pie, tilting it gently as you go, until the pie is completely filled with cider jelly
- Carefully put the pie back in the fridge and chill for at least 3 hours or overnight

TIP: You can use a digital food thermometer to make sure the pie is fully cooked. The meat should reach 65C / 150F inside

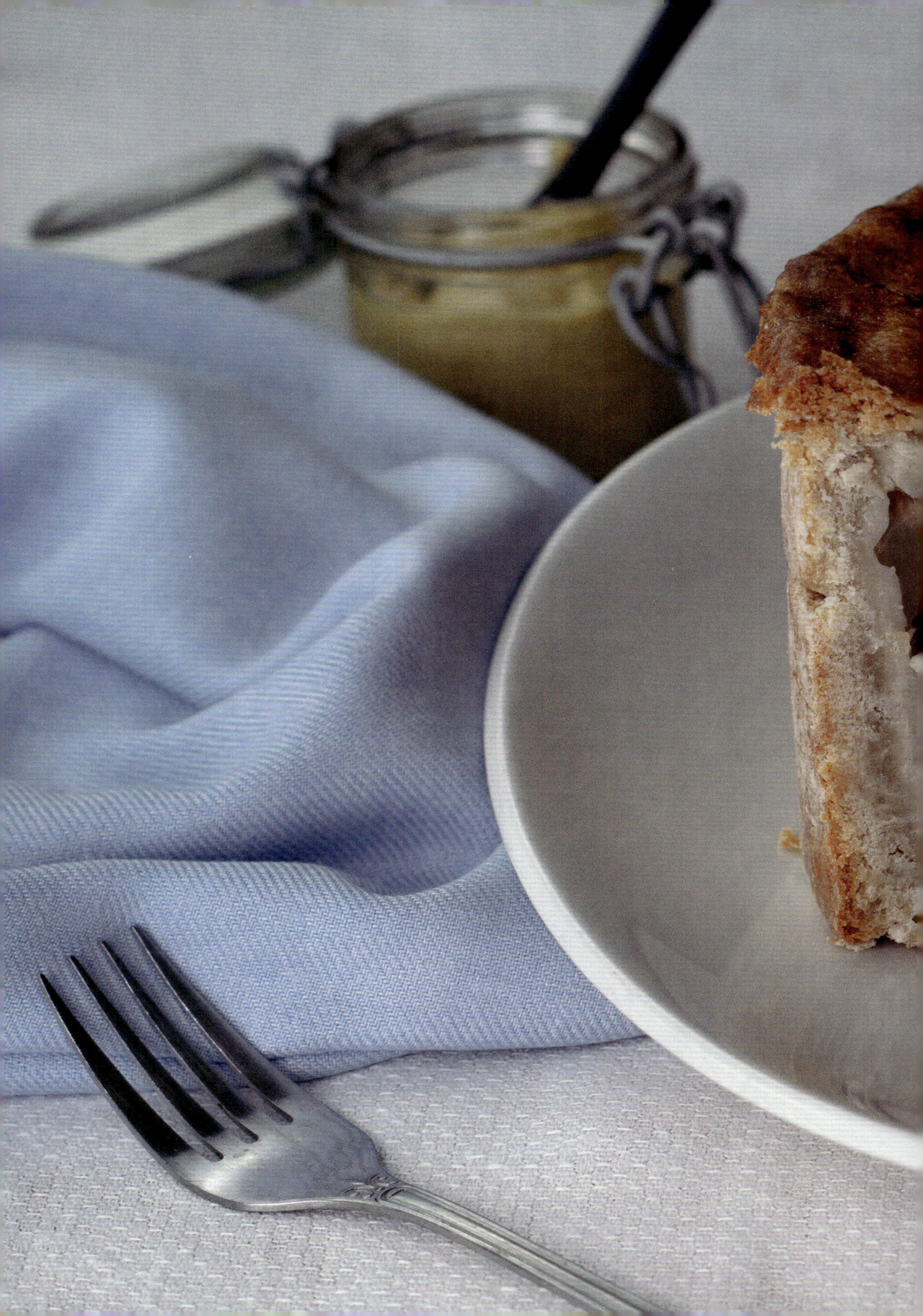

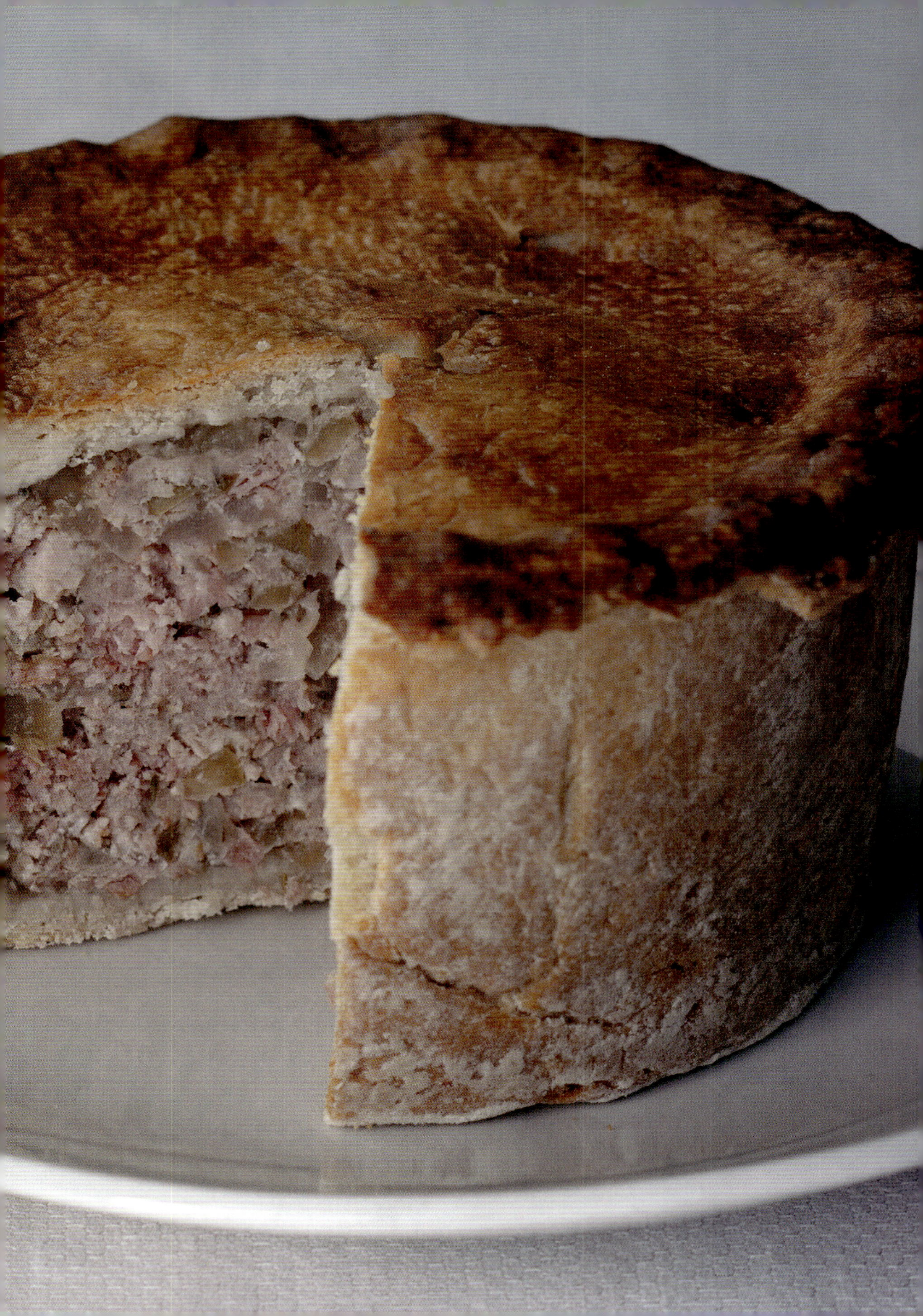

Goat's Cheese and Port Canapés

Makes 15-20 canapés — Prep time 40 minutes + cooling time — Difficulty ❸

Ingredients

80ml + 2 tbsp port

150g red or black seedless grapes

2 tbsp balsamic vinegar (1 tbsp for the chutney, 1 tbsp for the goat's cheese)

1 large sheet of ready rolled puff pastry (approx. 320g)

1 tbsp runny honey

100g soft goat's cheese

120g cream cheese

Plain flour for rolling

Salt

Equipment

2 x small saucepans

2 x baking trays

Baking paper

Rolling pin (or use an empty wine bottle)

Whisk

Piping bag (optional)

Perfect for satisfying a crowd, these beautiful canapés provide a delicious contrast of textures and flavours, with crisp pastry, soft port-infused cheese, and a perfectly tart grape and port chutney. The fruity sweetness from port goes brilliantly with tangy goat's cheese, providing a moreish mouthful that is perfect to serve at a party.

For peace of mind, all of the elements of this dish can be prepared up to 2 days in advance - just make sure to assemble them shortly before serving to ensure the pastry stays crisp. This recipe makes 15-20 fairly large canapés, or 30-40 smaller ones if you prefer.

For the grape chutney

- Put the grapes in a small saucepan together with 2 tbsp port, 1 tbsp balsamic vinegar and a pinch of salt. Cook over a medium heat with the lid on for 10 minutes, then remove the lid and cook for a further 10 minutes or until the grapes have split and the liquid has reduced. Remove from the heat and allow to cool

For the pastry

- Preheat your oven to 200C / Gas Mark 6 / 400F, and line 2 baking trays with baking paper

- Lay out the puff pastry on a clean floured surface and using a rolling pin, roll it to around 3mm (⅛ inch) thick. Slice the puff pastry sheet into 15-20 squares approx. 10cm (4 inches) wide, then take opposite corners of each square and fold them into the middle, pressing down with a finger

- Place the pastry shapes onto the prepared baking trays and bake for 15-20 minutes until golden, puffy and baked through. Cool on a wire rack or plate, then store in an airtight container until nearly ready to serve

For the goat's cheese

- Pour 80ml port into a small saucepan together with the honey. Simmer over a low heat for 10-15 minutes until the liquid has reduced to a thick syrup. Remove from the heat and cool for 5 minutes while you prepare the cheese

- Crumble the goat's cheese into a bowl, add the cream cheese and beat well with a wooden spoon until smooth. Add the port syrup, 1 tbsp balsamic vinegar and a pinch of salt and beat with a whisk for a few minutes

Bringing it together

- Once the pastry and the grape chutney have cooled, you can begin to assemble the canapés. Spread or pipe a generous dollop of the goat's cheese on top, then add a spoonful of the grape chutney. Arrange on a platter to serve

TIP: For smaller canapés, slice the pastry into 30-40 squares approx. 5cm (2 inches) wide

SAVOURY BAKING

Cider Soda Bread

Makes 1 loaf — Prep time 15 minutes — Cook time 35 minutes — Difficulty ①

Ingredients

330ml dry apple cider

450g plain flour (or a mix of plain and wholemeal), plus extra for sprinkling

2 eating apples - peeled, cored and grated

1 tsp bicarbonate of soda

Salt

No-knead soda bread is one of the quickest ways to make bread, and you can have a delicious crusty loaf on the table within the hour. Traditional soda bread is made with bicarbonate of soda and buttermilk - the acidic buttermilk reacts with the soda, and the resulting bubbles rise the bread. Instead of buttermilk, our recipe calls for cider, which is also mildly acidic and creates bread with a tender crumb and delicious depth of flavour.

You can customise this soda bread by adding fresh herbs, a handful of grated cheese or some diced onion. Serve with sharp cheddar cheese and a mug of your favourite cider, or alongside the Parsnip and Cider Soup on page 24. If cider isn't your tipple of choice, beer is also mildly acidic and works just as well in this recipe.

- Preheat the oven to 200C / Gas Mark 6 / 400F and place a baking tray in the oven to heat up for at least 20 minutes to help oven spring (rising) as it bakes
- In a large mixing bowl combine the flour, grated apple, bicarbonate of soda and 1 ½ tsp salt. Mix well
- Pour in the cider then mix lightly together with your hands until you have a sticky dough - it's ok if there are still a few dry bits. Turn the dough out onto a clean floured surface and shape it into a ball
- Take the hot tray out of the oven and sprinkle it generously with flour, then carefully place your bread loaf onto the hot tray. Use a sharp knife to make a deep cross in the dough, pressing down almost but not all the way to the tray, then put the bread in the oven
- Bake for 35 minutes or until the bread is deep golden brown all over and makes a hollow sound when tapped on the bottom. Leave to cool for at least 10 minutes, then slice and serve

TIP: You can use a digital food thermometer to tell when your bread is cooked - it should register 95C / 200F inside

Equipment

Baking tray

Large mixing bowl

Grater

SAVOURY BAKING

Stout and Rye Bread

Makes 1 large loaf — Prep time 3 hours including rising time — Cook time 50 minutes Difficulty ❸

Ingredients

400ml stout or porter

350g rye flour

250g strong white bread flour, plus extra for kneading and shaping

7g fast-action dried yeast

A few handfuls of seeds, walnuts or rye flakes

1 tbsp runny honey

Salt

Equipment

Large mixing bowl

Flat baking tray

Deep roasting tray

Stout and rye is a particularly lovely flavour combination - both are ingredients prized for their deep, earthy flavour and slight bitterness. Rye is a naturally tangy grain, dark and wholesome in the best possible way, and when balanced with the addition of a little honey it makes a chewy, comforting loaf with delicious depth. Stout adds to the dark, treacly flavour of the loaf while also working with the yeast as a natural leavening agent, helping the bread to rise.

We chose to use a mix of rye and white flours here for a slightly lighter loaf than traditional rye bread, and to help it rise a bit quicker. The bread will be easier to slice once it's had a chance to cool. Use for toast, sandwiches, alongside soups or stews, or topped Scandinavian-style with smoked fish and pickles.

- Combine the rye flour, bread flour, yeast and 1 tsp salt in a large mixing bowl, together with a few handfuls of seeds, walnuts or rye flakes
- Add the honey then slowly pour in the stout. Mix it all together by hand, gradually incorporating all the flour to make a dough, until the mixture resembles wet cement
- Sprinkle a clean surface with flour and knead the dough for 3-5 minutes until it's feeling a bit softer and smoother
- Put the dough back in the bowl then cover with cling film or a tea towel, and leave in a warm place for an hour and a half until significantly increased in size
- To shape the loaf, sprinkle a clean surface with flour and turn the dough out onto it. With floured hands shape the dough gently into a ball, and then tuck the sides underneath to tighten the top surface of the dough, trying to keep as much air in the dough as possible. Cover and leave to prove for another hour (or if you prefer to bake it later, after 40 minutes you can pop it in the fridge for up to 6 hours)
- Preheat the oven to 200C / Gas Mark 6 / 400F and place a flat baking tray into the oven to heat up for at least 30 minutes. Put a deep roasting tray in the bottom of the oven and boil a mugful of water in the kettle
- Take the baking tray out of the oven and sprinkle it generously with flour. Gently place the bread loaf onto the tray and use a sharp knife to make a few cuts in the top of the bread - this encourages it to rise up and out
- Pour the boiled water into the roasting tray at the bottom of the oven, then put the bread in the steamy oven

- Bake for 40-50 minutes until the loaf is deep brown and crusty all over, and makes a hollow sound when tapped on the bottom. If you have a digital food thermometer, you can use this to tell when your bread is cooked - it should register 95C / 200F inside
- Cover the bread with a tea towel to cool, then slice and serve

TIP: To knead the dough, push down on the dough and fold it over itself, and keep repeating. This stretches the dough and gradually it will become smoother and softer. Add a sprinkle more flour if the dough is too sticky to work with

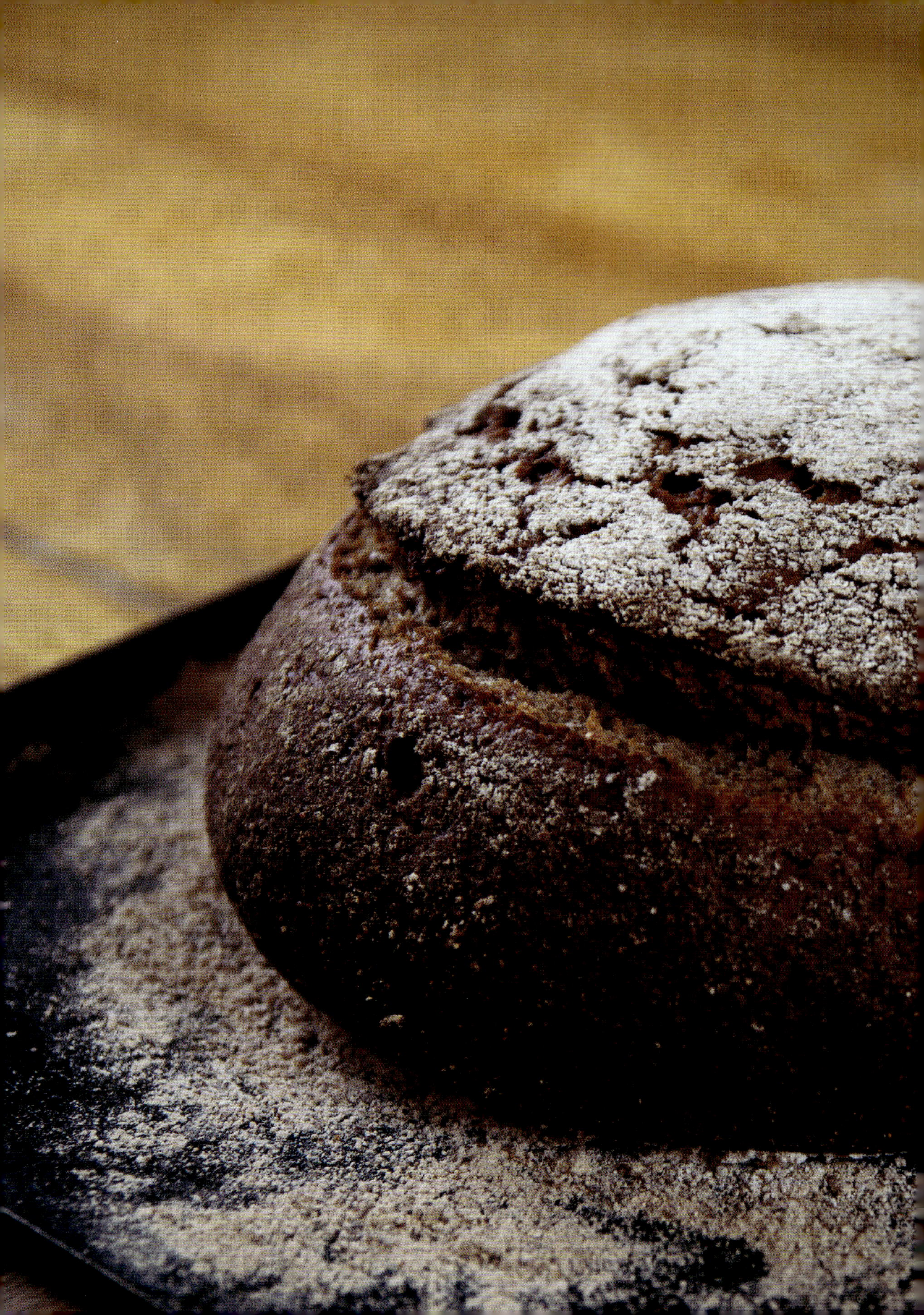

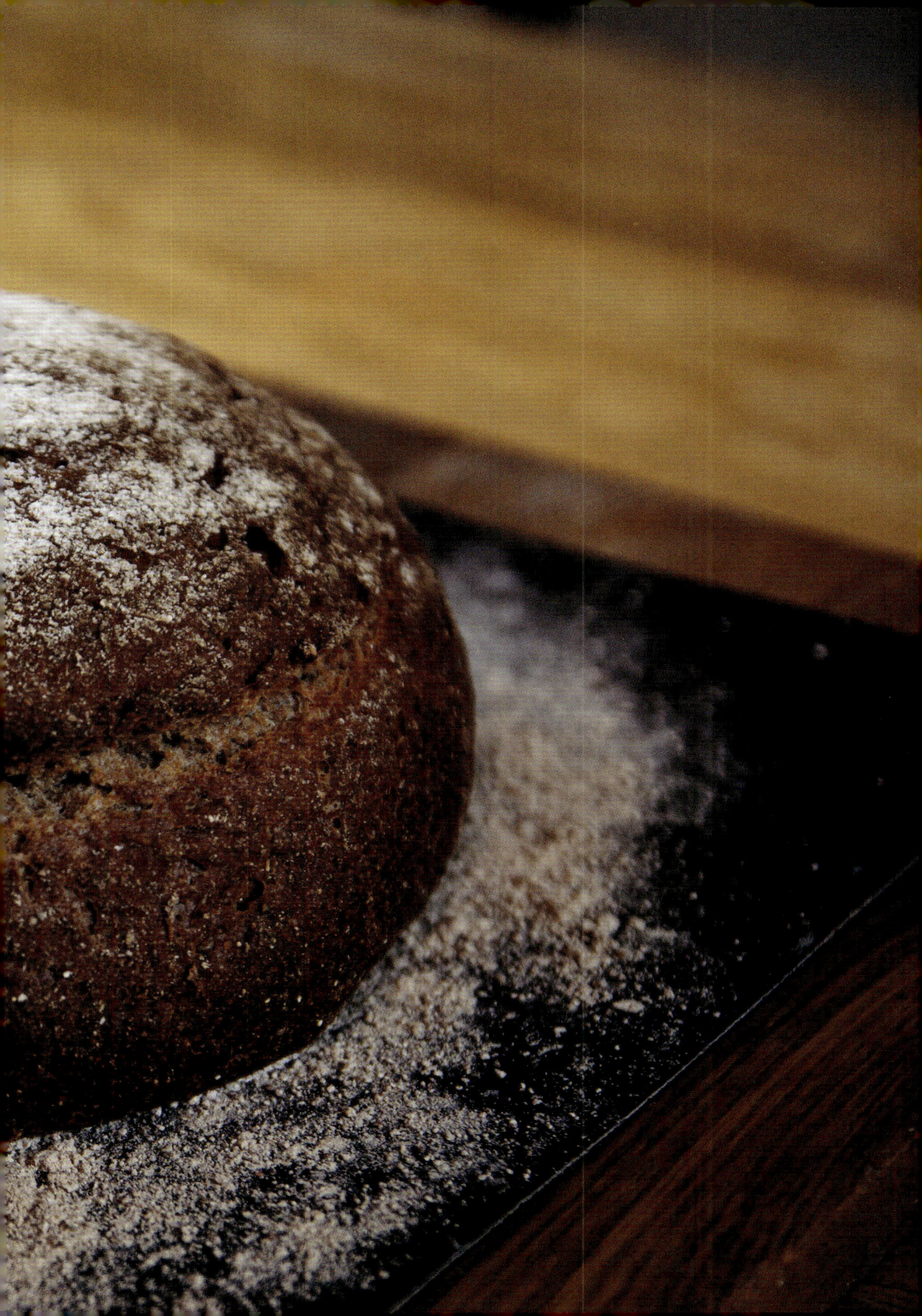

COOKING WITH ALCOHOL

Red Wine Focaccia

Makes 1 large or 2 medium focaccia breads — Prep time 3 hours including rising time Cook time 30 minutes — Difficulty ❷

Ingredients

160ml red wine

12g fast-action dried yeast

1 tsp white sugar

160ml lukewarm water

400g strong white bread flour

Extra virgin olive oil

Salt

Flaky sea salt and rosemary to garnish

Equipment

Large mixing bowl

1 or 2 baking trays

As keen breadmakers, the idea of adding alcohol to bread dough was intriguing. After a lot of research and testing we've created this red wine focaccia, which has a deliciously chewy and flavoursome crumb, and a crisp crust drizzled with olive oil and rosemary. The addition of alcohol slows the activity of the yeast, so it takes a little longer to rise than normal focaccia, but the wine adds a complex, gently fruity flavour and, of course, an eye-catching colour!

Focaccia bread is not particularly hard to make - unlike most bread you don't have to knead it a lot. It's a very soft dough, and occasional stretching and folding while the dough rises helps to create the typical large holes of focaccia. Drizzle with olive oil and serve as a starter, as part of a tapas spread, or to make a truly incredible sandwich. Top simply with sea salt or customise it to your preference - in the recipe below we sprinkle the focaccia with rosemary before baking, but you could also add black olives or thinly sliced red onion.

- In a large mixing bowl combine the yeast, sugar and lukewarm water. Mix well then leave it to sit for 10 minutes until the mixture is very bubbly

- Into the same bowl add the flour, red wine, 2 tbsp olive oil and 8g salt. Stir the mixture together then mix well with your hands or a wooden spoon until you have a wet, sticky dough. Cover with cling film or a tea towel and let it prove for 30 minutes

- After 30 minutes, drizzle your hands and the dough with some olive oil. Leaving the dough in the bowl, lift part of the dough and stretch it up over itself. Turn the bowl 90 degrees and repeat, pulling the dough up and over itself. Keep turning and pulling the dough over itself a few more times - it should start to hold its shape in a ball. Cover again and leave for about an hour, or until the dough has doubled in size

- Meanwhile, drizzle 1 or 2 baking trays liberally with olive oil

- Unstick the dough from the bowl, then repeat the process of stretching and folding the dough over itself. If you want two medium focaccia, split the dough in half now

- Turn the dough out onto an oiled tray then stretch it with your hands until it is wide and fairly flat - don't worry if it tears a bit! Cover again, and leave to rise for 1 hour until the dough is noticeably risen and puffy

- Preheat the oven to 220C / Gas Mark 7 / 425F for at least 30 minutes

- Drizzle the top of the focaccia with a bit more olive oil, then use the tips of your fingers to press down hard into the dough to make little dimples all over

- Sprinkle the top generously with sea salt and rosemary then bake for 20-25 minutes until golden brown all over, and the bottom is firm and dry to the touch

SAVOURY BAKING

BEER AND BAILEYS DOUGHNUTS, PAGE 266

SWEET BAKING

Cider Apple Cake	230
Chocolate Stout Cake	231
White Wine Pound Cake	234
Baileys Muffins	236
Limoncello Polenta Cake	238
Dark 'n' Stormy Cake	242
Plum and Brandy Cake	244
Coconut Rum and Raspberry Cupcakes	246
Whisky and Maple Cupcakes	248
Peanut Butter and Bourbon Cookies	250
Whisky Shortbread	252
Lemon and Ouzo Cookies	254
Salted Caramel Spiced Rum Brownies	256
Chocolate and Port Tiffin	260
Alcoholic Bakewell Tart	261
Limoncello Tart	264
Beer and Baileys Doughnuts	266
Kahlua Fudge	270
Apple Cider Pancakes with Cider Caramel	272
Orange and Spiced Rum Marmalade	274
Apricot and Amaretto Jam	278
Apple and Bourbon Butter	280

And finally, to finish this book with a flourish - **Sweet Baking**. There are some of our absolute favourites in this chapter, such as **Beer and Baileys Doughnuts**, **Alcoholic Bakewell Tart**, **Plum and Brandy Cake**, and the **Salted Caramel Spiced Rum Brownies** (we really couldn't pick just one favourite), as the varied flavours of alcohol are used in so many ways here.

To keep things simple, the recipes in this chapter are organised by type - we've started with cakes, then followed this with biscuits and cookies, tarts, dough, and finally spreads. The challenge of baking with alcohol is in adding liquid to something that should become solid as it bakes. The liquid that we add brings moisture, tenderness and flavour to the finished product - and in this chapter we'll explore the techniques that make this possible. It has very much been a process of trial-and-error for us - over half of the "discarded, not good enough" recipes that we developed in the last five years have been baked goods!

Baking with alcohol is a balancing act to get the precise combination of ingredients for a great bake and consistency, and ensure that the flavour of the alcohol is a central element of the dish.

There are two main ways to achieve this harmony. First, we can use small quantities of a strong-flavoured spirit that won't add a lot of liquid. Second, we can choose baking techniques that traditionally use a larger quantity of liquid, including certain cake recipes, fruit infusions or syrups.

Traditional 'wet batter' cake styles, or cakes made by stirring melted ingredients into dry ingredients, are the easiest bakes in which to incorporate alcohol. These cakes tend to be very easy to mix together, and as a larger quantity of liquid is used to give a runnier batter, we have chosen to use alcohols with a lower proof like wine, beer and liqueurs.

Examples in this book are the **White Wine Pound Cake**, or the Depression-era 'wacky cake' recipe that's the basis of our **Chocolate Stout Cake**. Muffins, too, often include milk, so our recipe uses Baileys Irish Cream with coffee.

For sponge cakes, with their lighter batter, we've found that extra liquid produces a heavier cake. Here, we've found it most effective to include a smaller quantity of higher strength alcohol in the cake batter, and adding additional flavour impact from a glaze, drizzle or icing.

This ensures that the moisture level of the cake can be carefully controlled, and that every bite will be full of flavour and fragrance. In addition, the sugar included in a glaze or icing counteracts any harsh alcohol notes from the spirit, so that the other aromatic compounds can really shine - a great example of this is the **Whisky and Maple Cupcakes**.

The same small quantities of alcohol are crucial in recipes for biscuits and cookies, where extra moisture is the enemy. There are recipes here for three different styles of biscuit: chewy cookie, buttery shortbread, and almond-laced macaroon.

Again, we've opted for spirits with prominent flavours, which are enhanced by the addition of other ingredients - lemon is a perfect partner for the bright aniseed notes of ouzo in our **Lemon and Ouzo Cookies**, while we found that vanilla extract is essential in our **Peanut Butter and Bourbon Cookies**, where it enhances the warming, spicy bourbon aromas. Meanwhile, our **Chocolate and Port Tiffin** uses a technique most often seen in festive baking, where dried fruits are infused with alcohol and stirred into the mixture for added moisture and rich flavour.

Flavoured caramel is another amazing way to include alcohol in your baking, as it's essentially a way of incorporating the flavours of alcohol into sugar. This technique can be used in a fudge, to make a caramel sauce, or added to a recipe - in our **Salted Caramel Spiced Rum Brownies**, rum-spiked caramel is dolloped over a rich rum brownie batter.

Towards the end of the book, we return again to the functional side of alcohol in cooking - it's a secret trick for making perfectly light, buttery pastry. That's because flour doesn't absorb alcohol in the same way as water, so it doesn't form gluten (which makes pastry tough). We've used this method for pastry-making in two tart recipes: an **Alcoholic Bakewell Tart** and a zesty **Limoncello Tart**.

Both of these also have fillings that use alcohol, where sweet liqueurs like amaretto, sloe gin and limoncello add a beautiful, fruity flavour, while providing the perfect level of moisture.

In our doughnut batter, the natural yeasts in beer help to create a light and fluffy texture, while also contributing to the rich and malty flavour of our **Beer and Baileys Doughnuts**. In a pancake batter, on the other hand, apple cider acts in the same way as buttermilk does, reacting with the baking soda to create light and fluffy pancakes.

And finally, there are three spread recipes at the end of the chapter: jam, marmalade and apple butter. In each of these, we add some of the alcohol right at the end, which ensures that the volatile molecules in the spirit carry the flavours and aromas to our noses and taste buds. It's exactly what toast needs.

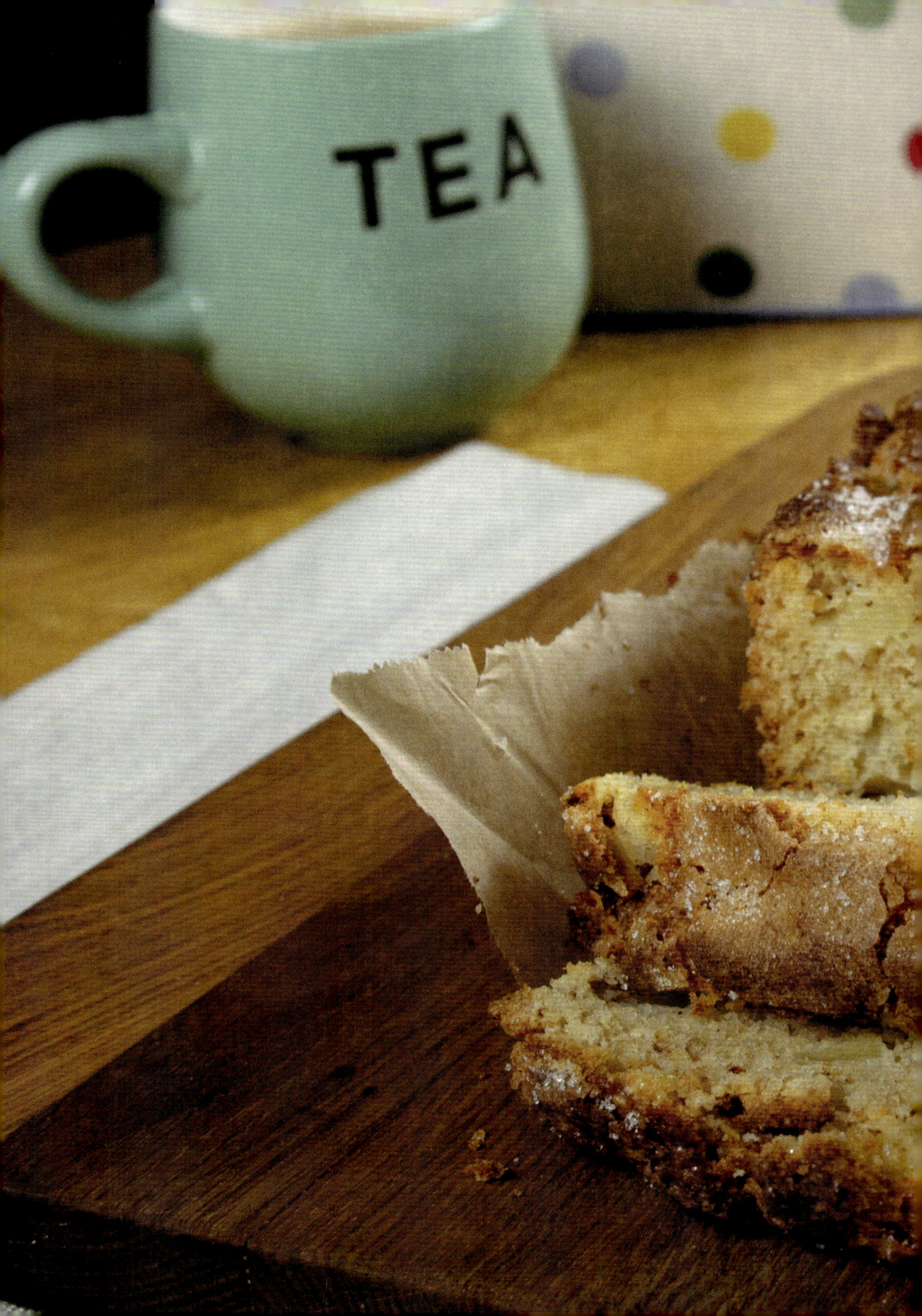
TEA

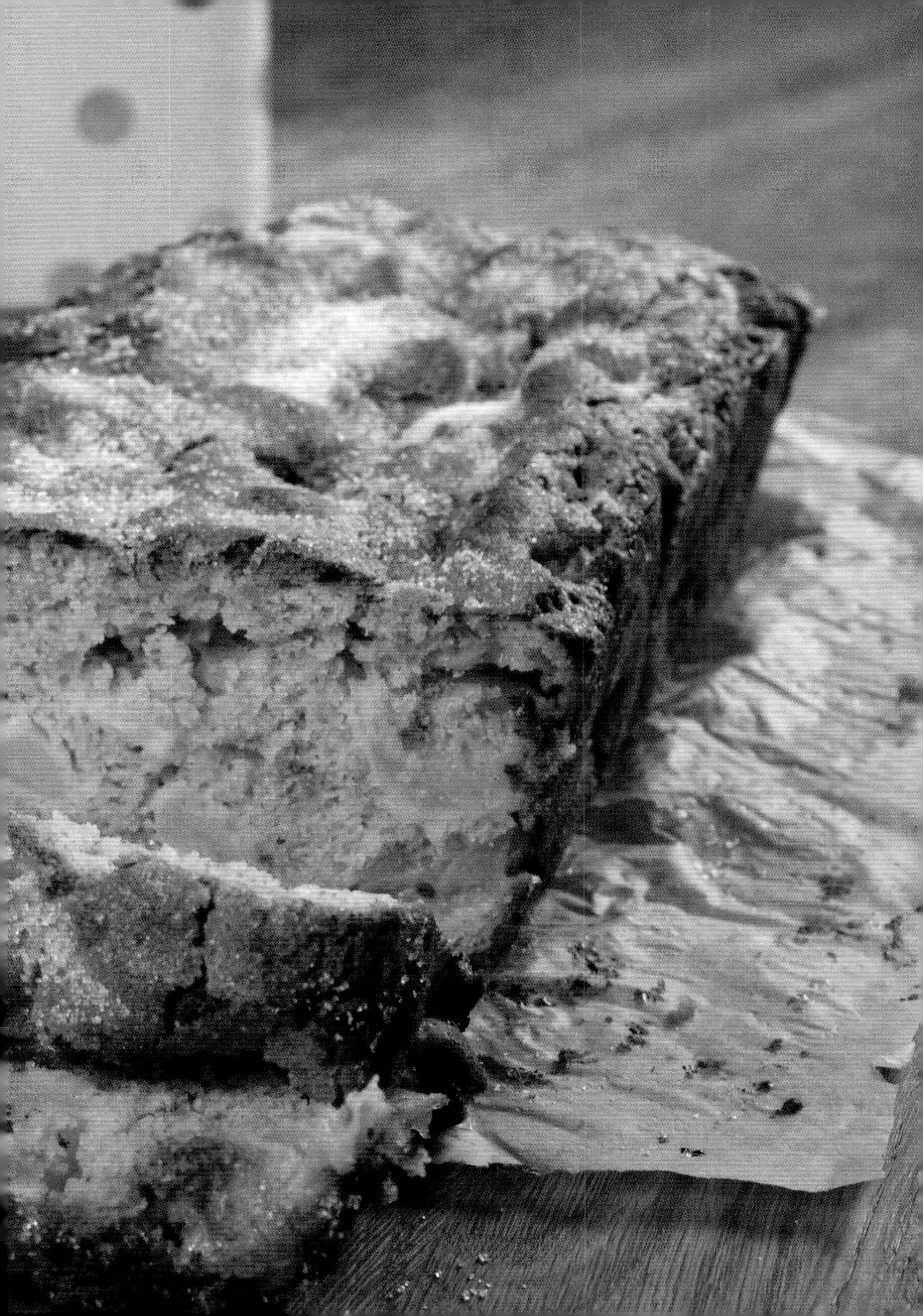

Cider Apple Cake

Serves 10 — Prep time 45 minutes — Cook time 45 minutes — Difficulty ②

Ingredients

300ml apple cider

100g butter

175g white sugar + 1 tbsp to sprinkle on top

2 eggs

250g self-raising flour (or use 240g plain flour mixed with 3 heaped tsp baking powder)

1 tsp ground cinnamon

½ tsp mixed spice or pumpkin spice

1 tsp vanilla extract

400g apples - peeled, cored and diced

Salt

We started making apple cakes years ago, when an apple tree in the garden gave us more windfalls than we knew what to do with. This is a homely cake with a really comforting texture, a crisp golden brown top and generous chunks of apple inside. Use any type of apples that you like - cooking apples, eating apples or a mixture are fine.

This rustic cake is deliciously moist inside thanks to the high quantity of apples and the addition of a thick cider syrup in the spiced cake batter. The moistness contrasts with the crunchy sugar-crusted top, and means that this cake works equally well for a teatime treat or served with custard for dessert.

- Pour the cider into a small saucepan and simmer for around 20 minutes until it has reduced by at least two thirds. Leave to cool for at least 10 minutes
- Preheat the oven to 180C / Gas Mark 4 / 350F. Grease a loaf tin and line it with baking paper
- Combine the butter and sugar in a large mixing bowl and beat well until the mixture is smooth and pale. Add one egg and 1 tbsp of the flour and beat well, then add the other egg along with 1 tbsp flour and beat again
- Fold in the rest of the flour along with the cinnamon, mixed spice, vanilla extract and a pinch of salt, then stir in the reduced cider and chopped apples
- Spoon the mixture into the prepared tin and smooth the top with a spoon, then sprinkle with the final 1 tbsp sugar
- Bake for 35-45 minutes or until a skewer comes out clean when poked into the centre of the cake. Cool in the tin for 10 minutes then transfer to a rack to cool completely

Equipment

Small saucepan

Loaf tin

Baking paper

Large mixing bowl

Electric beater or wooden spoon

Chocolate Stout Cake

Serves 10 — Prep time 30 minutes — Baking time 25 minutes — Difficulty ❸

This moist vegan chocolate cake is based on a Depression-era 'wacky cake'. Originally conceived as a cake mixture you could make without perishable ingredients like eggs and dairy, wacky cakes get their rise from oil and vinegar. This makes a scrumptious and rich chocolate cake that mixes together quickly, and it doesn't contain any unusual ingredients. The cake batter may be runnier than you are used to, but don't let this worry you.

We love to top this cake with a simple mousse made with dark chocolate and stout. The malty bitterness of stout shines through in delicious contrast to the sweet cake - for those with a sweeter tooth, you may prefer to switch some of the stout for water in the mousse. Although the mousse doesn't contain any dairy, store it in a cool place or the fridge to ensure that the mousse holds its shape.

For more alcoholic chocolate mousse inspiration, take a look at the many other variations on pg 174.

Ingredients

- 500ml stout
- 250g self-raising flour (or use 240g plain flour mixed with 3 heaped tsp baking powder)
- 250g + 4 tsp caster sugar
- 50g cocoa powder
- 120ml vegetable or sunflower oil
- 4 tsp vinegar
- 2 tbsp golden syrup
- 200g dark chocolate (min. 80% cocoa solids) - broken into pieces
- A few large handfuls of ice
- Salt
- Chopped hazelnuts to decorate

For the cake

- Preheat the oven to 180C / Gas Mark 4 / 350F
- Grease two cake tins with a little oil and line each with a circle of baking paper
- In a large bowl, mix together the flour, 250g sugar, cocoa powder and a pinch of salt
- Add the oil, vinegar, golden syrup and 300ml stout to the bowl. Mix well until smooth, then divide the batter between the prepared cake tins
- Bake for 20-25 minutes or until a skewer comes out clean when poked into the centre of the cake
- Cool the cakes for 10 minutes in the tins, then remove from the tins and cool completely on a rack

For the mousse topping

- Put an inch or two of water into a saucepan and heat over a medium heat until the water is barely simmering. Alongside it, prepare a large bowl of cold water with a few generous handfuls of ice
- Break the chocolate into a metal heatproof bowl, and add the remaining 4 tsp sugar and 200ml stout. Place the metal bowl over the saucepan of hot water, ensuring that the bowl doesn't touch the hot water, and stir gently until the chocolate has melted and the mixture is smooth

Equipment

- 2 x 20cm (8 inch) diameter cake tins
- Baking paper
- Medium saucepan
- Large bowl
- Metal bowl
- Piping bag and nozzle (optional)

Continued on the next page

SWEET BAKING

- Take the bowl out of the saucepan and place it into the bowl of iced water, which will begin to chill it from the outside. Immediately begin whisking the mixture and continue for a few minutes as the chocolate cools and begins to thicken. This will take about 5 minutes in total
- Stop whisking when the chocolate has reached the texture of whipped cream, being careful not to overmix (it will firm up a little more after you have stopped whisking)

To decorate the cake
- Make sure the cakes are completely cool before you begin to decorate
- Spread one third of the chocolate mousse mixture over one cake, then put the second cake on top. Pipe or swirl the rest of the mousse topping onto the cake, then sprinkle with chopped hazelnuts to decorate

TIP: If the mousse mixture is overbeaten it can become grainy or stiff instead of light and smooth. This can easily be fixed by heating the mixture to re-melt it, then cooling & beating again

TIP: Using a metal mixing bowl for the mousse mixture will help it to cool more quickly when placed in the ice water. This rapid cooling helps the mousse to emulsify and thicken. If you don't have a metal bowl, you could use a small metal saucepan instead

SWEET BAKING

COOKING WITH ALCOHOL

White Wine Pound Cake

Serves 10 — Prep time 20 minutes — Cook time 40 minutes — Difficulty ❶

Ingredients

250ml dry white wine (150ml for the cake, 100ml for the glaze)

3 eggs

150ml vegetable or sunflower oil

50ml milk

1 tsp vanilla extract

50g light soft brown sugar

200g white sugar

200g self-raising flour

1 tsp ground cinnamon

40g butter

100g icing sugar (powdered sugar)

Equipment

Bundt tin or loaf tin approx. 1.5L capacity

Large mixing bowl

Whisk or electric beater

Cooling rack

Small saucepan

The name 'pound cake' best describes the moist, tender crumb and rich buttery flavour of this cake, and this easy recipe is one you'll make time and again. The cake has a gentle, fruity flavour from the wine, with hints of warming cinnamon, vanilla and brown sugar. Choose a dry white wine that you enjoy drinking, as you'll have the rest of the bottle left over!

This cake is very quick to mix together, as the ingredients are simply whisked together in one large bowl. Drizzled liberally with white wine glaze, it's best eaten on the same day as baking. Serve on its own or with fresh summer berries for dessert.

- Preheat the oven to 170C / Gas Mark 3 ½ / 350F
- Grease the cake tin with a little oil, then sprinkle it with flour (if your mould is made of silicone, you don't need to flour it)

For the cake

- In a large mixing bowl, whisk together the eggs, oil, milk, vanilla extract, brown sugar, white sugar and 150ml of the white wine
- Add the flour and cinnamon and whisk again until you have a smooth and runny cake batter
- Pour the batter into the prepared cake tin, ensuring that you only fill it two-thirds full (this gives it space to rise). If you have extra batter that won't fit, bake it separately in a muffin tin or greased ramekin
- Bake the cake for 40 minutes or until a skewer comes out clean when poked into the centre of the cake. Cool the cake in the tin for 10 minutes then turn it out onto a rack to cool

For the glaze

- While the cake is cooling, pour the remaining 100ml white wine into a small saucepan. Bring to the boil then reduce the heat to low, and simmer for 10-20 minutes until it has reduced by about two thirds and is a thick, syrupy liquid
- Remove the pan from the heat and stir in the butter until melted, followed by the icing sugar. Mix until smooth
- With the cake still on the cake rack, slowly drizzle the glaze over the warm cake until it's sticky and glossy all over

TIP: If you're not sure how big your tin is, pop it on the scales and pour water inside it. The weight of the water inside shows the capacity of your tin (1kg water = 1 litre)

COOKING WITH ALCOHOL

Baileys Muffins

Makes 9-12 muffins (depending on their size!) — Prep time 20 minutes
Baking time 20 minutes — Difficulty ❶

Ingredients

140ml Baileys Irish Cream

70ml vegetable or sunflower oil

50g natural yogurt

50g white sugar

75g demerara sugar + 2 tbsp to sprinkle on top

1 tsp instant coffee dissolved in 1 tbsp boiling water (or use a shot of espresso)

1 egg

250g self-raising flour (or use 240g plain flour mixed with 3 heaped tsp baking powder)

100g chocolate chips

Salt

Muffins are very quick to make and are always best eaten fresh and warm from the oven. For a treat you'll want to make again and again, there's nothing better than chocolate and Baileys. The sweet stickiness of Irish cream is complemented by a hint of coffee, and the chocolate chips bring out the cocoa notes of the liqueur.

The trick to perfectly fluffy muffins is mixing in the flour as little as possible, to avoid developing much gluten (which makes muffins chewy). So use a light touch, give it a quick stir and pop them in the oven. These are perfect for brunch or a mid-morning cake break, or even for a late night snack!

- Preheat the oven to 180C / Gas Mark 4 / 350F
- Put 12 paper muffin cases into the muffin tray, or grease the tray with a little oil
- In a mixing bowl combine the oil, yogurt, Baileys, white sugar, 75g demerara sugar, the coffee and the egg
- Sift the self-raising flour and a pinch of salt over the mixture. Add the chocolate chips, then mix it all together until just combined (it's ok if there are still a few floury bits)
- Scoop the mixture into the muffin cases and sprinkle the tops with a little extra demerara sugar
- Bake for 20 minutes, until the tops are golden and crisp and a skewer comes out clean

Equipment

Muffin tray

9-12 paper muffin cases (optional)

Mixing bowl

Sieve

SWEET BAKING

Limoncello Polenta Cake

Serves 8-10 — Prep time 25 minutes — Baking time 40 minutes — Difficulty ②

Ingredients

220ml limoncello

280g butter

330g caster sugar (280g for the cake, 50g for the topping)

2 unwaxed lemons - zested and juiced

170g ground almonds

4 eggs

1 ½ tsp baking powder

200g fine polenta

Mascarpone or cream to serve

This bright yellow cake is soft, moist, full of lemony flavour, and naturally gluten free. Golden and crumbly polenta, although fairly flavourless by itself, has the wonderful ability to absorb lots of flavour and liquid - and what better liquid to use than limoncello!

The process of limoncello-making extracts the essential oils from the lemon peels, producing an intensely lemony cordial. Here there's limoncello in the cake batter to be absorbed by the polenta as it bakes, and we're drizzling the cake with even more limoncello and lemon juice at the end for freshness, fragrance and stickiness. Serve by itself, or with a generous dollop of mascarpone cheese or cream.

- Preheat the oven to 170C / Gas Mark 3 ½ / 350F
- Grease the loaf tin with butter, and line with baking paper
- In a large mixing bowl, combine the butter with 280g caster sugar and the lemon zest (reserving the lemon juice for later), and beat for 5 minutes until pale and fluffy
- Weigh out your ground almonds into a small bowl. Beat the eggs into the butter and sugar mixture one at a time, adding a spoonful of the ground almonds together with each egg, and beating well in between each addition
- Gently fold in the rest of the ground almonds together with the baking powder, polenta and 120ml of the limoncello
- Pour the cake mixture into the greased lined tin and smooth with a spoon
- Bake for 35-40 minutes until golden brown on top and a skewer poked into the cake comes out clean. Leave the cake in the tin while you prepare the drizzle
- When the cake is fresh out of the oven, heat the remaining 100ml limoncello with the juice of 2 lemons in a small saucepan until steaming. Drizzle the hot cake with the lemony liquid, then sprinkle with the remaining 50g caster sugar
- Serve warm or cold with a dollop of sweetened mascarpone or cream

Equipment

Loaf tin

Baking paper

Electric beater or wooden spoon

Large mixing bowl

Small bowl

Small saucepan

SWEET BAKING

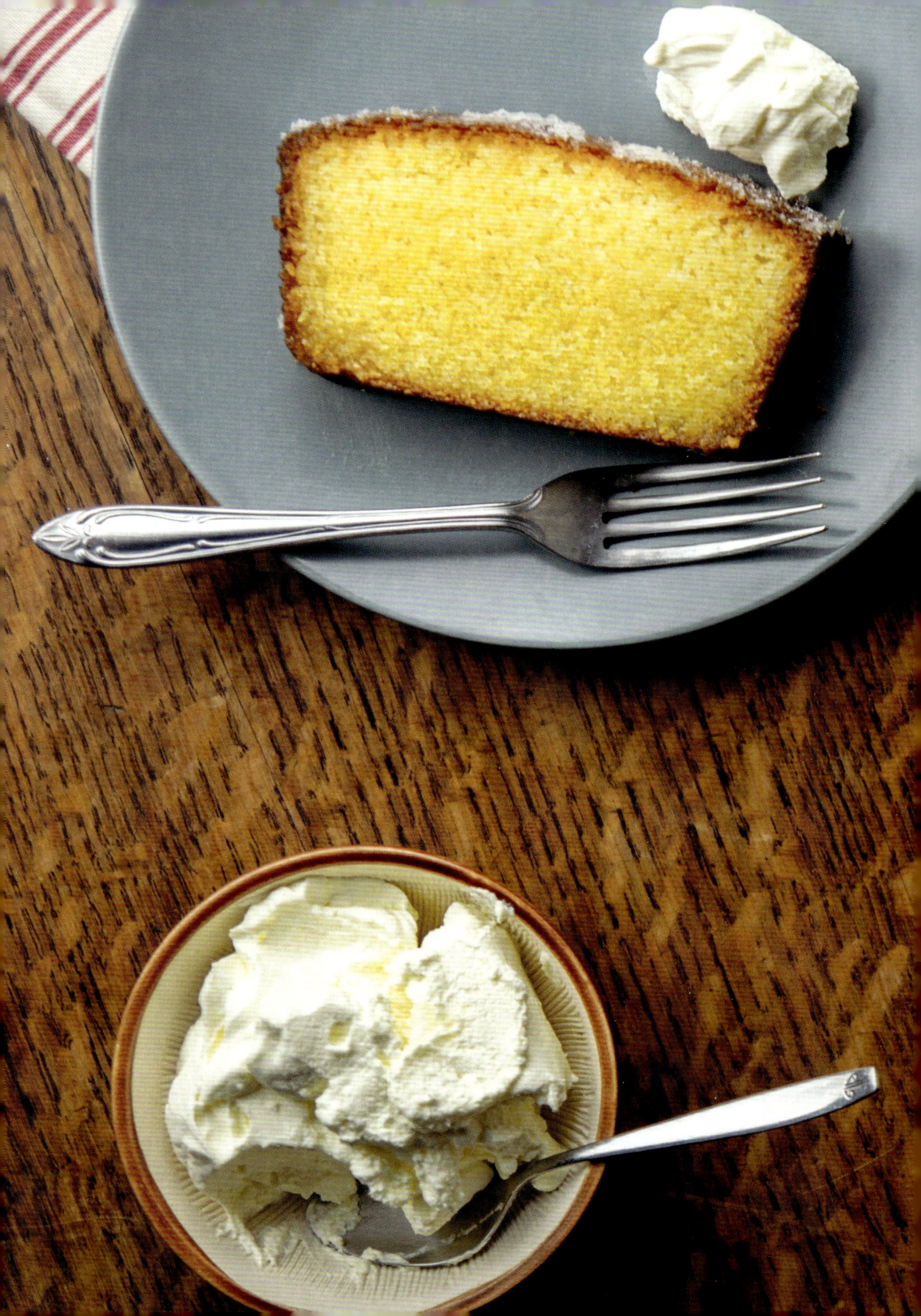

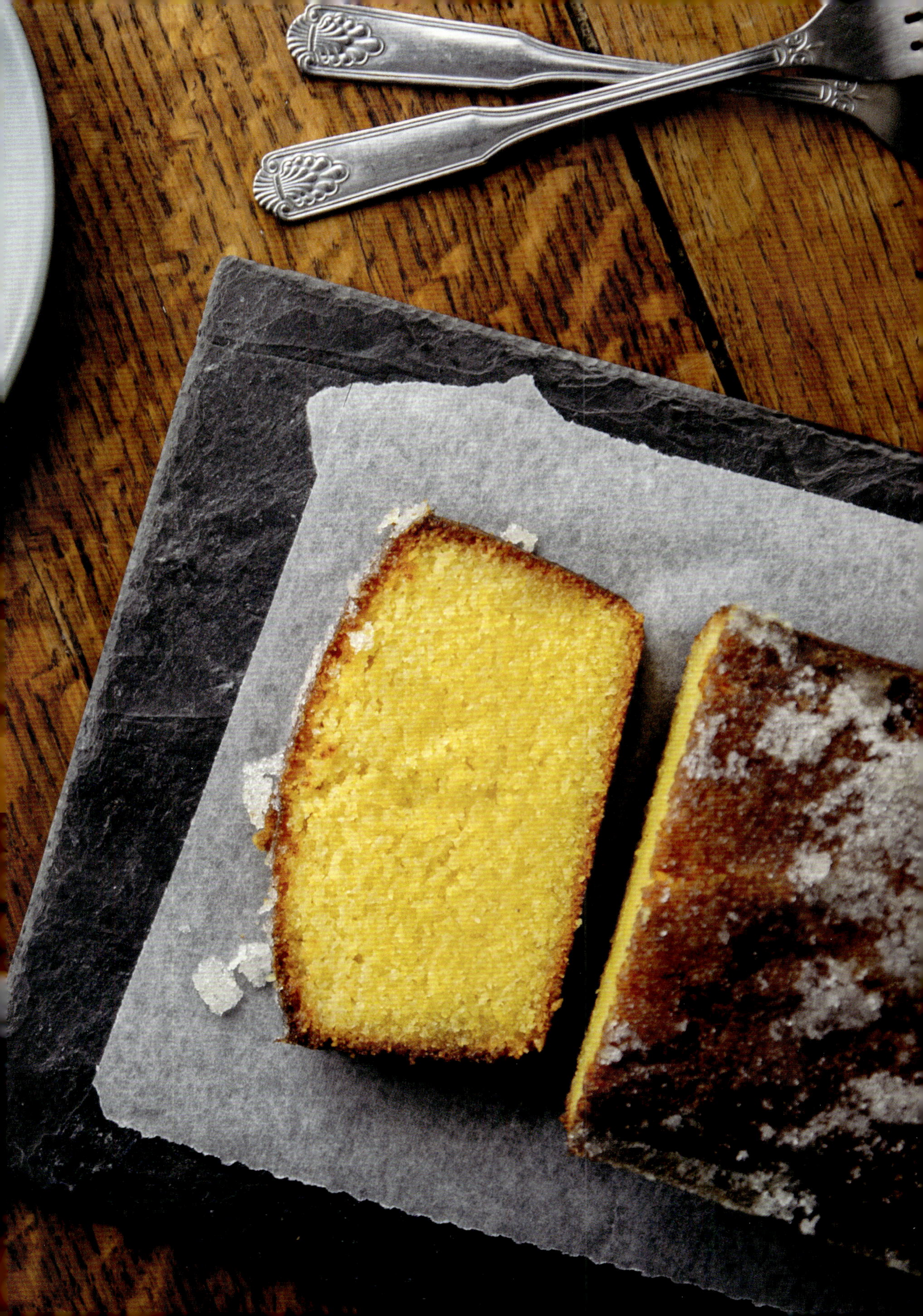

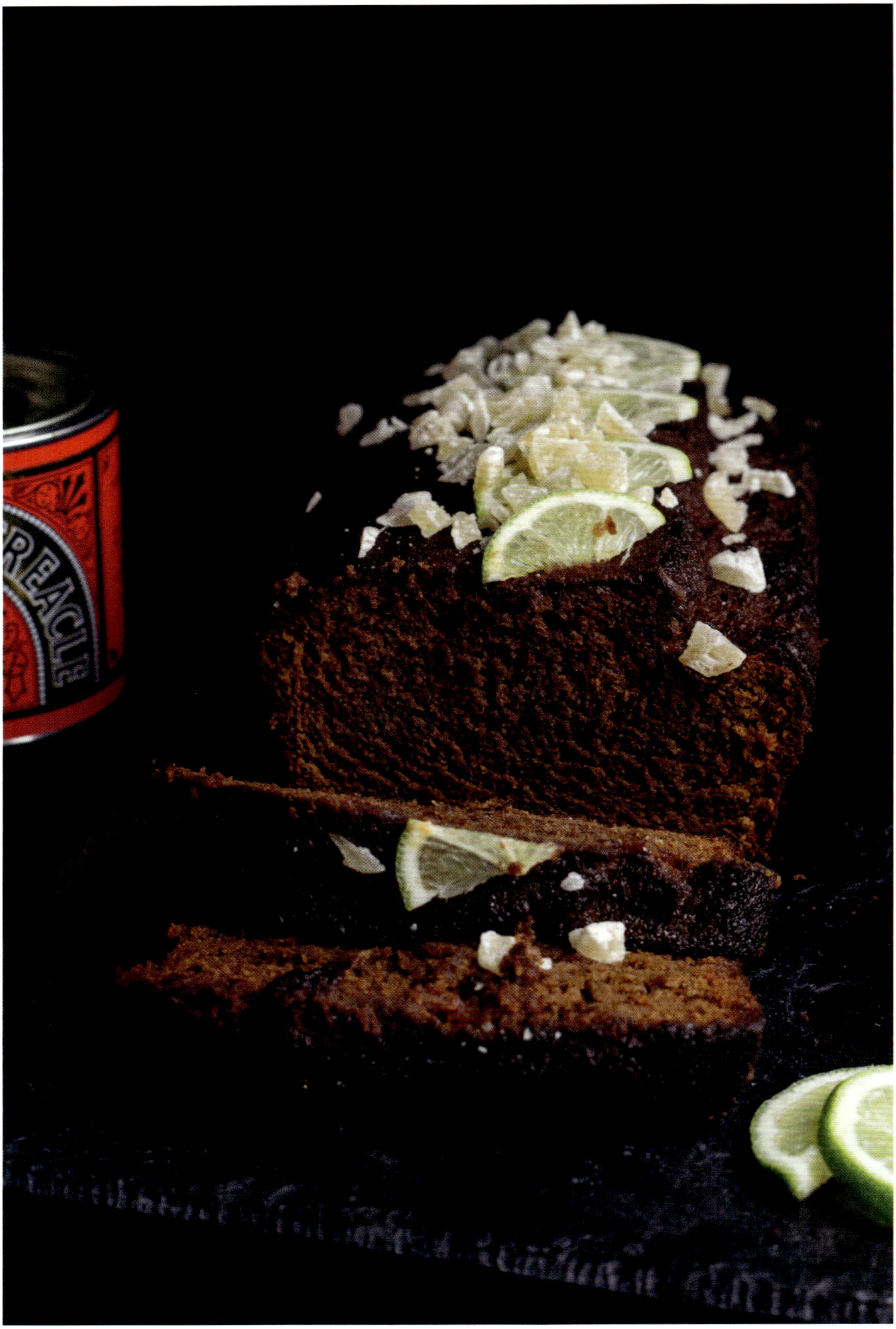

Dark 'n' Stormy Cake

Serves 10 — Prep time 20 minutes — Cook time 1 hour — Difficulty ❷

This decadent cake is our homage to the classic Dark 'n' Stormy cocktail - a sticky rum and ginger cake flavoured with treacle, spices and lime. It's spicy, citrusy, sweet, dark and - of course - alcoholic!

The batter here is quite runny, but don't let that worry you. The addition of rich, dark treacle with the brown sugar helps to trap the water molecules from the rum, resulting in a moist and tender crumb and a delicious depth of flavour from the caramelised sugars. This cake keeps really well, thanks to the moisture, so it can be made a day ahead of time. It's also fairly straightforward to make.

Ingredients

150ml dark or spiced rum (100ml for the cake, 50ml for the drizzle)

130g butter

200g black treacle

200g light or dark soft brown sugar (150g for the cake, 50g for the drizzle)

230g self-raising flour

2 ½ unwaxed limes - 2 zested and juiced, and the remaining ½ lime for decoration

2 tbsp ground ginger

1 ½ tsp mixed spice or pumpkin spice

50ml milk

2 eggs

Salt

30g crystallised ginger to decorate

- Preheat the oven to 180C / Gas Mark 4 / 350F
- Grease a loaf tin and line with baking paper
- Heat the butter, treacle and 150g brown sugar together in a small saucepan for 5 minutes until melted and smooth
- Separately, stir together the flour, lime zest, ground ginger, mixed spice and a pinch of salt
- Stir the melted treacle mixture into the flour, followed by the milk, eggs and 100ml dark rum. Mix well until you have a smooth runny batter
- Pour the batter into the prepared cake tin
- Bake for 30-40 minutes until the top of the cake is cracking and it's cooked through in the centre - the cake is done when a sharp knife comes out clean when poked into the centre
- While the cake is still fresh out of the oven, stir together the lime juice, remaining 50g brown sugar and 50ml rum in a small bowl. Mix well then pour this all over the top of the cake. Allow the cake to cool in the tin for at least 15 minutes then transfer to a rack to cool completely
- Decorate with crystallised ginger and thin slices of the extra half lime

Equipment

Loaf tin
Baking paper
Small saucepan
Small bowl

SWEET BAKING

COOKING WITH ALCOHOL

Plum and Brandy Cake

Serves 10 — Prep time 35 minutes — Cook time 1 hour — Difficulty ❷

This dense, almondy cake is studded with juicy plums throughout, and is a perfect way to enjoy a late summer abundance of fruit. Brandy has an affinity for sweetness and, while the brandy itself is a key flavour in this cake, it also lifts and enhances the subtle caramel flavour of the sticky baked plums on top of the cake. Brushed with a sweet, sticky brandy glaze, it's incredibly moreish.

Serve thick slices of this cake with a cup of tea, or enjoy it warm for dessert with a dollop of custard.

Ingredients

190ml brandy (70ml for the cake, 50ml for the top, 70ml for the glaze)

270g self-raising flour (or use 255g plain flour mixed with 4 level tsp baking powder)

70g ground almonds

½ tsp mixed spice or pumpkin spice

400g ripe plums - stoned, and half diced, half sliced

310g white sugar (250g for the cake, 60g for the glaze)

125g butter

1 tsp vanilla extract

3 eggs

50ml milk

1 tbsp plum, apricot or raspberry jam

- Preheat the oven to 180C / Gas Mark 4 / 350F
- Grease your cake tin and line with baking paper
- In a large mixing bowl combine the flour, ground almonds, mixed spice and the diced plums (reserving the sliced plums for later)
- In a separate bowl, beat together 250g of the sugar with the butter and vanilla until light and fluffy. Beat in the eggs one at a time, adding a spoonful of the flour mixture together with each egg, and beating well between each addition
- Fold in the rest of the flour and plum mixture, together with 70ml brandy and the milk
- Spoon the cake mixture into the prepared tin and smooth the top with the back of a spoon. Arrange the sliced plums in a pattern on the top
- Bake the cake for 50 minutes to 1 hour, rotating it after 40 minutes, until deep golden brown all over and a skewer comes out clean when poked into the centre of the cake
- While the cake is still in the tin, sprinkle the top with 50ml brandy then allow it to cool in the tin for 10 minutes. Then remove the cake from the tin and cool on a rack

For the glaze

- While the cake is cooling, combine the remaining 70ml brandy, 60g sugar and 1 tbsp jam in a small saucepan. Cook over a low heat for 5 minutes, stirring occasionally, until the sugar has dissolved and the glaze is syrupy
- Strain the glaze to remove any seeds or pieces of fruit, then brush the warm cake liberally with the glaze

Equipment

23cm (9 inch) diameter cake tin

Baking paper

2 x large mixing bowls

Small saucepan

Sieve or tea strainer

Coconut Rum and Raspberry Cupcakes

Makes 12-20 cupcakes (depending on the size) — Prep time 25 minutes Cook time 20 minutes — Difficulty ❷

Ingredients

150ml coconut rum

215g butter - softened (125g for the cupcakes, 90g for the icing)

170g caster sugar

125ml coconut milk

2 eggs

170g self-raising flour

40g desiccated coconut

½ tsp baking powder

200g icing sugar (powdered sugar)

150g fresh raspberries

Cupcakes are such a great place to use alcohol. The characteristic combination of icing and light sponge seems to taste so much better spiked with something a little stronger than vanilla! We've opted for the summery flavours of raspberries and coconut rum with this recipe, but if you enjoy these we highly recommend you try out the Whisky and Maple Cupcakes on page 248.

These playful treats owe their beautiful sweet flavour to coconut three ways: rum, milk, and desiccated. The fats from coconut milk carry the rich coconut flavour, while sprinkles of desiccated coconut add texture and sweetness. Coconut rum is added to the batter and then drizzled over the warm cakes, topping up the tropical flavours and carrying the coconut scent.

We love to poke a fresh raspberry inside each cupcake before cooking, as we find that the slight acidity balances the coconut sweetness. Topped with fluffy raspberry buttercream, it's impossible to eat just one!

For the cupcakes

- Preheat the oven to 180C / Gas Mark 4 / 350F
- Place cupcake cases into a cupcake or muffin tray
- In a large mixing bowl, beat together 125g butter with the sugar and coconut milk until pale, light and fluffy
- Add one egg and 1 tbsp of the self-raising flour and beat well, then add the other egg along with 1 tbsp flour and beat again
- Fold in the rest of the flour along with the desiccated coconut, baking powder and 3 tbsp coconut rum
- Scoop the mixture into your cupcake cases, then poke a raspberry or two into the centre of each cake
- Bake for 15-20 minutes until golden brown all over and a sharp knife comes out clean when poked into the centre. While the cakes are still warm, spoon 1 tsp coconut rum over each cake, then allow to cool

For the icing

- Combine the remaining 90g butter and about 10 raspberries in a large mixing bowl. Beat for a few minutes until smooth and soft and the raspberries have broken down. Stir in the icing sugar along with 1 tbsp coconut rum, then beat for a few minutes until pale and smooth
- Once the cakes have cooled, generously spread or pipe on the icing

Equipment

Cupcake or muffin tray

12-20 cupcake cases (depending on how big you want the cakes!)

2 x mixing bowls

Electric beater or wooden spoon

Piping bag and nozzle (optional)

SWEET BAKING

Whisky and Maple Cupcakes

Makes 12 cupcakes — Prep time 20 minutes — Baking time 15 minutes — Difficulty ❷

Whisky and maple syrup is a flavour pairing most often seen in cocktail-making, but cupcake-making is the next best thing! The smooth, sweet, slightly woody flavour of whisky goes beautifully with the butterscotch notes of maple syrup. We find that a strong-flavoured or smoky whisky is best here, ensuring that it shines through the sweetness of the cake. Make sure to use a whisky that you enjoy, as the flavour will be noticeable.

Adding a liquid like whisky to a cake mixture makes it a bit heavier, so a little extra baking powder adds lightness to these cupcakes. An electric beater is helpful as it allows you to get extra air into the batter - however, a wooden spoon and some elbow grease will do the job!

Ingredients

- 5 tbsp whisky
- 215g butter - softened (140g for the cupcakes, 75g for the icing)
- 140g caster sugar
- 2 eggs
- 150g self-raising flour
- 1 tsp baking powder
- 1 tbsp milk
- 200g icing sugar (powdered sugar)
- 1 tbsp maple syrup
- Salt

For the cupcakes

- Beat together 140g butter with the sugar in a large mixing bowl for 2-3 minutes until pale and creamy
- Add the eggs one at a time, beating well and scraping down the sides of the bowl in between each addition
- Gently fold in the flour, baking powder and a pinch of salt, followed by 4 tbsp whisky and the milk
- Divide the mixture between the cupcake cases
- Bake for 12-15 minutes until golden brown and a skewer inserted into the cake comes out clean. Transfer to a wire rack to cool completely

For the icing

- Beat the remaining 75g butter for 2-3 minutes until soft and light, then gently stir in the icing sugar to avoid a cloud of sugar
- Add the maple syrup and 1 tbsp whisky and beat again until smooth and light
- Pipe or spread the icing onto the cooled cupcakes to decorate

Equipment

- 12 hole cupcake tray
- 12 paper cupcake cases
- Large mixing bowl
- Electric beater or wooden spoon
- Piping bag and nozzle (optional)

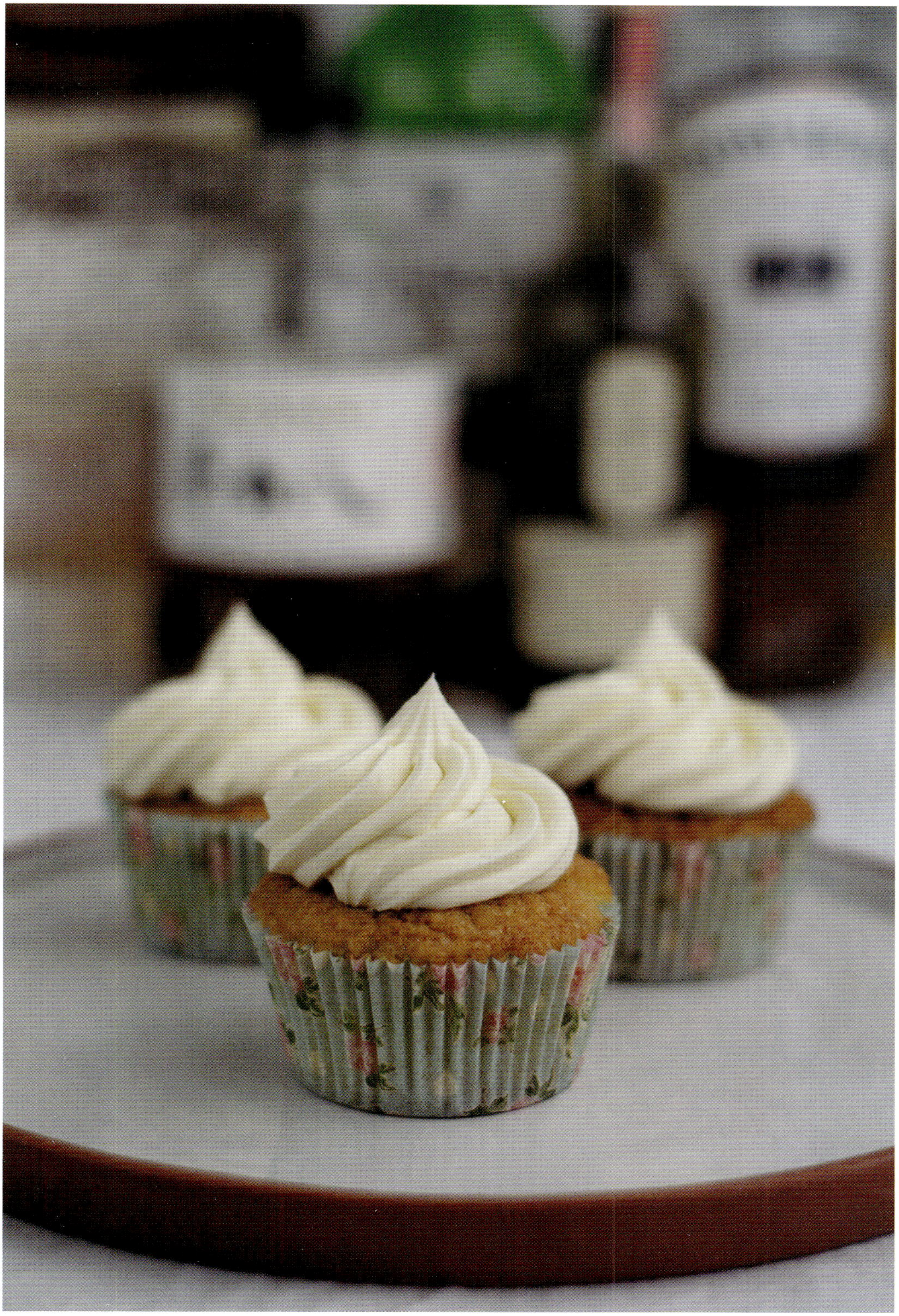

Peanut Butter and Bourbon Cookies

Makes 16-24 cookies depending on their size — Prep time 30 minutes + 1 hour chilling time — Baking time 9 minutes per batch + 10 minutes cooling time — Difficulty ❸

Ingredients

40ml bourbon

150g salted butter

2 eggs

1 tsp vanilla extract

140g caster sugar

140g light soft brown sugar

100g peanut butter (crunchy or smooth, your choice!)

240g plain flour

1 tsp bicarbonate of soda

Flaky sea salt to finish

We love cookies. These cookies are crisp on the outside, soft in the centre, and the sweet-salty flavour combination makes them so delicious that it's impossible to eat just one. The recipe may look quite intricate, but that's because getting the perfect balance of chewy, golden exterior and soft, gooey centre is more science than art.

To build the flavour in this cookie, butter is browned for a richer and more intense flavour than regular butter. Chilling time in the fridge is essential for the texture of the cookies, and gives the flavours time to develop - you can even make the mixture a day in advance for the very best results. Vanilla extract heightens the sweet notes of the bourbon, while a sprinkle of sea salt at the end sets off the peanut butter. Feel free to add chocolate or caramel chips if you fancy them!

If you don't have time to make browned butter (or can't be bothered), just use 130g salted butter.

For the brown butter

- Heat the butter and bourbon in a small saucepan over a low heat until the butter has melted. Simmer on a medium to high heat for about five minutes, swirling or whisking constantly, until the butter begins to turn golden brown. Remove the pan from the heat and pour the butter into a bowl to stop it cooking further and burning

For the cookie dough

- In a large mixing bowl beat together the eggs, vanilla and caster sugar for about 5 minutes until the sugar is dissolved and the mixture forms a smooth ribbon when you lift the beater

- Beat in the brown sugar, peanut butter and the browned bourbon butter until incorporated

- In a separate mixing bowl, whisk together the flour and bicarbonate of soda to ensure the bicarbonate of soda is evenly distributed. Add the flour mixture to the egg mixture and stir until just combined. A bit of flour here and there is ok, as you want to avoid overmixing it

- Cover the dough then chill in the fridge for at least an hour, or up to 24 hours. This deepens the flavour and helps the centre of the cookies stay soft and chewy

Equipment

Small saucepan

2 x mixing bowls

Electric beater or wooden spoon

Baking tray

Baking paper

Ice cream scoop (or large spoon)

Cooling rack

To bake

- Preheat the oven to 190C / Gas Mark 5 / 375F

- Place baking paper on your baking tray, then scoop balls of the cookie mixture and place them on the baking paper - an ice cream scoop is ideal for this

- Tear the dough balls in half to show a rougher surface, then stick them back together, with the rough edge now on the outside. This will help give the cookies a lovely bumpy texture on the outside

- Bake for 7½ to 9 minutes or until golden brown on the outside but still pale and soft in the middle. Give them a little poke in the centre - they should be quite soft, as they will firm up as they cool
- Sprinkle the cookies with a little flaky sea salt while they're still warm. Leave to cool for at least 10 minutes on the tray before removing to a cooling rack. Enjoy!

TIP: Each oven is different, so keep a close eye on the cookies as they bake. If you really want perfection, bake a small batch first and let them cool, then check that they are just right before baking the rest

Whisky Shortbread

Makes approx. 20 shortbread fingers — Prep time 40 minutes — Cook time 20 minutes
Difficulty ❶

Ingredients

75ml whisky

200g butter - softened

80g caster sugar

250g plain flour, plus extra for rolling

100g rice flour

Salt

There's something so satisfying about the crisp snap of a shortbread biscuit. Dense and buttery, with a crumbly texture and slight sweetness, shortbread is an underrated member of the biscuit tin. In our recipe, the addition of whisky adds a malty depth of flavour, making these just perfect served with a large cup of tea - or a dram of your favourite Scotch!

We use a combination of plain and rice flours in this recipe - rice flour doesn't contain any gluten, and in shortbread this provides a slightly coarser texture with a satisfying crunch. You can usually find it in the Asian or gluten-free sections of a large supermarket.

- Preheat the oven to 170C / Gas Mark 3 ½ / 350F
- Place baking paper on two baking trays
- Beat the butter, sugar and whisky together for a few minutes in a mixing bowl until pale and creamy
- Stir in the flour, rice flour and a pinch of salt, and knead the mixture gently until it comes together into a ball (if it's too sticky, add a little extra flour). Cover the bowl and chill for 20 minutes to firm up - this helps the biscuits retain their shape in the oven
- Sprinkle a clean surface with flour and gently roll the dough out into a rectangle just over 1cm (½ inch) thick. Slice the dough into fingers with a sharp knife
- Prick the shortbreads with a fork, then place on the trays
- Bake for 15-20 minutes until just turning golden brown. Allow to cool for 5 minutes on the tray before moving to a cooling rack

Equipment

2 x baking trays (or bake the mixture in 2 batches)

Baking paper

Mixing bowl

Electric beater or wooden spoon

Rolling pin (or use an empty wine bottle)

SWEET BAKING

Lemon and Ouzo Cookies

*Makes 18-25 cookies — Prep time 30 minutes + 30 minutes resting
Cook time 15 minutes — Difficulty* ❷

Ingredients

1 ½ tbsp ouzo

2 egg whites

1 unwaxed lemon - zested

160g caster sugar + 3 tbsp for rolling

220g ground almonds

3 tbsp icing sugar (powdered sugar) for rolling

These melt-in-the-mouth cookies are our take on traditional Italian ricciarelli. Made with egg whites and almonds, these macaroon-like treats are beautifully fragrant and chewy, and naturally gluten and dairy-free. The cookies have an endearingly crisp sugary shell which is surprisingly easy to achieve by rolling them in sugar and leaving them to dry a little before baking.

Our version is flavoured with lemon zest and the gentle aniseed flavour of ouzo, and although these are traditionally enjoyed at Christmas, we love them all year round, served with coffee or a glass of prosecco. For a variation, try making these with orange zest and amaretto liqueur.

If you really enjoy cookies, we recommend you make a double batch, as one batch of these normally lasts about 30 minutes in our house.

- Place a sheet of baking paper on each baking tray
- In a large, scrupulously clean mixing bowl beat the egg whites with the lemon zest for approximately 5 minutes until very stiff - when you lift the beater out it should leave peaks
- Fold in half the caster sugar and ground almonds with a spatula, trying to keep some of the air in the egg whites. Once this is all mixed in, add the rest of the caster sugar, the ground almonds and the ouzo and fold it together. You will have a thick sticky mixture
- Pour 3 tbsp of caster sugar into a small bowl, and 3 tbsp icing sugar into another bowl. Take spoonfuls of the sticky cookie mixture and roll by hand into balls. Roll the balls in the caster sugar and then in the icing sugar, before placing on the baking paper. Leave the cookies to rest uncovered for half an hour - this allows them to dry out a little, giving them a crisp exterior
- Preheat the oven to 170C / Gas Mark 3 ½ / 350F
- Just before baking, gently press down the top of each cookie to slightly flatten them - they will crack around the edges
- Bake for 12-15 minutes until pale golden brown all over, then allow to cool on the tray for 5 minutes before transferring to a plate or cooling rack

Equipment

2 x baking trays (or bake the mixture in 2 batches)

Baking paper

Large mixing bowl

Electric beater or whisk

2 small bowls (cereal bowls are ideal)

TIP: Make sure that your mixing bowl is very clean, otherwise the egg whites may have trouble forming stiff peaks

SWEET BAKING

Salted Caramel Spiced Rum Brownies

Makes approx. 20 brownies — Prep time 40 minutes — Cook time 40 minutes
Difficulty ❸

Ingredients

7 tbsp dark or spiced rum

200g condensed milk (½ a standard can)

300g butter (75g for the caramel, 225g for the brownies)

75g light or dark soft brown sugar

200g dark chocolate (min. 70% cocoa solids)

1 tsp vanilla extract

75g self-raising flour

350g white sugar

60g cocoa powder

1 tsp mixed spice or pumpkin spice

½ tsp chilli powder

4 eggs - beaten

Salt

Flaky sea salt to garnish

Equipment

Shallow metal baking tin approx. 20 x 30cm (8 x 11 inches)

Baking paper

2 x small saucepans

Heatproof bowl

Mixing bowl

These brownies are a real household favourite, and quite possibly our friend Chloe's favourite food in the world. Generously spiked with rum throughout, swirled with sweet caramel and with a hint of warming spice, these brownies are as beautiful as they are delicious. We've also added a sprinkle of sea salt at the end, which enhances the sweetness of the caramel.

Our recipe includes cocoa powder for a deep chocolate flavour, and a little bit of self-raising flour to get the perfect crisp brownie crust with a rich, gooey centre. Resist temptation and allow them to cool in the pan for at least 30 minutes so the caramel has time to set. The brownies are perfect on their own, but for extra indulgence a scoop of ice cream alongside wouldn't go astray.

- Preheat the oven to 180C / Gas Mark 4 / 350F
- Grease the baking tin and line with baking paper

For the caramel

- Empty the condensed milk into a small saucepan along with 75g butter, the brown sugar and ¼ tsp salt. Heat gently, stirring continuously so it doesn't burn on the bottom, for 5-10 minutes until the caramel is has begun to thicken, leaving a clear trail on the saucepan as you stir. Remove from the heat and set to one side to cool

For the brownie mixture

- Put an inch or two of water into a saucepan, and heat over a medium heat until the water is barely simmering
- Break the chocolate into a heatproof bowl, and add the remaining 225g butter, the vanilla extract and 3 tbsp of the rum. Place the bowl over the saucepan of hot water, ensuring that the bowl isn't touching the hot water, and stir gently until the chocolate has melted and the mixture is smooth. Set to one side to cool for a few minutes
- In a separate mixing bowl, stir together the flour, white sugar, cocoa, mixed spice, chilli powder and a large pinch of salt. Pour in the melted chocolate mixture and stir well, then add the beaten eggs, stirring well until smooth. Pour the batter into the prepared tin

Bringing it together

- Stir 1 tbsp of rum into the cooled caramel until smooth, then dollop large spoonfuls of caramel on top of the brownie batter. Swirl the top gently with a knife to make pretty caramel swirls on top of the brownie
- Bake for 30-40 minutes or until the brownies are crisp and firm on top but the caramel is still a little bit gooey and wobbly in the middle (it will firm up as it cools). While the brownies are fresh out of the oven, sprinkle a further 3 tbsp rum over the top followed by a large pinch of flaky sea salt. Allow to cool for at least 30 minutes before slicing

SWEET BAKING

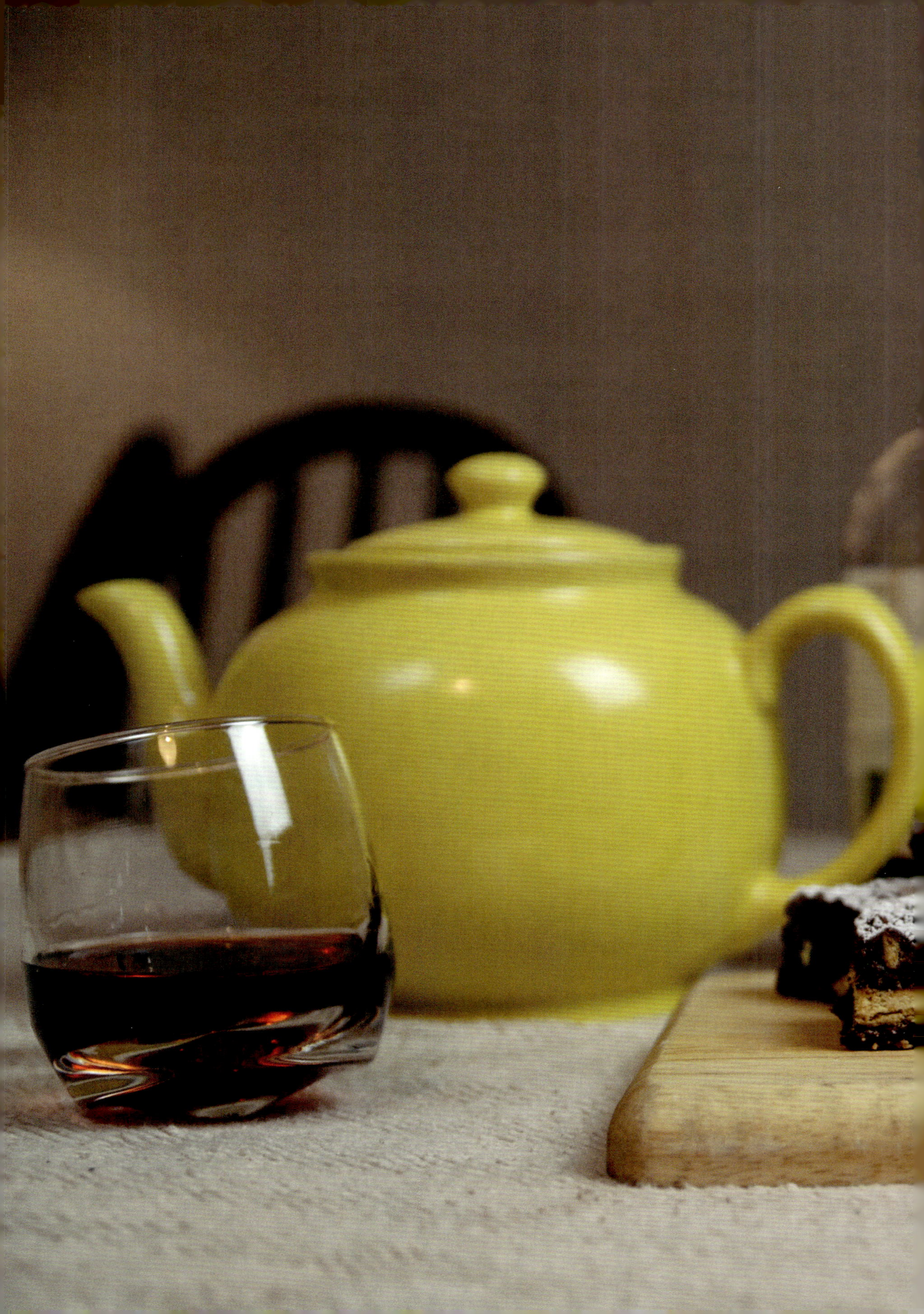

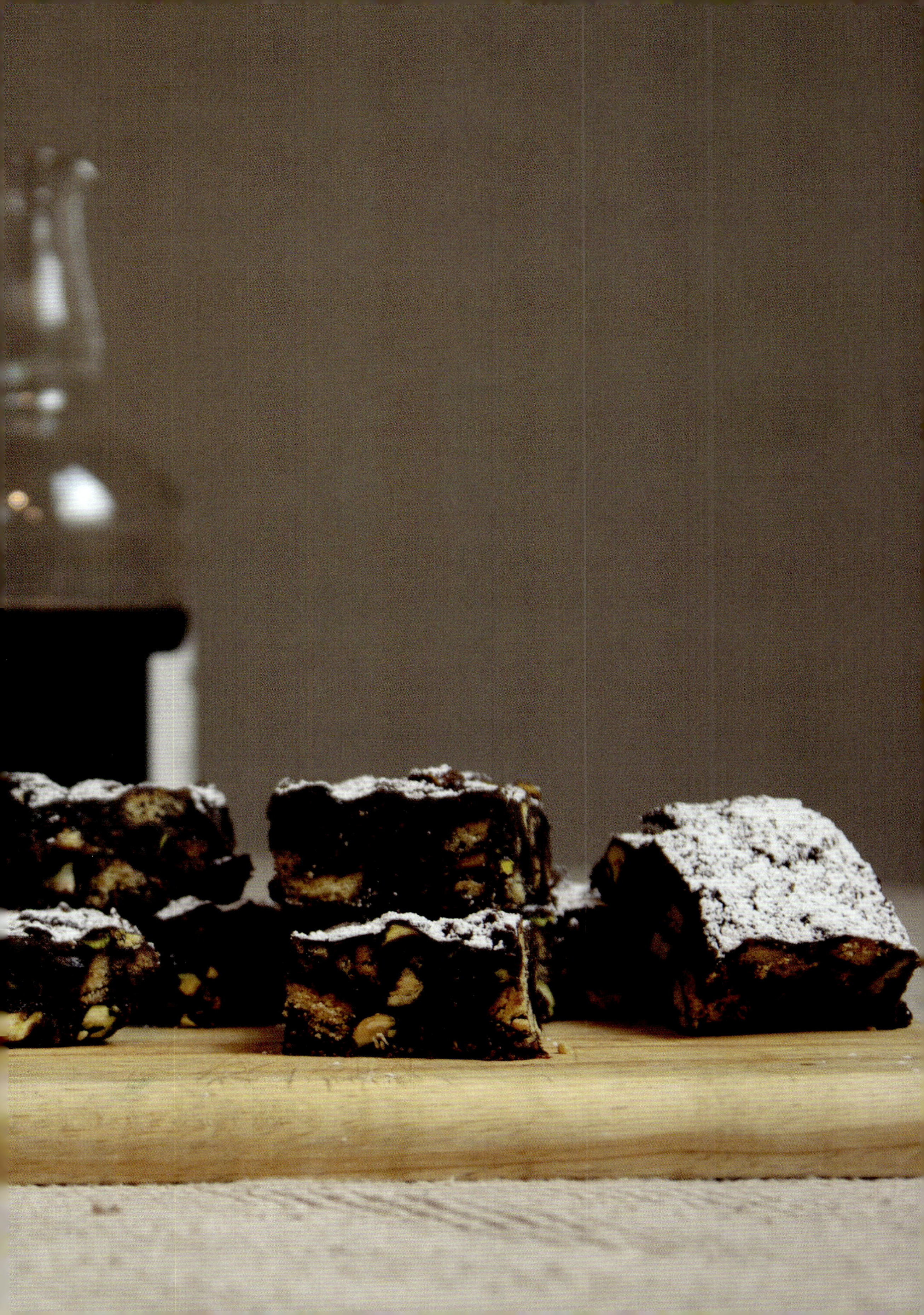

Chocolate and Port Tiffin

Makes approx. 16 pieces — Prep time 30 minutes + 3 hours chilling — Difficulty ❶

Ingredients

200ml port

200g dried cranberries or raisins (or a mixture)

250g digestive biscuits

300g milk chocolate

150g golden syrup

100g butter

30g cocoa

1 tsp vanilla extract

60g shelled unsalted pistachios - roughly chopped

Salt

Icing sugar (powdered sugar) to decorate

Equipment

Shallow baking tin approx. 20 x 30cm (8 x 11 inches)

Baking paper

2 x small saucepans

Food processor or a freezer bag and rolling pin

Mixing bowl

Heatproof bowl

Sieve or tea strainer

Chocolate tiffin, also known as chocolate biscuit cake or fridge cake, is an addictively straightforward no-bake treat. A few ingredients are melted together and stirred into dried fruit and biscuits, then it sets in the fridge. Our version is packed with boozy fruit and pistachios, which take it to the next level.

The succulent texture of this tiffin comes from cranberries simmered in port until sticky and plump, providing rich, fruity flavour in every bite. Sprinkled with icing sugar to decorate, this grown-up slice goes perfectly with a glass of port or sloe gin. If you can bear to give them away, they're also a fun homemade gift.

Add your own twist to this recipe by substituting some of the port for another alcohol - cointreau and brandy both work well.

- Grease your tin with butter, and line with baking paper
- Combine the dried fruit and port in a small saucepan and cook over a low heat for 20 minutes, stirring occasionally, until the fruit has absorbed most of the liquid and is very sticky. Set to one side
- Put the digestive biscuits into a resealable freezer bag, push the air out and then whack them with a rolling pin to crush them into small pieces - alternatively, blitz them in a food processor to fine crumbs. Transfer to a mixing bowl, together with the chopped pistachios
- Put an inch or two of water into a saucepan and heat over a medium heat until the water is barely simmering
- Combine the chocolate, golden syrup, butter, cocoa, vanilla extract and a pinch of salt in a heatproof bowl. Place the bowl over the pan of simmering water, ensuring that the bowl doesn't touch the hot water. Stir the mixture gently until the chocolate has melted and the mixture is smooth, then remove from the heat
- Stir the soaked fruit into the melted chocolate mixture, then add to the bowl with the crushed biscuits and chopped pistachios and stir it all together
- Pour the mixture into the prepared tin then smooth it with the back of a spoon. Place the tin in the fridge and chill for at least 3 hours until solid. Sieve icing sugar over the top to decorate

Alcoholic Bakewell Tart

Serves 8-10 — Prep time 1 hour 30 minutes — Cook time 30 minutes — Difficulty ❸

Our version of the classic Bakewell tart has all the elements you would expect - pastry, jam, frangipane, and a drizzle of icing. Of course, all the elements in this version are enriched with alcohol, and the final result is well-balanced with the right level of sweetness, and incredibly moreish. There's fragrant amaretto in the pastry and frangipane layers, a delicious and easy homemade sloe gin jam, and a drizzle of tart limoncello icing.

If you don't have time or don't want to make all the separate elements, you can use a store-bought tart case or jam. We won't tell, and it will still contain booze!

Ingredients

- 6 tbsp amaretto liqueur
- 3 tbsp sloe gin or other fruit liqueur
- 1-2 tbsp limoncello (or the same quantity of lemon juice)
- 175g plain flour
- 250g butter - 100g chilled, 150g softened
- 75g icing sugar (powdered sugar) (25g for the pastry, 50g for the icing)
- 4 eggs (1 for the pastry, 3 for the frangipane)
- 200g raspberries or mixed berries (frozen and defrosted are fine)
- 170g caster sugar (40g for the jam, 130g for the frangipane)
- 150g ground almonds
- 1 tsp vanilla extract
- Flaked almonds to decorate

Equipment

- Food processor (optional)
- 2 x mixing bowls
- Small saucepan
- Sieve or tea strainer (optional)
- 23cm (9 inch) tart tin, preferably with a removable base
- Rolling pin (or empty wine bottle)
- Baking paper
- Baking beans (or dried rice or pasta)
- Electric beater or whisk

For the pastry

- If you have a food processor, put the plain flour, 25g icing sugar and 100g chilled butter in the food processor, and blitz until the mixture forms crumbs. Add 1 egg and 2 tbsp amaretto liqueur and pulse until the mixture forms a ball of pastry (if it doesn't stick together, add an extra 1 tbsp of amaretto)
- Alternatively, grate 100g chilled butter into a mixing bowl. Add the flour and 25g icing sugar, and use your fingers to rub the butter into the flour until it forms crumbs. Then add 1 egg and 2 tbsp amaretto liqueur and mix together gently until you have a soft ball of dough (if it doesn't stick together, add an extra 1 tbsp of amaretto)
- Cover the pastry and chill in the fridge for at least 15 minutes.

For the jam

- While the pastry is chilling, combine the berries, sloe gin and 40g caster sugar in a small saucepan. Cook over a medium heat for 10-15 minutes, stirring occasionally, until the fruit has broken down and most of the liquid has evaporated. The jam is ready when a spoon stirred through leaves a trail across the bottom of the pan
- Remove from the heat and allow to cool. If you prefer a seedless jam, strain through a sieve or tea strainer, pressing it through with the back of a spoon

For the pastry

- Grease the tart tin with plenty of butter, and sprinkle with flour
- Roll out the chilled pastry on a clean floured surface into a circle approximately 3mm (⅛ inch) thick and 30cm (11 inches) in diameter, a bit wider than your tart tin. Gently transfer the pastry to the tin and press it to the sides, making sure that you don't stretch the dough. Chill in the fridge for a further 30 minutes
- Preheat the oven to 180C / Gas Mark 4 / 350F
- When the oven is hot, remove the tart case from the fridge. Scrunch up a piece of baking paper, then smooth it out and place inside your tart case. Fill with baking beans (or dried rice or pasta)

SWEET BAKING

- Place in the oven and bake for 12 minutes, then carefully remove the baking beans and paper and bake for a further 5 minutes until the pastry is pale golden brown
- Gently trim off the excess pastry with a sharp knife to neaten the edges, then allow to cool

For the frangipane
- While the pastry is chilling, combine 150g softened butter with 130g caster sugar in a large mixing bowl, and beat well for a few minutes until pale and light. Add 3 eggs one at a time, beating in well, then fold in the ground almonds, 3 tbsp amaretto, and the vanilla until just combined

Bringing it together
- Spread the jam across the cooled pastry, then scoop the frangipane on top and smooth it out with the back of a spoon
- Bake for 25-30 minutes until the top is firm and deep golden brown and the pastry is cooked through. Remove from the oven and allow to cool

To decorate
- In a small bowl combine 50g icing (powdered) sugar with 1 tbsp limoncello. Mix well then add more limoncello a little at a time until you have a smooth runny consistency. Drizzle the icing across the tart then sprinkle with flaked almonds

SWEET BAKING

Limoncello Tart

Serves 8-10 — Prep time 1 hour 30 minutes — Cook time 30 minutes — Difficulty ❸

Ingredients

75ml limoncello

3-4 tbsp vodka

175g plain flour

25g icing sugar (powdered sugar), plus extra to decorate

100g butter - chilled

5 eggs + 1 egg yolk

200g caster sugar

3 unwaxed lemons - zested and juiced

125ml double (heavy) cream

Equipment

Food processor (optional)

Mixing bowl

23cm (9 inch) tart tin, preferably with a removable base

Rolling pin (or empty wine bottle)

Baking paper

Baking beans (or dried rice or pasta)

Electric beater or whisk

Sweet and sour lemon tart is a classic addition to a high tea spread, and never fails to impress. We've created a version that includes limoncello, which has an intense lemony flavour with just a hint of bitterness, thanks to essential oils from lemon peels. Added to this quick custard filling, together with fresh lemon zest and juice, it delivers a bright and zesty taste of Italian sunshine.

We like to use vodka instead of water to make shortcrust pastry. The alcohol content of vodka doesn't allow the flour to develop gluten structure in the same way that water does, so it's easier to get a soft, crumbly pastry. If time is short you can use a ready made tart case - simply add the limoncello filling and bake until just set.

For the pastry

- If you have a food processor, put the flour, icing sugar and cubes of the chilled butter in the food processor, and blitz it until the mixture forms crumbs. Add 1 egg yolk and 3 tbsp vodka, and pulse until the mixture forms a ball of pastry (if it doesn't stick together, add an extra 1 tbsp of vodka)

- Alternatively, grate the chilled butter into a mixing bowl. Add the flour and icing sugar, and use your fingers to rub the butter into the flour until it forms crumbs. Then add 1 egg yolk and 3 tbsp vodka, and mix together gently until you have a soft ball of dough, adding extra vodka to bring it together if necessary

- Cover the pastry and chill in the fridge for at least 15 minutes

- Grease the tart tin with plenty of butter, and sprinkle with flour

- Roll out the chilled pastry on a clean floured surface into a circle approximately 3mm (⅛ inch) thick and 30cm (11 inches) in diameter, a bit wider than your tart tin. Gently transfer the pastry to the tin and press it to the sides, making sure that you don't stretch the dough. Chill in the fridge for a further 30 minutes

- Preheat the oven to 190C / Gas Mark 5 / 375F

- When the oven is hot, remove the tart case from the fridge. Scrunch up a piece of baking paper, then smooth it out and place inside your tart case. Fill with baking beans (or dried rice or pasta)

- Place in the oven and bake for 12 minutes, then carefully remove the baking beans and paper, and bake for a further 5 minutes until the pastry is pale golden brown

- Gently trim off the excess pastry with a sharp knife to neaten the edges, then allow to cool

For the filling

- While the pastry is cooling, gently beat 5 eggs together in a large mixing bowl. Add the caster sugar, limoncello, lemon zest, lemon juice and the cream, then mix it all together well

Bringing it together
- Place the cooled tart case onto the oven shelf, then carefully pour the filling into the tart case and close the oven door
- Bake for 25-30 minutes until the tart is just set with a slight wobble and starting to brown in places on top
- Cool the tart for at least 30 minutes then carefully remove it from the tin. Dust with icing sugar and serve warm or cold

Beer and Baileys Doughnuts

Makes 12 doughnuts — Prep time 2 hours 30 minutes including rising time
Cook time 30 minutes — Difficulty ❸

Ingredients

For the doughnuts

150ml lager, wheat beer or pale ale

40ml milk

40g butter

450g strong white flour, plus extra for kneading

9g fast-action dried yeast

200g caster sugar

2 eggs

1.5L vegetable or sunflower oil

Salt

For the filling

3 tbsp Baileys Irish Cream

150ml double (heavy) cream

1 tbsp hot chocolate powder

Equipment

Small saucepan

2 x large mixing bowls

Dough scraper or palette knife (optional)

Baking paper

Large heavy bottomed saucepan

Tongs

Digital food thermometer

Cooling rack

Whisk or electric beater

Piping bag and nozzle

If you've never made doughnuts before, it's time to start! These light, tender beer doughnuts are a world apart from the shop-bought variety, and they are sure to be the highlight of your weekend. Fried until crisp and golden, rolled in sugar and then filled with luscious Baileys cream, you'll struggle not to eat three!

Beer has been used as a raising agent in bread recipes for centuries. The yeast in the beer reacts with the starches in the flour, releasing carbon dioxide which helps the dough to rise. Together with baking yeast, this creates doughnuts with a light and fluffy texture that are rich in complex malty flavours. Any beer is fine here, but avoid anything too hoppy or bitter. A wheat beer provides hints of citrus, while lager has a slightly maltier note.

These doughnuts will keep for a day or two unfilled, but once filled they should be eaten as soon as possible. We love the Baileys Irish Cream filling used here but you could also try them with custard, jam or lemon curd.

Some tips on deep frying
A food thermometer is important here for maintaining the right oil temperature. If the temperature is too high the outside of the doughnut will cook faster than the inside, but if it's too low the batter will absorb some oil so the doughnuts will taste a little oily. If the oil starts to smoke, turn it off. **Don't leave the room while you're cooking, as hot oil can be dangerous!**

- Combine the milk and butter in a small saucepan and heat over a low heat until the butter has melted. Cool the mixture until lukewarm (you should be able to stick a finger into the liquid comfortably)

- Separately, mix together the flour, yeast, 40g of the caster sugar and ½ tsp salt until combined. Pour in the beer, then add the melted butter mixture and the eggs and mix well until you have a soft sticky dough

- Sprinkle a clean surface with flour, and knead the dough for 10-15 minutes until soft and smooth. You may need a dough scraper or palette knife to help scrape the surface as you go. If it is still very sticky after 15 minutes, add another sprinkling of flour to the surface and knead a little longer

- Lightly grease the mixing bowl with oil and put the dough in it, then cover with cling film or a tea towel and leave to rest for an hour in a warm place. The dough should have noticeably increased in size

- Turn out the dough onto a very clean surface and divide into 12 even sized pieces (weighing about 70g each). Roll the dough into smooth tight balls with your hands then place them onto oiled baking paper at least 2 inches apart. Cover loosely with oiled cling film and leave to rest for 45 minutes or until nearly doubled in size

- Fill a large heavy bottomed saucepan with 1.5L of oil, making sure the saucepan is no more than ⅓ full

- Heat the oil until it reaches 170C / 340F, then gently lower a few doughnuts into the oil. Fry for 3 minutes on each side until the doughnuts are deep golden brown all over, then use tongs to transfer to a wire rack. Allow the oil to reheat to 170C / 340F before you fry the next batch of doughnuts
- While the doughnuts are still warm, pour the remaining 70g caster sugar into a bowl and roll each doughnut in sugar until coated all over. Allow to cool before filling

For the filling
- Beat the cream, Baileys and hot chocolate powder together with a whisk or electric beater until it holds soft peaks. Scoop the filling into a piping bag
- Use a sharp knife to cut a hole in the side of each doughnut. Place the nozzle of the piping bag right into the doughnut and squeeze the filling in firmly until the cream starts to come back out of the hole

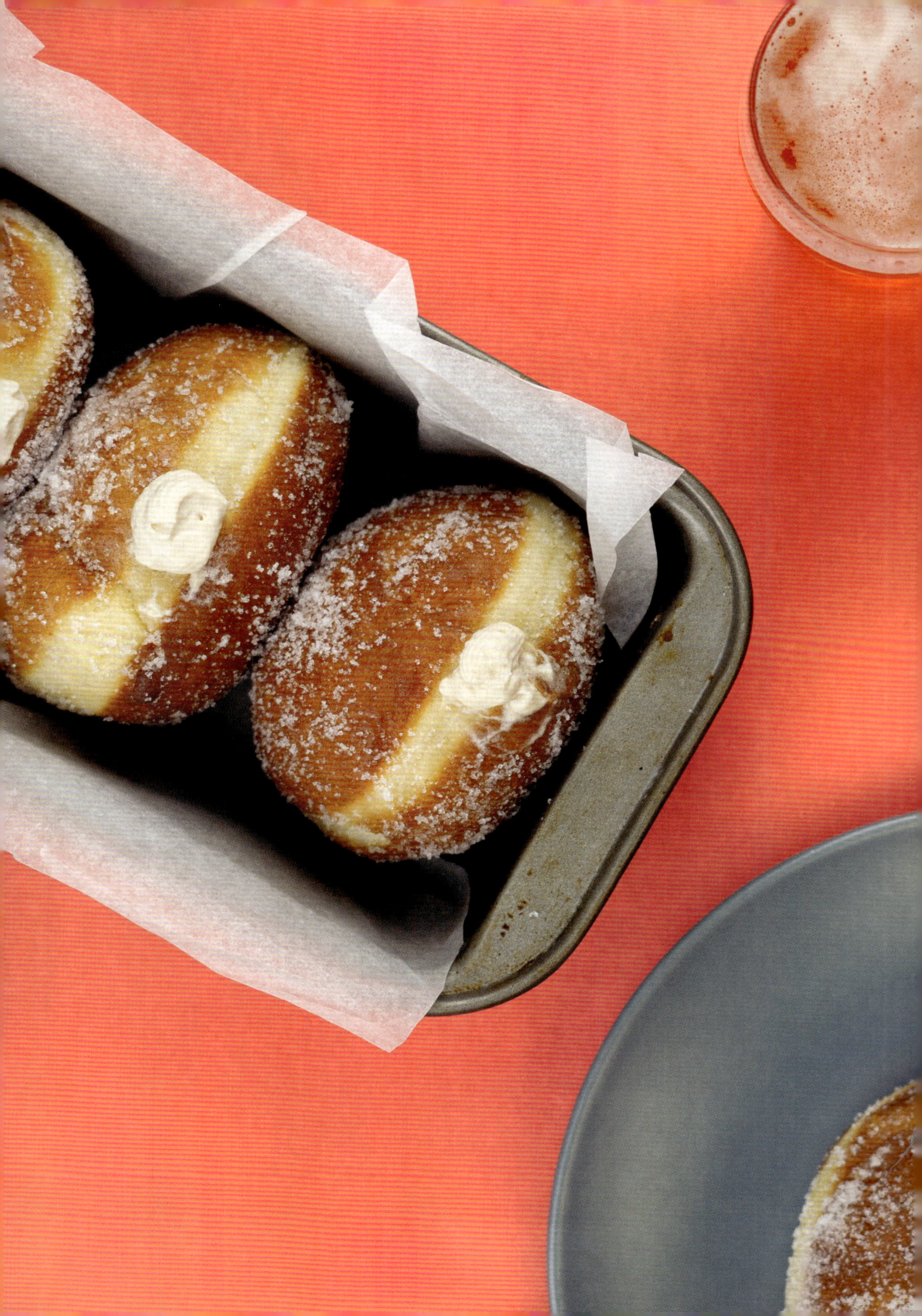

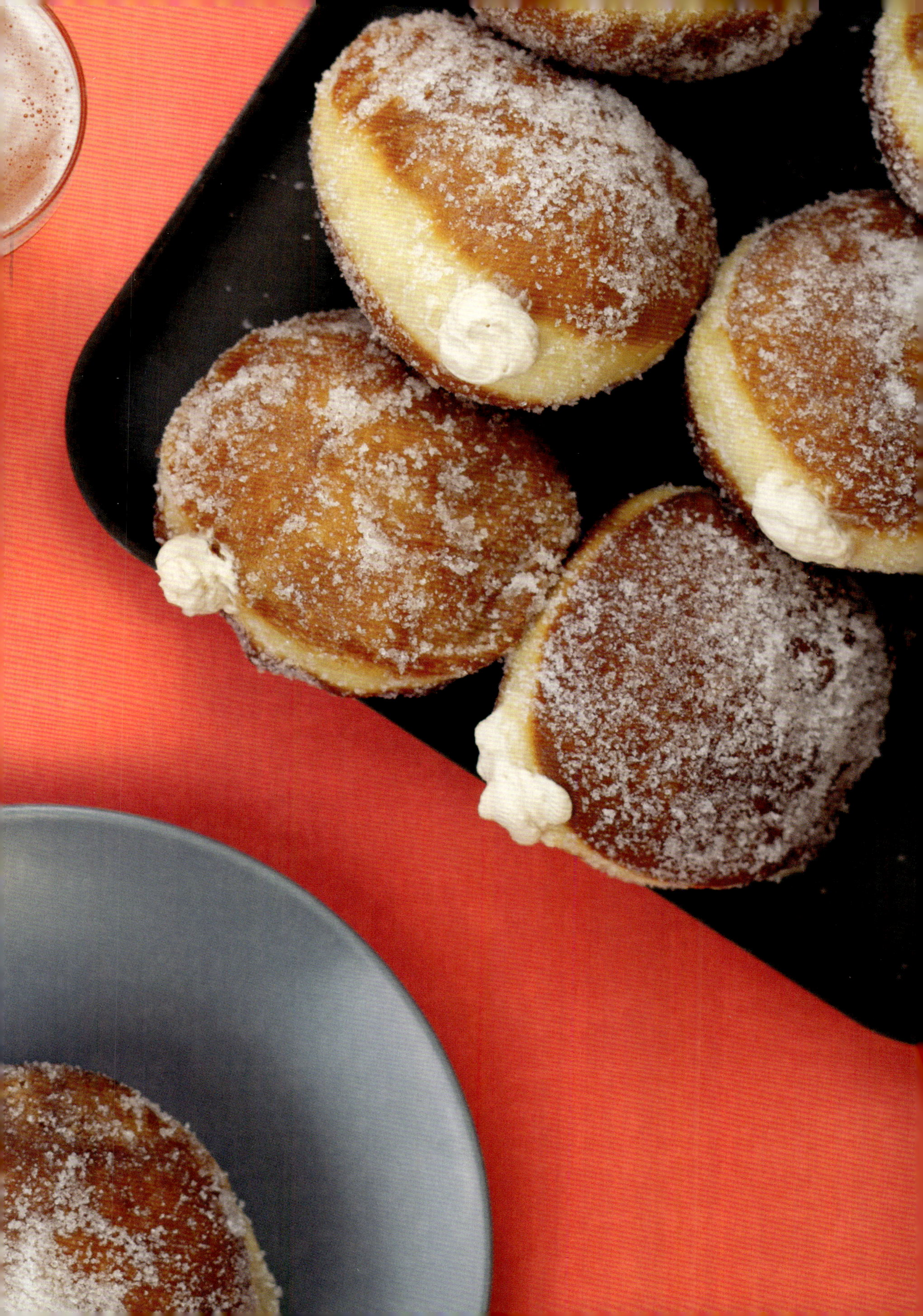

Kahlua Fudge

Makes approx. 25 pieces — Prep time 20 minutes + 4 hours chilling — Difficulty ❶

Ingredients

60ml kahlua liqueur

200g condensed milk (½ a standard tin)

250g white chocolate - broken into pieces

30g butter

Salt

This is a really easy version of fudge - it's made with white chocolate, condensed milk and a generous helping of kahlua coffee liqueur. There's no sugar to dissolve, so it takes just a few minutes to melt the ingredients together, and the mixture sets into a chewy, creamy fudge. We like to make just a small batch, but you can easily double this recipe if you prefer. Serve with coffee, as an after dinner treat, or wrap in wax paper and give it as a gift.

If you don't like coffee, try making this recipe with Irish cream liqueur instead!

- Grease a small piece of baking paper with a little oil, and then line the bottom and sides of your dish with the baking paper
- Empty the condensed milk, kahlua liqueur, butter and a pinch of salt into a small saucepan and heat for a few minutes until it comes to the boil
- Turn the heat to low for 5 minutes, stirring constantly so it doesn't burn on the bottom, until the mixture is a light caramel colour and thick enough that the spoon leaves a clear trail on the saucepan as you stir
- Remove the pan from the heat and add the white chocolate pieces, stirring until the chocolate has melted and the mixture is smooth
- Pour the mixture into the prepared dish, then place it in the fridge. Chill for at least 4 hours or overnight until set
- When the fudge has set, run a knife around the edge of the dish, then turn the fudge out onto a board or plate. Slice it into small squares and store in a container in the fridge for up to 2 weeks

Equipment

Dish or lunchbox approx. 10 x 20cm (4 x 8 inches)

Baking paper

Small saucepan

SWEET BAKING

Apple Cider Pancakes with Cider Caramel

Serves 4 — Prep time 20 minutes — Cook time 20 minutes — Difficulty ❷

Ingredients

350ml medium-sweet apple or pear cider (250ml for the caramel, 100ml for the pancakes)

75g light soft brown sugar

75g butter, plus extra to serve

75ml double (heavy) cream

150ml milk

200g self-raising flour

½ tsp bicarbonate of soda

2 tbsp white sugar

1 small eating apple - peeled, cored and grated

1 tsp mixed spice or pumpkin spice

2 eggs

Salt

2 tbsp vegetable or sunflower oil, plus extra to fry the pancakes

Squirty cream to serve

Equipment

Small saucepan

Jug

Small bowl

Mixing bowl

Non-stick frying pan

Try these delicious, fluffy, American-style apple pancakes - perfect for a cosy weekend breakfast. With homely aromas of warm spices and tart apple, drizzled with a thick cider caramel, these are a really great way to start the day. Serve with tea or coffee - it is breakfast, after all!

Many pancake recipes call for buttermilk, which is slightly acidic. Here, cider acts in its place - the interaction between acidic cider and alkaline bicarbonate of soda creates bubbles that give the pancakes a perfectly fluffy texture, as well as a delicious apple flavour.

Any leftover cider caramel keeps well in the fridge for up to two weeks, just give it a stir before using. It's great on crêpes, as an ice cream topping, drizzled over warm chocolate brownies, or even with fresh fruit.

For the cider caramel

- Pour 250ml of the cider into a small saucepan and place over a low-medium heat. Simmer for approximately 20 minutes, checking on it and swirling the pan occasionally, until the cider has reduced by about ¾ and is thick and syrupy
- Add the brown sugar and butter to the reduced cider and stir until melted and smooth. Stir in the double cream then transfer the caramel sauce to a jug

For the pancakes

- Combine the milk and the remaining 100ml cider in a jug or small bowl and leave to one side for 5 minutes. It will thicken and go lumpy - don't worry, it's meant to!
- Meanwhile mix together the flour, bicarbonate of soda, 2 tbsp sugar, grated apple, mixed spice and a pinch of salt in a large mixing bowl. Add the eggs, oil and the thickened milk and stir well
- Heat 1 tsp oil in a non-stick pan over a medium heat. Ladle in small quantities of pancake batter and fry the pancakes until the small bubbles in the centre stay there, and the edges start to look firm and golden
- Flip the pancakes and cook for a further minute on the other side. Stack the cooked pancakes on a plate covered with a clean tea towel and repeat the process, adding more oil to the pan in between batches, until you have used all the batter
- Serve the pancakes topped with cider caramel, and butter or squirty cream

SWEET BAKING

Orange and Spiced Rum Marmalade

Makes 5-6 jars — Prep time 30 minutes — Cook time 2 hours — Difficulty ❸

Ingredients

- 120ml dark spiced rum
- 800g Seville oranges - halved, with the knobbly ends sliced off
- 1 large unwaxed lemon - halved, with the knobbly ends sliced off
- 1.8L cold water
- 1.6Kg granulated sugar

Equipment

- Muslin bag, or a clean piece of cotton to tie into a little bundle
- A wide deep saucepan e.g. stock pot
- Large deep ovenproof dish
- 5-6 jam jars with lids
- Baking tray
- Digital food thermometer (optional)
- Wide funnel or jam funnel (optional)

Homemade marmalade is about 900% tastier than most store-bought marmalade, and the citrus scent which will fill your house makes for an incredibly snug winter ritual. It takes time and a little patience, particularly while slicing up the orange peel by hand, so pop some good music on and enjoy.

We stir in spiced rum at the end while the marmalade cools. This adds a lovely kick of warming spice, and ensures that the alcohol doesn't boil off. Alcohol is volatile, so as you spread it on your toast the aromas are carried to your senses - it's just what breakfast needs!

Seville oranges are usually only available during January, and their sharp, bitter flavour makes them the traditional fruit for making marmalade. By heating the sugar in a low oven before adding it to the pan, you reduce the cooking time and preserve the bright flavour of these oranges. If you can't wait until January, substitute with 500g eating oranges and 300g grapefruit.

- Juice the fruit, removing the pips and tying them inside a muslin bag. Put the juice into a wide deep saucepan, along with the muslin bag (the pectin in the pips helps the marmalade to set)
- Chop the orange and lemon peel finely with a very sharp knife into little slices 1-3mm wide and up to 3cm (1 inch) long. Shredding by hand takes a while, but it ensures that you get pieces of peel at your desired thickness
- Scoop the peel into the saucepan along with 1.8L of cold water. Bring it to a boil then simmer, uncovered, for 1 hour 30 minutes to soften the peel
- After 1 hour 10 minutes, heat your oven to 120C / Gas Mark ½ / 250F. If you are not using a digital thermometer, place a small plate in the fridge to chill now
- Pour the sugar into a large deep ovenproof dish and put it in your preheated oven for 10 minutes to warm - this helps the sugar to dissolve quicker. Leave the oven on as you will use it again shortly
- Remove the muslin bag from the saucepan, and add the warm sugar. Stir until the sugar has all dissolved, then turn the heat up and boil the marmalade rapidly for 15 minutes. **Be very careful and keep a close eye on it** to make sure it doesn't overflow, and stir once or twice to ensure that the bottom isn't burning
- After 15 minutes, test the temperature of your marmalade with the thermometer. The marmalade is ready (at setting point) when it reaches 104C (220F)
- If you aren't using a thermometer, scoop a small amount of the mixture onto your chilled plate. Wait a moment, then push it gently with a teaspoon - if the surface of the marmalade wrinkles, it's ready. If it stays runny, boil for 3 more minutes then test it again

COOKING WITH ALCOHOL

- When the marmalade has reached its setting point, turn the heat off, put the lid on and allow it to sit in the saucepan for 30 minutes. This cools the marmalade a little and stops the peel from floating to the top of your jars
- Meanwhile, wash the jars and lids in very hot soapy water and rinse well, then place the jars on a tray in the oven for 20 minutes to sterilise them
- Stir the spiced rum into the marmalade then carefully ladle it into the hot jars. If you're worried about burning yourself, washing up gloves are a good precaution
- Wipe the edges of each jar carefully with a damp cloth or paper towel, then close the lids tightly and leave to cool completely, preferably overnight. You may hear the occasional 'pop' as the seal on top of the jar closes
- Label the jars then store in a cool dark place. The marmalade may darken over time. Once opened, store in the fridge

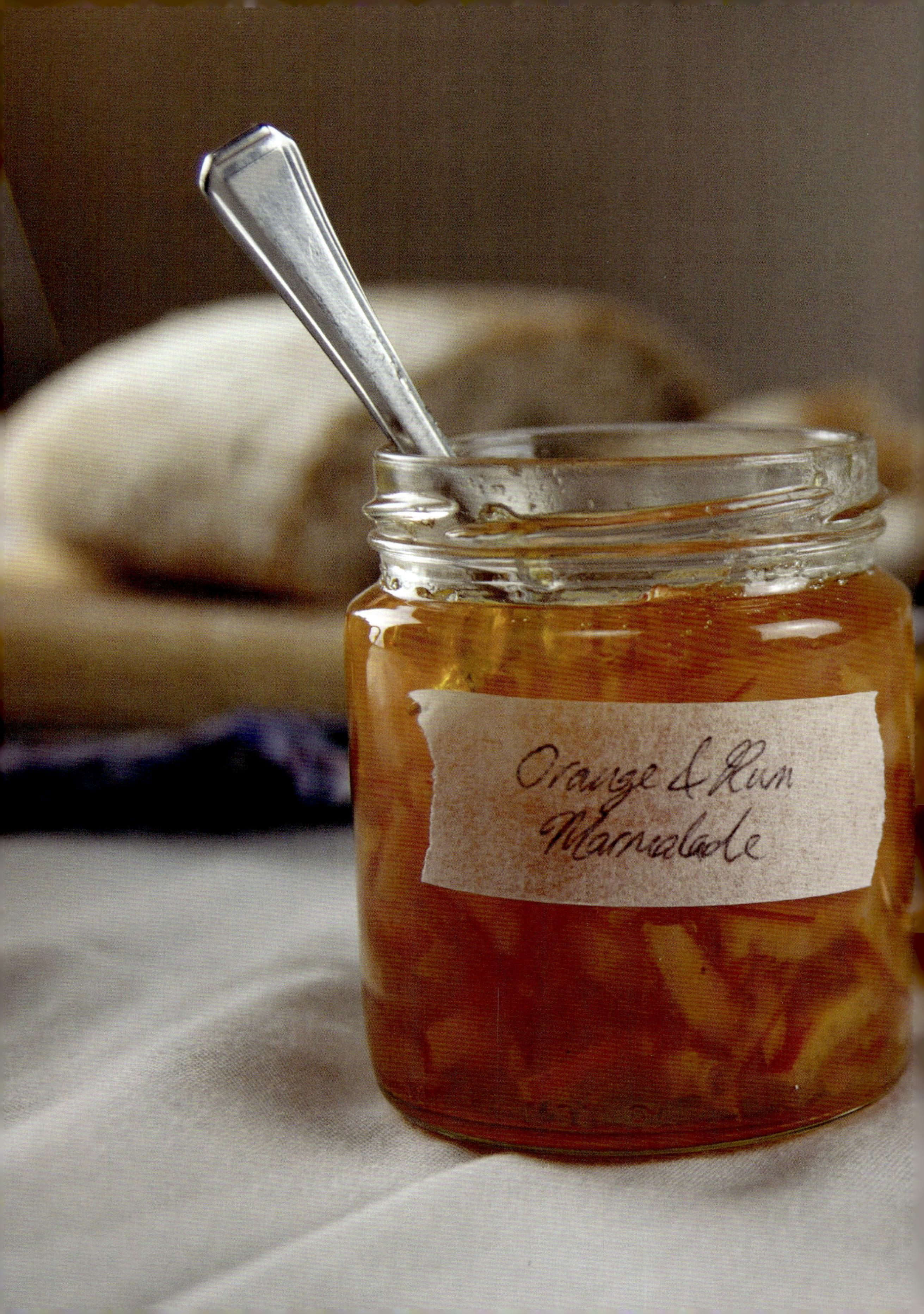
Orange & Rum
Marmalade

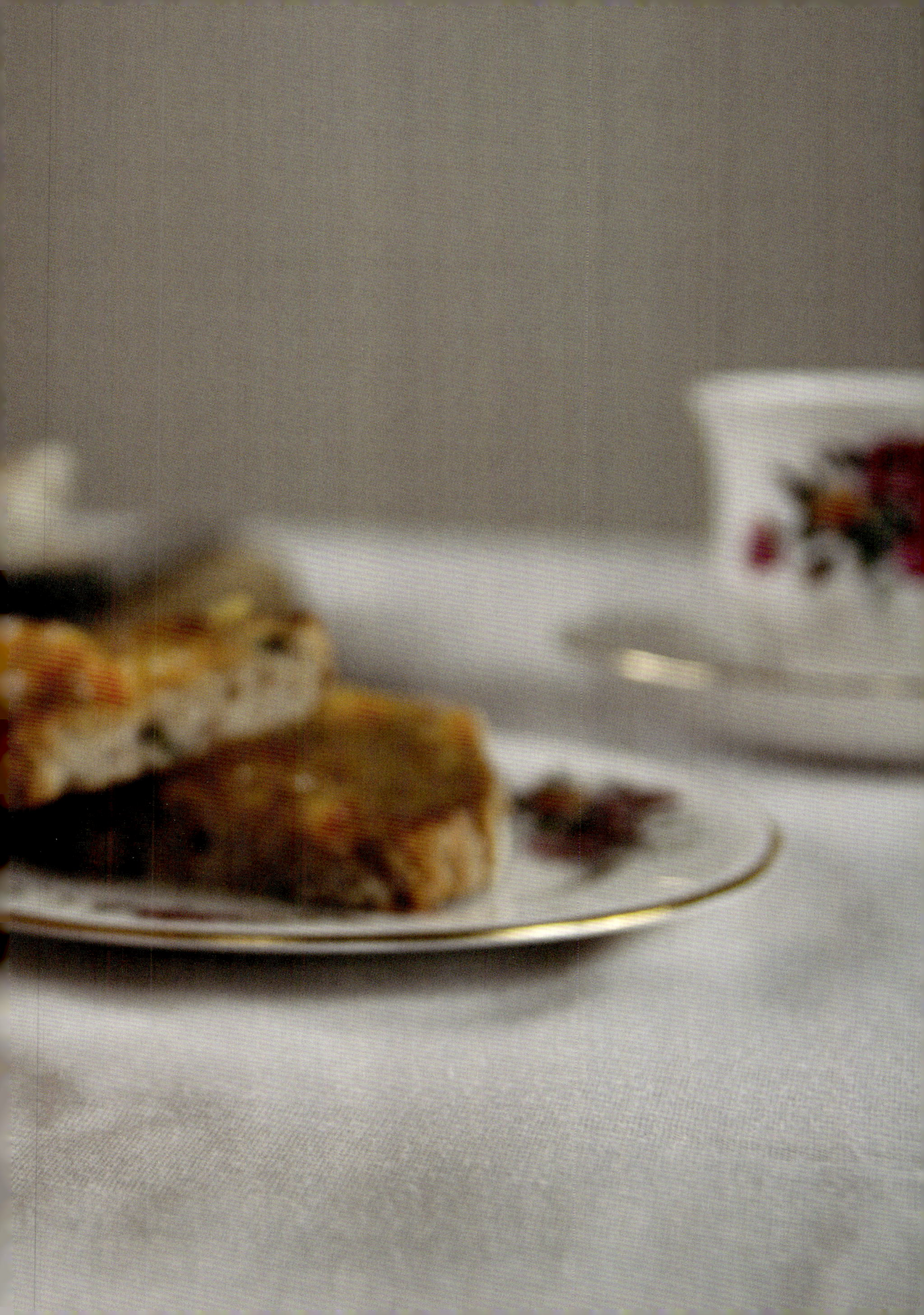

Apricot and Amaretto Jam

Makes 3 jars — Prep time 20 minutes — Cook time 30 minutes — Difficulty ❸

Ingredients

5 tbsp amaretto liqueur

500g apricots - stoned and roughly chopped

350g jam sugar

1 lemon - juiced (approx. 2 tbsp lemon juice)

Apricots and almonds are in the same botanical family, and the flavours go together beautifully in this preserve. We're using amaretto liqueur to add a sweet, nutty fragrance to this sunny orange jam, which is perfect for toast, on scones, or dolloped over yogurt with a nutty granola.

If you haven't made jam before, don't be intimidated - we're just making three jars of jam and it doesn't require any specialist equipment. The jam only cooks for a short time, so it retains its bright apricot flavour, and the extra pectin in the jam sugar ensures that it sets perfectly.

- If you don't have a digital thermometer, place a small plate in the fridge to chill
- Heat your oven to 120C / Gas Mark ½ / 250F. Wash three jars and lids in very hot soapy water and rinse well, then place the jars on a tray in the oven for 20 minutes to sterilise them while you make the jam
- Combine the apricots, jam sugar, lemon juice and 2 tbsp of the amaretto liqueur in a large saucepan. Cook over a low heat, stirring gently until the sugar has dissolved, then turn the heat up to medium
- Boil the jam for 5-10 minutes, keeping an eye on it and stirring occasionally to ensure that it doesn't burn on the bottom. The jam is ready (at setting point) when it reaches 105C (220F) on your digital thermometer
- If you aren't using a thermometer, after 5 minutes of boiling scoop a teaspoon of the jam onto the chilled plate. Wait a moment, then push it gently with a teaspoon - if the surface of the jam wrinkles, it's ready. If it stays runny, boil the jam for 2 more minutes then test it again
- Once the jam has reached its setting point, turn off the heat and wait for 5 minutes - this will ensure that the pieces of fruit don't all float to the top of the jar. Stir the remaining 3 tbsp of amaretto liqueur into the jam, then carefully ladle it into the hot jars
- Wipe the edges of each jar carefully with a damp cloth or paper towel, then close the lids tightly and leave to cool completely
- Label the jars then store in a cool dark place. Once opened, store in the fridge

Equipment

3 jam jars with lids

Large saucepan

Baking tray

Digital food thermometer (optional)

COOKING WITH ALCOHOL

SWEET BAKING

Apple and Bourbon Butter

Makes 2 jars — Prep time 20 minutes — Cook time 1 hour 30 minutes — Difficulty ❸

Ingredients

120ml bourbon

750g large cooking apples - peeled, cored and roughly chopped

100g light or dark soft brown sugar

100g white sugar

1 tsp vanilla extract

Salt

This thick, rich spread is traditionally known as apple butter, but it's really more like apple jam. It's made by cooking apples gently over a very low heat until the sugars caramelise and turn a deep rich brown. The flavour deepens, too, creating a concentrated spread that is sweet, tangy and fragrant with bourbon and vanilla.

The high sugar concentration in apple butter means that it keeps really well, so it's a great way to use a glut of apples and preserve the flavours of autumn. Serve on toast, crumpets, granola, porridge, pancakes, ice cream, muffins… or eat it straight from the jar!

- In a large wide saucepan, cook the apples with 50ml water over a low heat, with the lid on, for 20-30 minutes until the apples are thoroughly soft and broken down, stirring occasionally to ensure that they aren't sticking

- Add the brown sugar, white sugar, ½ tsp salt and the bourbon and cook over a very low heat, stirring frequently to ensure that it doesn't stick and burn, until all the sugar has dissolved. You may want to have the lid on at an angle to avoid it splattering out of the pan

- Cook over a very low heat for around 45 minutes, stirring occasionally, until the mixture is thick, glossy and dark brown. The apple butter is ready when a spoon leaves a clear wide trail across the bottom of the saucepan when you stir it, and the mixture looks shiny and jammy on the spoon

- Meanwhile, heat your oven to 120C / Gas Mark ½ / 250F. Wash two jars and lids in very hot soapy water and rinse well, then place the jars on a tray in the oven for 20 minutes to sterilise them

- Stir the vanilla extract into the apple butter, then carefully scoop the mixture into the hot jars

- Wipe the edges of each jar carefully with a damp cloth or paper towel then close the lids tightly and leave to cool completely.

- Label the jars then store in the fridge for up to a month, although you'll likely eat it before then!

Equipment

Large wide saucepan

2 small jam jars with lids (or 1 very large jar)

Baking tray

SWEET BAKING

Index — Recipe Difficulty

To help you navigate this book, and to know what to expect before cooking, there's a difficulty rating at the top of each recipe.

❶ Recipes rated as a "1" will be uncomplicated, usually suitable for a busy weeknight. These recipes require basic kitchen skills, and don't involve too many steps. These recipes will be suitable for a novice cook.

❷ Recipes rated as a "2" will require a bit more skill or time, with a few more steps or techniques involved. These recipes are suitable for an established home cook.

❸ Recipes rated as a "3" are more complex - they either have a few different component parts or steps, or use techniques that we wouldn't have energy for on a weeknight. These are best suited to a confident or accomplished home cook.

Recipes rated ❶

Starters and Light Meals
- Chorizo in Red Wine and Honey, 18
- Parsnip and Cider Soup, 24
- Mushroom and White Wine Soup, 26
- Cheese Fondue Tear-and-Share Bread, 30
- Bloody Mary Prawn Cocktail, 36

Mains
- Dark Beer and Aubergine Chilli, 58
- Rickard Family Jägermeister Chicken, 66
- Port Pesto with Rigatoni, 92
- Fennel and White Wine Tagliatelle, 94
- Tomato, Gin and Rosemary Pasta, 98
- Cheddar and Stout Risotto, 100

Side Dishes and Condiments
- Cider Braised Leeks, 122
- Shallots Glazed in White Wine, 124
- Beer Basmati, 126
- Bourbon and Bacon Corn-on-the-Cob, 128
- Spiced Rum Barbecue Pineapple, 130
- Gin Slaw, 132
- Prosciutto, Melon and Sherry Salad, 134
- Port Marinated Olives, 136
- Bourbon Glazed Carrots, 138
- Sherry and Lemon Gravy, 139
- Cider Mustard, 144
- Ale Pickled Eggs, 150

Hot Desserts
- Roasted Apricots in Madeira, 158
- Rhubarb and Gin Crumble, 160

Cold Desserts
- Rum, Raisin and Pistachio Posset, 184
- Chocolate and Amaretto Ganache Pots, 186
- Orange and Tequila Sorbet, 196
- Piña Colada Sorbet, 198
- Roasted Plum and Port Ripple Ice Cream, 200

Savoury Baking
- Cider Soda Bread, 214

Sweet Baking
- White Wine Pound Cake, 234
- Baileys Muffins, 236
- Whisky Shortbread, 252
- Chocolate and Port Tiffin, 260
- Kahlua Fudge, 270

Recipes rated ❷

Starters and Light Meals
- Prawn, Feta and Ouzo Saganaki, 20
- Jamaican Rum Chicken with Mango Hot Sauce, 22
- Irish Onion Soup, 28
- Tequila Fish Tacos with Pink Onions, 32
- Mussels in Stout, Bacon and Whisky, 40

Mains
- Beef and Ale Stew with Ale Dumplings, 50
- Chicken with Brandy and Apricots, 54
- Coq au Cidre, 56
- Lamb, Gin and Juniper Stew, 60
- Mojito Chicken, 64
- Sweet and Spicy Tequila Lime Pork, 68
- Trout with Dill and Ouzo, 70
- Sangria Chicken, 72
- Salmon with Cava Sauce and Crushed Lemon Potatoes, 80
- Sticky Cider Sausages with Mustard Mash, 82
- Tequila and Habanero Salmon with Salsa Fresca and Black Beans, 84
- Dark Rum and Orange Pork Chops, 86
- Mushroom and Sherry Pasta, 96
- Red Wine Risotto with Roasted Aubergine, 104
- Parsnip and Cider Tarte Tatin, 110

Side Dishes and Condiments
- Potato and Beer Dauphinoise (Beerphinoise), 120
- Red Wine Salt, 148

Hot Desserts
- Sloe Gin and Blackberry Cobbler, 156
- Red Wine Chocolate Fudge Pudding, 166

Cold Desserts
- Alcoholic Chocolate Mousse, 174
- Crema Catalana con Madeira, 180
- Gin, Lime and Elderflower Cheesecake, 188
- Prosecco Panna Cotta, 190
- Aperol Spritz Jellies, 192

Savoury Baking
- Red Wine Focaccia, 220

Sweet Baking
- Cider Apple Cake, 230
- Limoncello Polenta Cake, 238
- Dark 'n' Stormy Cake, 242
- Plum and Brandy Cake, 244
- Coconut Rum and Raspberry Cupcakes, 246
- Whisky and Maple Cupcakes, 248
- Lemon and Ouzo Cookies, 254
- Apple Cider Pancakes with Cider Caramel, 272

Recipes rated ③

Starters and Light Meals
    Tempura Aubergine with Unagi Sake Sauce, 34
    Chicken and Brandy Pâté, 38

Mains
    Bourbon Brined Beef Short Ribs, 52
    Philly Cheese Steak with Beer Sauce, 78
    Chicken, Amaretto, and Saffron Biryani, 102
    Mushroom and Stout Pasties, 108
    White Wine Chicken Pot Pie, 112

Side Dishes and Condiments
    Red Wine and Caramelised Onion Chutney, 146

Hot Desserts
    Pear and Amaretto Frangipane Tart, 162
    Chocolate and Rum Fondants with Raspberry Sauce, 164
    Whisky Sticky Toffee Pudding, 168

Cold Desserts
    Tequila Key Lime Pie, 178
    Amaretto and Ginger Cheesecake, 182
    Rosé and Raspberry Trifles, 194

Savoury Baking
    Three Cheese and Onion Vodka Tarts, 206
    Cider Crust Pork Pie, 208
    Goat's Cheese and Port Canapés, 212
    Stout and Rye Bread, 216

Sweet Baking
    Chocolate Stout Cake, 231
    Peanut Butter and Bourbon Cookies, 250
    Salted Caramel Spiced Rum Brownies, 256
    Alcoholic Bakewell Tart, 261
    Limoncello Tart, 264
    Beer and Baileys Doughnuts, 266
    Orange and Spiced Rum Marmalade, 274
    Apricot and Amaretto Jam, 278
    Apple and Bourbon Butter, 280

Index — Ingredient

A

Ale
- Beef and Ale Stew with Ale Dumplings, 50
- Dark Beer and Aubergine Chilli, 58
- Potato and Beer Dauphinoise (Beerphinoise), 120
- Ale Pickled Eggs, 150

Amaretto
- Chicken, Amaretto, and Saffron Biryani, 102
- Pear and Amaretto Frangipane Tart, 162
- Chocolate and Rum Fondants with Raspberry Sauce, 164
- Amaretto and Ginger Cheesecake, 182
- Chocolate and Amaretto Ganache Pots, 186
- Alcoholic Bakewell Tart, 261
- Apricot and Amaretto Jam, 278

Aperol
- Aperol Spritz Jellies, 192

Apple
- Cider Apple Cake, 230
- Apple Cider Pancakes with Cider Caramel, 272
- Apple and Bourbon Butter, 280

Apricot
- Chicken with Brandy and Apricots, 54
- Roasted Apricots in Madeira, 158
- Apricot and Amaretto Jam, 278

Aubergine
- Prawn, Feta and Ouzo Saganaki, 20
- Tempura Aubergine with Unagi Sake Sauce, 34
- Dark Beer and Aubergine Chilli, 58
- Red Wine Risotto with Roasted Aubergine, 104

B

Bacon
- Mussels in Stout, Bacon and Whisky, 40
- Coq au Cidre, 56
- Bourbon and Bacon Corn-on-the-Cob, 128

Baileys Irish Cream
- Alcoholic Chocolate Mousse, 174
- Baileys Muffins, 236
- Kahlua Fudge, 270
- Beer and Baileys Doughnuts, 266

Bakewell
- Alcoholic Bakewell Tart, 261

Beans
- Dark Beer and Aubergine Chilli, 58
- Tequila and Habanero Salmon with Salsa Fresca and Black Beans, 84

Beef
- Beef and Ale Stew with Ale Dumplings, 50
- Bourbon Brined Beef Short Ribs, 52
- Philly Cheese Steak with Beer Sauce, 78

Beer - see Ale, Lager, Stout

Berry
- Sloe Gin and Blackberry Cobbler, 156
- Chocolate and Rum Fondants with Raspberry Sauce, 164
- Prosecco Panna Cotta, 190
- Rosé and Raspberry Trifles, 194
- Coconut Rum and Raspberry Cupcakes, 246

Biscuits
- Peanut Butter and Bourbon Cookies, 250
- Whisky Shortbread, 252
- Lemon and Ouzo Cookies, 254

Blackberry
- Lamb, Gin and Juniper Stew, 60
- Sloe Gin and Blackberry Cobbler, 156

Bourbon
- Bourbon Brined Beef Short Ribs, 52
- Bourbon Glazed Carrots, 138
- Bourbon and Bacon Corn-on-the-Cob, 128
- Peanut Butter and Bourbon Cookies, 250
- Apple and Bourbon Butter, 280

Brandy
- Chicken and Brandy Pâté, 38
- Chicken with Brandy and Apricots, 54
- Chocolate and Rum Fondants with Raspberry Sauce, 164
- Plum and Brandy Cake, 244
- Chocolate and Amaretto Ganache Pots, 186

Bread
- Cheese Fondue Tear-and-Share Bread, 30
- Cider Soda Bread, 214
- Stout and Rye Bread, 216
- Red Wine Focaccia, 220

Brownie
- Salted Caramel Spiced Rum Brownies, 256

C

Cabbage
- Gin Slaw, 132

Cake
- Chocolate Stout Cake, 231
- Cider Apple Cake, 230
- White Wine Pound Cake, 234
- Baileys Muffins, 236
- Limoncello Polenta Cake, 238
- Dark 'n' Stormy Cake, 242
- Plum and Brandy Cake, 244
- Coconut Rum and Raspberry Cupcakes, 246
- Whisky and Maple Cupcakes, 248

Caramel
- Whisky Sticky Toffee Pudding, 168
- Salted Caramel Spiced Rum Brownies, 256
- Apple Cider Pancakes with Cider Caramel, 272

Carrot
- Bourbon Glazed Carrots, 138
- Gin Slaw, 132

Cheese
- Cheese Fondue Tear-and-Share Bread, 30
- Philly Cheese Steak with Beer Sauce, 78

Cheese - cheddar
- Irish Onion Soup, 28
- Cheddar and Stout Risotto, 100
- Mushroom and Stout Pasties, 108
- Potato and Beer Dauphinoise (Beerphinoise), 120
- Three Cheese and Onion Vodka Tarts, 206

Cheese - feta
- Prawn, Feta and Ouzo Saganaki, 20
- Three Cheese and Onion Vodka Tarts, 206

Cheese - goat's
- Goat's Cheese and Port Canapés, 212

Cheese - paneer
- Chicken, Amaretto, and Saffron Biryani, 102

Cheese - soft
- Roasted Apricots in Madeira, 158
- Tequila Key Lime Pie, 178
- Amaretto and Ginger Cheesecake, 182
- Gin, Lime and Elderflower Cheesecake, 188
- Goat's Cheese and Port Canapés, 212

Cheesecake
- Amaretto and Ginger Cheesecake, 182
- Gin, Lime and Elderflower Cheesecake, 188

Chicken
- Jamaican Rum Chicken with Mango Hot Sauce, 22
- Chicken and Brandy Pâté, 38

Chicken with Brandy and Apricots, 54
Coq au Cidre, 56
Mojito Chicken, 64
Rickard Family Jägermeister Chicken, 66
Sangria Chicken, 72
Chicken, Amaretto, and Saffron Biryani, 102
White Wine Chicken Pot Pie, 112
Sherry and Lemon Gravy, 139

Chocolate
Chocolate and Rum Fondants with Raspberry Sauce, 164
Red Wine Chocolate Fudge Pudding, 166
Alcoholic Chocolate Mousse, 174
Chocolate and Amaretto Ganache Pots, 186
Chocolate Stout Cake, 231
Chocolate and Port Tiffin, 260
Salted Caramel Spiced Rum Brownies, 256

Chorizo
Chorizo in Red Wine and Honey, 18
Sangria Chicken, 72

Cider
Parsnip and Cider Soup, 24
Coq au Cidre, 56
Sticky Cider Sausages with Mustard Mash, 82
Parsnip and Cider Tarte Tatin, 110
Cider Braised Leeks, 122
Cider Mustard, 144
Cider Crust Pork Pie, 208
Cider Soda Bread, 214
Cider Apple Cake, 230
Apple Cider Pancakes with Cider Caramel, 272

Coconut
Piña Colada Sorbet, 198
Coconut Rum and Raspberry Cupcakes, 246

Coffee liqueur
Kahlua Fudge, 270

Cointreau
Alcoholic Chocolate Mousse, 174

Cookies
Peanut Butter and Bourbon Cookies, 250
Whisky Shortbread, 252
Lemon and Ouzo Cookies, 254

Corn
Dark Rum and Orange Pork Chops, 86
Bourbon and Bacon Corn-on-the-Cob, 128

Cream
Potato and Beer Dauphinoise (Beerphinoise), 120
Crema Catalana con Madeira, 180
Rum, Raisin and Pistachio Posset, 184
Chocolate and Amaretto Ganache Pots, 186
Gin, Lime and Elderflower Cheesecake, 188
Prosecco Panna Cotta, 190
Beer and Baileys Doughnuts, 266

D
Date
Whisky Sticky Toffee Pudding, 168
Dessert wine - see Madeira

E
Egg
Ale Pickled Eggs, 150
Elderflower
Gin, Lime and Elderflower Cheesecake, 188

F
Fennel
Fennel and White Wine Tagliatelle, 94
Fish
Tequila Fish Tacos with Pink Onions, 32
Trout with Dill and Ouzo, 70
Salmon with Cava Sauce and Crushed Lemon Potatoes, 80
Tequila and Habanero Salmon with Salsa Fresca and Black Beans, 84
Focaccia
Red Wine Focaccia, 220

G
Gin
Lamb, Gin and Juniper Stew, 60
Tomato, Gin and Rosemary Pasta, 98
Gin Slaw, 132
Rhubarb and Gin Crumble, 160
Sloe Gin and Blackberry Cobbler, 156
Gin, Lime and Elderflower Cheesecake, 188
Gin - Sloe
Sloe Gin and Blackberry Cobbler, 156
Alcoholic Chocolate Mousse, 174
Alcoholic Bakewell Tart, 261
Ginger
Amaretto and Ginger Cheesecake, 182
Dark 'n' Stormy Cake, 242

I
Ice cream
Roasted Plum and Port Ripple Ice Cream, 200
Irish Cream
Baileys Muffins, 236
Kahlua Fudge, 270
Beer and Baileys Doughnuts, 266

J
Jägermeister
Rickard Family Jägermeister Chicken, 66
Jam
Apricot and Amaretto Jam, 278
Jelly
Aperol Spritz Jellies, 192
Rosé and Raspberry Trifles, 194

K
Kahlua
Kahlua Fudge, 270
Kirsch
Cheese Fondue Tear-and-Share Bread, 30
Alcoholic Chocolate Mousse, 174

L
Lager
Tempura Aubergine with Unagi Sake Sauce, 34
Dark Beer and Aubergine Chilli, 58
Philly Cheese Steak with Beer Sauce, 78
Potato and Beer Dauphinoise (Beerphinoise), 120
Beer Basmati, 126
Beer and Baileys Doughnuts, 266
Lamb
Lamb, Gin and Juniper Stew, 60
Leek
Cider Braised Leeks, 122
Lemon
Trout with Dill and Ouzo, 70
Sherry and Lemon Gravy, 139

Limoncello Polenta Cake, 238
Lemon and Ouzo Cookies, 254
Limoncello Tart, 264

Lime
  Mojito Chicken, 64
  Sweet and Spicy Tequila Lime Pork, 68
  Tequila Key Lime Pie, 178
  Gin, Lime and Elderflower Cheesecake, 188
  Dark 'n' Stormy Cake, 242

Limoncello
  Limoncello Polenta Cake, 238
  Alcoholic Bakewell Tart, 261
  Limoncello Tart, 264

M

Madeira
  Roasted Apricots in Madeira, 158
  Crema Catalana con Madeira, 180

Mango
  Jamaican Rum Chicken with Mango Hot Sauce, 22

Maple syrup
  Bourbon Glazed Carrots, 138
  Whisky and Maple Cupcakes, 248

Marmalade
  Orange and Spiced Rum Marmalade, 274

Melon
  Prosciutto, Melon and Sherry Salad, 134

Mexican
  Tequila Fish Tacos with Pink Onions, 32
  Dark Beer and Aubergine Chilli, 58
  Sweet and Spicy Tequila Lime Pork, 68
  Tequila and Habanero Salmon with Salsa Fresca and Black Beans, 84

Mint
  Mojito Chicken, 64
  Prosciutto, Melon and Sherry Salad, 134

Mushroom
  Mushroom and White Wine Soup, 26
  Beef and Ale Stew with Ale Dumplings, 50
  Lamb, Gin and Juniper Stew, 60
  Mushroom and Sherry Pasta, 96
  Mushroom and Stout Pasties, 108

Mussels
  Mussels in Stout, Bacon and Whisky, 40

Mustard
  Sticky Cider Sausages with Mustard Mash, 82
  Cider Mustard, 144

O

Olive
  Port Marinated Olives, 136

Onion
  Irish Onion Soup, 28
  Bourbon Brined Beef Short Ribs, 52
  Sticky Cider Sausages with Mustard Mash, 82
  Red Wine and Caramelised Onion Chutney, 146
  Three Cheese and Onion Vodka Tarts, 206

Orange
  Sangria Chicken, 72
  Dark Rum and Orange Pork Chops, 86
  Orange and Tequila Sorbet, 196
  Roasted Plum and Port Ripple Ice Cream, 200
  Orange and Spiced Rum Marmalade, 274

Ouzo
  Prawn, Feta and Ouzo Saganaki, 20
  Trout with Dill and Ouzo, 70
  Lemon and Ouzo Cookies, 254

P

Pancake
  Apple Cider Pancakes with Cider Caramel, 272

Parsnip
  Parsnip and Cider Soup, 24
  Parsnip and Cider Tarte Tatin, 110

Pasta
  Fennel and White Wine Tagliatelle, 94
  Mushroom and Sherry Pasta, 96
  Port Pesto with Rigatoni, 92
  Tomato, Gin and Rosemary Pasta, 98

Pastry
  Mushroom and Stout Pasties, 108
  Parsnip and Cider Tarte Tatin, 110
  White Wine Chicken Pot Pie, 112
  Pear and Amaretto Frangipane Tart, 162
  Three Cheese and Onion Vodka Tarts, 206
  Cider Crust Pork Pie, 208
  Goat's Cheese and Port Canapés, 212
  Alcoholic Bakewell Tart, 261
  Limoncello Tart, 264

Peanut butter
  Peanut Butter and Bourbon Cookies, 250

Pear
  Pear and Amaretto Frangipane Tart, 162

Pie - see Pastry

Pineapple
  Alcoholic Chocolate Mousse, 174
  Spiced Rum Barbecue Pineapple, 130
  Piña Colada Sorbet, 198

Pistachio
  Rum, Raisin and Pistachio Posset, 184

Plum
  Roasted Plum and Port Ripple Ice Cream, 200
  Plum and Brandy Cake, 244

Polenta
  Limoncello Polenta Cake, 238

Pork
  Sweet and Spicy Tequila Lime Pork, 68
  Dark Rum and Orange Pork Chops, 86
  Sticky Cider Sausages with Mustard Mash, 82
  Cider Crust Pork Pie, 208

Port
  Port Pesto with Rigatoni, 92
  Port Marinated Olives, 136
  Alcoholic Chocolate Mousse, 174
  Roasted Plum and Port Ripple Ice Cream, 200
  Goat's Cheese and Port Canapés, 212
  Chocolate and Port Tiffin, 260

Porter - see Stout

Potato
  Parsnip and Cider Soup, 24
  Salmon with Cava Sauce and Crushed Lemon Potatoes, 80
  Sticky Cider Sausages with Mustard Mash, 82
  Chicken, Amaretto, and Saffron Biryani, 102
  Mushroom and Stout Pasties, 108
  Potato and Beer Dauphinoise (Beerphinoise), 120

Prawns
  Prawn, Feta and Ouzo Saganaki, 20
  Bloody Mary Prawn Cocktail, 36

Prosciutto or parma ham
  Prosciutto, Melon and Sherry Salad, 134

Prosecco
  Prosecco Panna Cotta, 190
  Aperol Spritz Jellies, 192

R

Raisin
  Rum, Raisin and Pistachio Posset, 184

Raspberry
- Chocolate and Rum Fondants with Raspberry Sauce, 164
- Prosecco Panna Cotta, 190
- Rosé and Raspberry Trifles, 194
- Coconut Rum and Raspberry Cupcakes, 246

Red wine
- Chorizo in Red Wine and Honey, 18
- Sangria Chicken, 72
- Red Wine Risotto with Roasted Aubergine, 104
- Red Wine and Caramelised Onion Chutney, 146
- Red Wine Salt, 148
- Red Wine Chocolate Fudge Pudding, 166
- Red Wine Focaccia, 220

Rhubarb
- Rhubarb and Gin Crumble, 160

Rice
- Cheddar and Stout Risotto, 100
- Chicken, Amaretto, and Saffron Biryani, 102
- Red Wine Risotto with Roasted Aubergine, 104
- Beer Basmati, 126

Risotto
- Cheddar and Stout Risotto, 100
- Red Wine Risotto with Roasted Aubergine, 104

Rum - coconut
- Alcoholic Chocolate Mousse, 174
- Coconut Rum and Raspberry Cupcakes, 246

Rum - dark or spiced
- Jamaican Rum Chicken with Mango Hot Sauce, 22
- Dark Rum and Orange Pork Chops, 86
- Spiced Rum Barbecue Pineapple, 130
- Chocolate and Rum Fondants with Raspberry Sauce, 164
- Rum, Raisin and Pistachio Posset, 184
- Chocolate and Amaretto Ganache Pots, 186
- Dark 'n' Stormy Cake, 242
- Salted Caramel Spiced Rum Brownies, 256
- Orange and Spiced Rum Marmalade, 274

Rum - white
- Mojito Chicken, 64
- Piña Colada Sorbet, 198

Rye
- Stout and Rye Bread, 216

S

Sake
- Tempura Aubergine with Unagi Sake Sauce, 34

Salmon
- Salmon with Cava Sauce and Crushed Lemon Potatoes, 80
- Tequila and Habanero Salmon with Salsa Fresca and Black Beans, 84

Salt
- Red Wine Salt, 148

Shallot
- Shallots Glazed in White Wine, 124

Sherry
- Mushroom and Sherry Pasta, 96
- Sherry and Lemon Gravy, 139
- Prosciutto, Melon and Sherry Salad, 134

Shortbread
- Whisky Shortbread, 252

Sorbet
- Orange and Tequila Sorbet, 196
- Piña Colada Sorbet, 198

Soup
- Parsnip and Cider Soup, 24
- Mushroom and White Wine Soup, 26
- Irish Onion Soup, 28

Sparkling wine
- Salmon with Cava Sauce and Crushed Lemon Potatoes, 80
- Prosecco Panna Cotta, 190
- Aperol Spritz Jellies, 192

Stout
- Irish Onion Soup, 28
- Mussels in Stout, Bacon and Whisky, 40
- Dark Beer and Aubergine Chilli, 58
- Cheddar and Stout Risotto, 100
- Mushroom and Stout Pasties, 108
- Alcoholic Chocolate Mousse, 174
- Stout and Rye Bread, 216
- Chocolate Stout Cake, 231

Sweet potato
- Dark Beer and Aubergine Chilli, 58
- Sangria Chicken, 72
- Sweet and Spicy Tequila Lime Pork, 68

T

Tapas
- Chorizo in Red Wine and Honey, 18
- Prawn, Feta and Ouzo Saganaki, 20
- Shallots Glazed in White Wine, 124
- Prosciutto, Melon and Sherry Salad, 134
- Port Marinated Olives, 136

Tequila
- Tequila Fish Tacos with Pink Onions, 32
- Sweet and Spicy Tequila Lime Pork, 68
- Tequila and Habanero Salmon with Salsa Fresca and Black Beans, 84
- Alcoholic Chocolate Mousse, 174
- Tequila Key Lime Pie, 178
- Orange and Tequila Sorbet, 196

Tiffin
- Chocolate and Port Tiffin, 260

Toffee - see Caramel

Tomato
- Prawn, Feta and Ouzo Saganaki, 20
- Port Pesto with Rigatoni, 92
- Tomato, Gin and Rosemary Pasta, 98

Trout
- Trout with Dill and Ouzo, 70

V

Vodka
- Bloody Mary Prawn Cocktail, 36
- Alcoholic Chocolate Mousse, 174
- Aperol Spritz Jellies, 192
- Three Cheese and Onion Vodka Tarts, 206
- Limoncello Tart, 264

W

Whisky
- Mussels in Stout, Bacon and Whisky, 40
- Whisky Sticky Toffee Pudding, 168
- Whisky and Maple Cupcakes, 248
- Whisky Shortbread, 252

White wine
- Mushroom and White Wine Soup, 26
- Cheese Fondue Tear-and-Share Bread, 30
- Fennel and White Wine Tagliatelle, 94
- White Wine Chicken Pot Pie, 112
- Shallots Glazed in White Wine, 124
- White Wine Pound Cake, 234

Wine - see Red wine, White wine, Rosé wine or Sparkling wine

Acknowledgements

To everyone who supported the idea of this book, and told us we could and should write it. Then kept asking about it, kept caring, and encouraged and celebrated each step along the way. Thank you.

To our friends who helped so much with tasting and testing, and loaning plates, prosecco glasses or a bit of perspective - we love you. In no particular order: Chloe S, Tabby, Hannah A, James W, Dan, Jenny, Simon, Beth, Lydia, Hannah E, Sam, Joe, Sophie, Sarah, Toby, Ralph, James N, JJ, Kate, Brian, Jennifer, Mariah, Chloe I and Tom, among others.

To our families for their love, support, testing, feedback, and for telling so many people about this book - the Rickard and Swinn parents, and Elizabeth, Neil, Joe and Hannah.

Paige Henderson, our truly wonderful editor - thank you for your patience, for believing in us, for letting us create the book that we dreamed of, and for pushing us to be better. Where would we be without your incredible editing skills, love of commas, and enthusiasm for this book?! We couldn't have done it without you.

Jamie McGarry - thank you for passing this project to Paige in the first place, and for your support and patience. Peter Barnfather, for the beautiful cover design. Louise Farmer, for taking some really lovely photos of us. To Pukka and Doddle, for supporting our non-work passion project.

And of course, the upstairs neighbours for taking excess baked goods off our hands. We appreciate it.

And finally, a big thank you to our Kickstarter supporters!

Without whom this book would not have been possible.

- Abi Harris
- Albert Porter
- Alyson Knezevich
- Alyssa "Twist" Light
- Anders Onnerfalt
- Andrea J
- Andrew T Davies
- Anisha Rhoden
- Anna, Phil & Dominic Wright
- Anne Fleckenstein
- Anonymous
- Antoine Authier
- Brooke
- Bryan Koepp
- C.K. Ingold
- Charlotte Foldys
- Chloe Sellick
- Chris
- Chris 'Micklex' Michler
- Chris Kuivenhoven
- Chris Remo
- Christina Owen
- ChuChuEn
- Clara A. Warner
- Collin Warden
- Courtney Dobbertin
- Dan & Jenny Pritchard
- Dan Ortiz
- Daniel "Joe" Jackson
- Darren Belding
- David Graf
- David Kreutz
- David Lawes
- David Sattlecker
- David William Such
- Del Vecchio D.
- Derek Bird
- DirtyPhoque
- Dominic Wittmer
- Dr Lucy Elkerton
- Eleanor Lee
- Elspeth Hinde
- Emma B
- Emma Sharp
- Evan R. Stanley
- Fenric Cayne
- Fred Milano
- Guy Fisher
- Harald Hanche-Olsen
- Harrison C. Lovell
- Helen Robinson
- HokutoDeCuisine
- Hrvoje Vrazic
- In honor of Chef Thom England
- Isaiah Whisner
- Isak Larsson
- Jack Walker
- Jacquelyn Stevens
- James Ransome
- Jeffrey and Christine Townsend
- Jennifer Busch
- Jérémy 'Salias' Cordier
- Jeremy Broglio
- Jin Wilson
- Joe Swinn
- Joel and Verity Gerard
- John McGettigan
- Jon Fallows
- Jon Toivo
- Jonathan Brady
- Jordan Bressman
- Jorrit Grob and Brian Meijer
- Joseph A Marshall
- Josh Sharp
- Justin Varney-Bennett
- Kathryn Hough

Katie and Keith
Katie M
Ki Tat
Korie Vee
Kseniya G
L Evans
L Kinghorn
L.J.
Laura Mansfield
Lauren Olinger
Linda K. Swinn
Liz R
M. Morrell
Maggie S
MAP
Marek J. Łaska
Marie Esclozas
Mark Bowell
Mark C Thomas
Markus Ast
Markus Wlasto
Marrio & Diana
Matt, Elizabeth, Oliver, Annabel & baby Alice
Matthew Beymer
Matthew Dang
Matthew Ware
Matthias Freise
Michael Schuerger & Corey Yaklin
Mikael Hjelm
Mike Rich
Mo! Langdon
Monty
MythSigh
Nathalie A Starr
Nathan Deems
Nathan Mitchell
Neil & Elizabeth Hamilton
Ole-Morten Larsen
Paige Henderson
Pernille Fladsrud
Philip Ma

Philip Swinn
PongZerHK
Raphael Dobmann
Ravi Pina
Richard Wilkin
Rodger Battersby
Rory, Felicity & Maisie
Sallie Buckner
Sam
Sam 'Jacko' Jackson
Sam & Sam
Sam and Hannah Eason
Sam Eu
Sam Heathfield
Sam Koppen
Sam Robertson
Sean Eveson
Seth and Kelly Manning
SH Tan
Sian Pearce
Tash & Rich
Terry & Dana Rickard
Terry & Lara Choo
The Cookes
Thomas Crown
Tim Baker
Tim Graves
Toby and Sarah
Tom & Shari Robertshaw
Tom Codrington
Tracy Popey
Trevor Keagbine
Trine Viveke Salvesen
Virginia Cartwright
Vladimir Zaytsev
Wendy & Ken Frankovich
Wilma Jandoc Win
Zachy46
Zack Cox & Donna Vu

...and many more!

About the Authors

Aaron and Susannah Rickard are passionate home cooks based in Bath in the south west of England.

Susannah works in the international business team for a herbal tea company. Australian-born and now UK-based, she spent a number of years working for a recipe kit company, writing and testing hundreds of recipes from around the world.

Aaron is a web developer in London and a keen food photographer. With an American heritage and a multicultural upbringing, a love of food from all over the world was encouraged from an early age.

Taking every opportunity to pick up brand-new techniques, Aaron and Susannah have researched, written and tested all of the recipes in **Cooking with Alcohol** together in their home kitchen. Susannah is responsible for the clear and approachable writing style, while Aaron's stunning photography and typesetting has been a real labour of love.

Find them on Instagram @rickardkitchen and at cookingwithalcohol.co.uk